> Keith—
> Thanks for the friendship + putting up with me at Bass. Thanks for all you've done + continue to do for Nashville. I think you're the best!
> Angie p.55

CLIMBING THE CHARTS

The Ascent of
NASHVILLE

―――★―――

Angie Lawless | Brandon Miller | Steve Morris

Copyright © 2021 Angie Lawless, Brandon Miller, and Steve Morris

Climbing the Charts: The Ascent of Nashville

Photographs by Holly Ray

All rights reserved.

Hardcover ISBN: 978-1-5445-0857-3
eBook ISBN: 978-1-5445-0856-6

To Ellis, Isaac, Levi, and Rosalie
Continue shining on Nashville, telling her with each passing day
that you came to make positive differences.

To Dylan and Townes
Daughters with namesakes inspired by Nashville Skyline,
may you continually inspire those around you,
and future skylines, wherever they be.

To Ava
Of all the big and great changes in our city since I moved here,
the biggest and greatest for me is you. Keep learning and growing.

Everybody now thinks that Nashville is the coolest city in America.
—Dave Grohl[1]

I belonged to Nashville before I belonged to anyone.
—Brandi Carlile[2]

I ain't bashful. I'm from Nashville.
—Bumper sticker displayed at Robert's Western World

One of the magical things about Nashville is just how many
incredibly talented people are here and the way they support each other.
—Callie Khouri, creator of the *Nashville* television series[3]

I guess Nashville was the roughest
But I know I've said the same about them all.
—Willie Nelson, "Me and Paul"

I got friends in Nashville, or at least they're folks I know
Nashville's where you go to see if what is said is so.
—Drive-By Truckers, "Carl Perkins' Cadillac"

CONTENTS

★

About the Photographer
xi

About Wagon Wheel
xiii

About the Authors
xv

Special Thanks
xvii

Introduction
xix

CHAPTER 1
Nashville Now
3

CHAPTER 2
A Bit of History
13

CHAPTER 3
Southern Hospitality
25

CHAPTER 4
Business Environment and Entrepreneurship
35

CHAPTER 5
Development and Real Estate
47

CHAPTER 6
Music
63

CHAPTER 7
Healthcare
81

CHAPTER 8
Public Sector and Politics
91

CHAPTER 9
Food and Drink
107

CHAPTER 10
Sports
123

CHAPTER 11
Education
135

CHAPTER 12
Keeping Busy
145

Conclusion
155

Endnotes
157

ABOUT THE PHOTOGRAPHER

★

Holly Ray is from Dallas, Texas. In 2019, she graduated from the University of Alabama, where she studied photography. She now lives in Nashville and has a passion for documenting the ever-changing cityscape.

ABOUT WAGON WHEEL

★

Wagon Wheel Title, founded in 2006, is a boutique real estate title and escrow company from Nashville, Tennessee. At Wagon Wheel, skilled attorneys and closing professionals conduct and coordinate our real estate closings. Wagon Wheel offers a full array of real estate title and escrow services to purchasers, sellers, and lenders on real estate related transactions. We have extensive experience in all of the following transactions:

- Purchase and/or sale of residential or commercial property

- Refinancing of residential or commercial property

- Condominium structure

- Equity lines of credit

- Title searches and title reports

- Construction loans

- Investment property transactions, including Section 1031 exchanges

- For sale by owner ("FSBO")

- Distressed property transactions, including foreclosures, short sales, and bank-owned property ("REOs")

Wagon Wheel Title aims to distinguish itself from other Nashville title companies by offering a unique level of personalized title and escrow service, market knowledge and legal expertise. Wagon Wheel Title is an agent of Chicago Title Insurance Company, First American, Westcor, and WFG.

ABOUT THE AUTHORS

Angie Lawless

Angie is from Mount Vernon, Kentucky. She graduated summa cum laude from Eastern Kentucky University with a BA in Speech Communication and BBA in General Business. After college, Angie moved to Nashville, where she attended Vanderbilt Law School, serving on the Moot Court Board and the Vanderbilt Law Review. After VULS, Angie practiced as a transactional attorney with Bass, Berry & Sims PLC. During her time at Bass, Angie co-founded a real estate investment company and discovered that her true career interest was in real estate. This revelation led to Angie co-founding Wagon Wheel Title and Lockeland Law Group.

In her spare time, Angie enjoys spending time with her husband and four children, Ellis, Isaac, Levi, and Rosalie. She loves to travel and hopes to visit Vietnam and South Africa soon. Her favorite thing about Nashville is the open-minded, accepting culture and the city's mindset of constant progress and innovation, with a sense of always reaching and striving for more, economically, culturally, and socially. She also loves the live music scene, especially the Station Inn, which is her favorite place in all of Nashville.

Brandon Miller

Originally from Cleveland, Tennessee, Brandon graduated summa cum laude from Dartmouth College, where he was elected to Phi Beta Kappa and awarded the Edwin F. Jones Prize for a history honors thesis about the attack on the 1961 Freedom Riders in Anniston, Alabama. After college, he road-tripped across the United States for almost a year until entering Harvard Law School. Upon graduating from Harvard in 2001, where his third-year paper focused on the portrayal of lawyers in the works of novelist Walker Percy, he returned to Tennessee to practice law with the Nashville law firm of Bass, Berry & Sims PLC. After co-founding a real estate investment company, he became increasingly interested in real estate and urban development, which led to his involvement in co-founding Wagon Wheel Title and Lockeland Law Group. A graduate of the Nashville Emerging Leaders (NEL) program and former board member of the Tomorrow Fund, Brandon currently serves as Board President of Rebuilding Together Nashville (RTN), a leading housing nonprofit focused on affordable housing solutions.

In his spare time, Brandon dabbles in reading and writing and enjoys playing (and winning) 3 Crow Bar trivia, listening to live music, tasting bourbon, and spreading the gospel of horology. He has two daughters, Townes and Dylan, named for Townes Van Zandt and Bob Dylan. His favorite thing about Nashville is the diverse cultural milieu, with all sorts of people, from rural farmers to celebrity A-listers to Vanderbilt scholars. His favorite place in Nashville is a three-way tie between 3 Crow Bar, an eclectic neighborhood bar, and Attaboy and Urban Cowboy, which both serve up craft cocktails in a speakeasy setting.

Steve Morris

Originally from Gleason, Tennessee, Steve graduated from Vanderbilt University with a BA in Philosophy and Political Science. After college, Steve attended Vanderbilt Law School, where he was the John S. Beasley Scholar and served as Articles Editor for the *Vanderbilt Law Review*. After graduating from law school in 2003, Steve moved to Memphis, where he served as a clerk for the Hon. Julia Smith Gibbons of the United States Court of Appeals for the Sixth Circuit. Upon completion of his clerkship in 2004, Steve returned to Nashville, where he worked as a transactional attorney with Bass, Berry & Sims PLC. In 2009, Steve joined Wagon Wheel Title and co-founded Lockeland Law Group. Steve enjoys the fast pace of real estate transactions and has extensive experience setting up and closing multi-unit projects. He says, "I love that this profession gives me a reason to see my friends and lots of opportunities to talk with new people."

When he's not closing real estate deals, Steve enjoys spending time with his daughter, Ava, as well as skiing, reading, and listening to live music. His favorite part of Nashville is the live music scene, from the intimate performances at living-room-size venues to the sold-out stadium concerts at Bridgestone Arena. His favorite place is the Five Points area, which is close to the Wagon Wheel office and where he is building a new house.

SPECIAL THANKS

★

In the course of any project as time-consuming and multifaceted as writing a book, there are more people deserving of thanks than there are thanks to go around.

Our author team would first and foremost like to thank all the various people—50-plus—who gave generously of their time to help shape the narrative of this work. While many of those we interviewed at least get a mention, some yet do not, but their input, opinions, and perspectives were still crucial to the development of this work. Many of the people we interviewed are truly the busiest people we know, and are the true movers and shakers of Music City. Our thanks also to photographer Holly Ray (Instagram: @hollyrayyy), for capturing the beauty and spirit of our city.

Moreover, family and friends, as well as work colleagues who took on extra burdens at times, played an especially critical part in helping inspire and, more importantly, sustain this project.

INTRODUCTION

NASHVILLE
A City on the Rise

In the past three decades, Nashville has been catapulted from relative obscurity to one of the media's favorite cities. We've experienced a three-pronged explosion of population, economy, and culture. In terms of population, Metro Nashville is now home to 1.9 million people from a diverse set of backgrounds. Economically, we have become a hub for businesses, especially in the healthcare sector, and many companies continue to open or move headquarters here. Culturally, we're one of the most unique cities in the United States. We have a thriving culinary scene, many galleries and museums, three major sports franchises, and, in our opinion and many others', the best live music scene in the world. There's a reason millions of people visit Nashville each year, with over 15 million visitors in 2018 alone.[4]

Here are a few highlights of Nashville's accomplishments in just the past few years:

- In 2016, despite having "no chance," Nashville was the first city selected to receive a Major League Soccer expansion team—the Nashville Soccer Club.

- In 2017, the Nashville Predators (who ESPN voted as the best franchise in not just the NHL but across all sports[5]) made it to the Stanley Cup finals for the first time.

- In 2018, Amazon announced it will be opening up an Operations Center for Excellence, which will bring a $230 million investment to the city, as well as 5,000 new jobs, with a focus on management and tech roles, with an average predicted salary of $150,000.[6]

- In 2019, Nashville hosted the NFL draft and smashed several records in the process, bringing in a record 600,000 attendees and generating a record $133 million in direct spending for the city; by comparison, Dallas, which hosted the draft in 2018, generated $74 million.[7]

- Also in 2019, Nashville was ranked as having one of the best job markets for major US cities, having the lowest unemployment rate of any top 50 metropolitan statistical area (MSA), at 2.4 percent.[8]

While Nashville's achievements might shock outsiders, they're no surprise to Nashville's residents. Nashville has certainly evolved, but more than the city itself, it is the *perception* of the city that has changed. As *Forbes* put it, "Nashville's current boom isn't so much of a rebirth as it is a Renaissance."[9] Yes, Nashville has a lot to offer right now, but as any Nashvillian can attest, it's *always* had a lot to offer. It's just taken a while for the rest of the country to realize and fully appreciate it. As locals, we love our city and have known that feeling for as long as we've been here.

This shift in perception is due in part to a change in media portrayals. One of the most illustrative examples of this is the stark differences between Robert Altman's 1975 film *Nashville* and the 2012 ABC TV series *Nashville*.

Nashville's Image Evolution: Rural Backwater to Progressive Cosmopolis

Robert Altman may be best known for his film *M*A*S*H*, which inspired the TV show by the same name, but *Nashville* is considered his masterpiece. In the words of critic Roger Ebert, "After I saw it, I felt more alive. I felt

I understood more about people. I felt somehow wiser. It's that good a movie."[10] *Nashville* received 11 Golden Globe nominations and 3 Oscar nods, including nominations for Best Picture and Best Director and a win for Best Original Song ("I'm Easy" by Keith Carradine, which also won a Golden Globe).[11] The acclaim continues today. In 2017, the film was ranked number 59 on the American Film Institute's 100 Years, 100 Movies, 10th Anniversary Edition List.[12]

Though *Nashville* enjoyed commercial and critical success, not everyone was a fan. The film was widely despised by the mainstream country music community. Many artists, especially Nashville natives, believed Altman's masterwork ridiculed their talent, sincerity, and the city itself, perpetuating negative and false stereotypes. After the local premiere of the film in Nashville, Minnie Pearl, a familiar and beloved face at the Grand Ole Opry, kept her comments brief: "It was interesting. Sure is good to see you tonight."[13] Ronnie Milsap, who was in the midst of a career that would produce 35 number 1 country hits and win 6 Grammys, said, "I've seen a lot of movies in my day, and this is one of them."[14] Despite the tongue-in-cheek southern diplomacy, the message was clear: this was a movie by and for outsiders; it was not a true picture of Nashville.

Despite having an ensemble cast, with 24 main characters, *Nashville* failed to represent the diverse complexity of Nashvillians. Nearly all the characters of the film were in the country music or gospel industry, and the majority were portrayed as unsophisticated yokels. Many argue that the film perpetuated an image of the South as a rural, backward place of rednecks and simpletons. For those who loved the city and had a vision of building Nashville into a booming cosmopolitan center, the film was the ultimate slap in the face. It was also ironic that those portraying Nashville as a place of ignorance were in fact the ignorant ones, creating an anachronistic, inaccurate picture of the city.

That was how Nashville was framed in 1975. Flash-forward to 2012, to the ABC TV series *Nashville* created by Callie Khouri (who had actually lived in Nashville), and you get a vastly different perspective. Like Altman's *Nashville*, Khouri's *Nashville* revolves around the music business, with many of the characters being aspiring artists. Truly, no story about Nashville is complete without proper attention paid to music.

However, Khouri's *Nashville* also has strong political and economic themes. The show features political intrigue and paints Nashville as a city of movers and shakers. The characters are not portrayed as country bumpkins but as well-educated, sophisticated, and complex individuals. In addition to talented musicians and songwriters, the show also features savvy businesspeople and shrewd politicians. The show reflects the reality of Nashville as a hotbed of innovators and creators, be they musicians, entrepreneurs, or real estate developers.

The city of Nashville had already begun its climb when Khouri's *Nashville* began airing, but the show played a critical role in framing Nashville as a tastemaker city that sets trends.

Love it or hate it, the show, with its millions of viewers and billboards across the country, did much to change popular perceptions of Nashville. It also didn't hurt Nashville's tourism industry, which has been booming over the past decade, with many giving Khouri's *Nashville* partial credit. As Butch Spyridon, CEO of the Nashville Convention and Visitors Corporation, said, "We couldn't have asked for any better treatment of Nashville."[15]

The way filmmakers and TV producers have told Nashville's story has shaped the popular imagination in terms of what Nashville is like as a city. Just as influential as these fictional portrayals is the news media spin, which has also played a key role in Nashville's rise.

The "It" City: A Marketing Story

There is no single inflection point marking Nashville's meteoric rise in perception from one-trick country music pony to cosmopolitan darling. Rather, there has been steady cultural growth and a series of smart political and community decisions. Ultimately, Nashville is responsible for its own ascent. That said, one single instance that began to change the national media conversation on Nashville was the *New York Times'* 2013 front-page article, "Nashville's Latest Big Hit Could Be the City Itself," which declared Nashville the new "it" city.[16] With that article, Nashville was thrust into the spotlight across the country in a big

xxii ★ *Climbing the Charts: The Ascent of Nashville*

way. From that point on, how Nashville was perceived as a city changed.

The spark of the *New York Times* article soon grew into roaring flames, thanks in large part to smart PR moves by the city. In many ways, the story of Nashville is a story of marketing. For every city that rises or falls, a big factor is how the city is marketed. The key power players of Nashville have capitalized on positive publicity and done a tremendous job of marketing the city. Predators CEO Sean Henry credits Butch Spyridon in particular, saying, "He built a brand for this city."[17] We have crafted an identity for ourselves founded on our unique cultural milieu of music, southern hospitality, and economic dynamism.

This isn't just a story about a city. There are plenty of cities in the United States. Nashville's story is one that is worthy of attention for those interested in a master class in how to grow and market a city in a sustainable, forward-thinking way.

A Unique Perspective: Outsiders Turned Insiders

We are uniquely positioned to tell the story of Nashville's dramatic transformation because we can give both the insiders' and the outsiders' perspective. Like so many others, we are Nashville immigrants, having moved here near the turn of the millennium. We love this city even more because we *chose* it. The fact that we've lived elsewhere also gives us greater context for how Nashville ranks in the grand scheme of things.

Though none of us was born in Nashville, we are all from the Upland South, hailing from Tennessee or Kentucky. We work and live here. We are entrepreneurs, investors, and citizens here. We are a part of the community. Nashville is our *home*. We are Nashvillians, down to the core, and our lives are wrapped up in the city.

Both professionally and personally, we have been perfectly situated to observe and participate in the city's growth. For many years, local ordinances restricted new residential developments downtown. Once the laws changed to allow for new construction, Angie and Brandon were among the first to purchase condos in downtown. As pioneers in Nashville's urban living experiment, they have been firsthand witnesses to the downtown rejuvenation.

Professionally, all three of us previously worked at one of the city's premier law firms, Bass, Berry & Sims. We are now partners at Lockeland Law Group, PLC, and Wagon Wheel Title, a boutique title and escrow services firm. We are also investors and have built and owned multiple commercial and residential spaces. Our office is just a mile and a half from downtown, in East Nashville, giving us a front-row seat to the rise of East Nashville and a finger on the city's heartbeat. Plus, working in the real estate space, we are intimately familiar with the city's growth and development. If a new development project pops up in Nashville, we're among the first to know.

Ultimately, we're stakeholders in this city. We care what happens to it. We are proud of all that Nashville has accomplished, but even more than most, we're looking to the future and what comes next for Nashville.

Still Climbing the Charts

Nearly a decade ago, Mayor Karl Dean said, "It's good to be Nashville right now."[18] His words are as true today as they ever were.

When it comes to Nashville, you don't need to worry about whether you've missed the boat because we're still climbing the charts. The changes in Nashville that make us so special are only accelerating. In fact, we fully expect some of the information in this book to be out of date within months of publication. We see that as a good thing because it means we're still growing. Ultimately, while the specific facts and statistics will change, the higher-level themes and narrative of the city will remain constant. One of those integral themes is that each year, we continue to set our sights higher. As Butch Spyridon said, "We don't ever spend much time looking backward…we try to spend 90 percent of our time looking forward, 'how do we keep climbing that mountain?'"[19]

Nashville isn't going to be giving up its world-class status anytime soon. If you've been thinking about moving to Nashville, doing business here, or visiting, now is the perfect time. We hope that the following pages will give you a closer look inside what we believe is the most wonderful city in the world. So put on your favorite record, sit back, relax, and read on.

Wagon Wheel Title: The Storybehind the Name

When we left our law firm to start Wagon Wheel, we knew we wanted our company's name to be something iconic that reflected Nashville's rich history. Our office is just a few blocks from Woodland Studios, so we figured it should be related to music. At the time of our founding, "Wagon Wheel" (the Old Crow Medicine Show version) was Angie's favorite song. Plus, the imagery of a wheel made sense. As attorneys, we are at the center of the real estate transaction process, connecting all the different spokes.

"Wagon Wheel" is a great representation of Nashville. The evolution of the song captures the music ecosystem in Nashville that looks to the past for inspiration while making something fresh and current. "Wagon Wheel" began with the obscure 1973 western film *Pat Garrett and Billy the Kid*. Bob Dylan had his first film role in this movie and wrote the soundtrack. "Wagon Wheel" did not actually appear in the movie, but an unfinished, unedited outtake of the song—then entitled "Rock Me, Mama"—was released on a bootleg version of the movie's soundtrack.

Ketch Secor, of Old Crow Medicine Show, got his hands on one of these bootleg recordings and became obsessed with the song. The song was really just a sketch at the time, with some chords and lyric fragments. Secor couldn't get the tune out of his head, though, and more than two decades after Dylan first started the song, Secor wrote verses to complete it. Old Crow Medicine Show began performing the song, and it took off. When they decided to license and release the song in 2004, they worked out a copyright agreement that listed both Dylan and Secor as 50-50 cowriters.

Then, about a decade later, Darius Rucker heard a student performance of the song at his daughter's school and fell in love with it. He decided to record it, and in 2013, the song became a number one country hit.

From obscure outtake almost lost on the cutting room floor to bluegrass hit to national earworm, "Wagon Wheel" has undergone a remarkable transformation that epitomizes more than just the music of Nashville. From real estate developers to chefs to entrepreneurs, Nashvillians embrace the past but treat it like a living thing that can evolve. Like jazz artists, we are always looking for ways to change and improvise to create something new and special.

Today, we cannot imagine a better name for our company than Wagon Wheel Title. However, we must admit that at the beginning, our name was a disadvantage. The higher echelon legal community didn't take us as seriously as they would have if we'd chosen a more traditional name. At the time, we actually shared our name with a bar—the alcoholic kind, not the legal kind. But instead of taking the easy, conventional route of stringing our names together, we did what felt right to us. That is the Nashville way. Just as Nashville has found success while remaining true to its roots, so have we. Now that we have some name recognition, people love that we're Wagon Wheel Title instead of Lawless, Miller & Morris.

Once, because of our name, some Canadian tourists even stopped by to visit. They'd heard that Darius Rucker had recorded "Wagon Wheel" in our office. (He didn't, but the Canadians had a great time visiting us anyway.) We're probably the only title and escrow company that has attracted tourists!

PART I

★

TRENDING UP
A Portrait of Nashville

CHAPTER 1

NASHVILLE NOW

In a relatively short amount of time, Nashville has transformed from the country's "biggest small town" into the "Now City." Metro Nashville is currently home to about 1.9 million people, with projections of 2.5 million people living in the Nashville area by 2040.[20] In 2016, Nashville gained a net 69 new people each day on average, and just a year later, in 2017, the city gained an average of 100 new residents every day, primarily due to people moving to the city.[21] Per *Forbes*' 2018 list, Nashville is the seventh-fastest growing American city, just behind Las Vegas and just ahead of Austin.[22] (For context in just how much these changes have been accelerating, in 2017, Nashville was only number 20 on *Forbes*' list of fastest-growing cities.[23])

With such rapid growth, Nashville has needed to learn how to handle the growing pains that come along with a city's development. Our recent hosting of the NFL draft is a great example of how we've managed to navigate these challenges.

The Cherry Tree Crisis: A "Both/And" Mentality

Here in Nashville, we love football. (Go Titans!) Naturally, people were excited for Nashville to host the NFL Draft.

With the draft, not only would we get a front-row seat to one of the biggest football events of the year, but the draft would also bring in a nice chunk of change, with an estimated 100,000 visitors and $125 million economic impact.[24] What more could you want? Well, if you were a Nashvillian, you wanted all of the above without anyone laying a finger on your beloved cherry trees.

A few weeks before the draft, it was announced that 21 cherry trees in downtown Nashville would be removed to make room for a temporary stage for the event. Some of the trees would be transplanted, but some would be cut down and turned into mulch. The announcement could not have been more poorly timed. The cherry trees were just beginning to bloom, and the annual Cherry Blossom Festival was two weeks away.

Nashvillians weren't having it. The Loraxes of Nashville jumped to the trees' defense, with 66,000 people signing an online petition to stop the trees' removal.[25]

At this point, there's nothing special about this story. This happens all the time: sacrifices are made in the name of economic improvement. Trees might make a city beautiful, but money is what keeps it alive. Twenty-one trees in exchange for $125 million is a fair price—that's about $6 million per tree. But here's where Nashville is different: when the people protested cutting down the trees, *the city listened*. People first found out about the trees on a Friday evening, and by that following Monday, the day the trees were originally slated to be cut down, the city had revised its plans. Instead of removing 21 trees, they would remove just 10 trees, all of which would be transplanted elsewhere, not turned to mulch. Plus, the Nashville Convention and Visitors Corporation and the NFL would donate 100 cherry trees each—200 total—to Metro Parks.[26]

According to some, the uproar over the trees highlighted a growing rift between "old" and "new" Nashville: the "it" city versus "our" city.[27] But part of Nashville's secret sauce is that we aren't one or the other; we are *both*. This isn't a story about old fighting new; it's a story about compromise, about Nashvillians standing up for their city so that we can continue to grow while retaining what made us special in the first place. In a time when red tape and government bureaucracy make the wheels of change grind slowly, it's also a story about how Nashville gets things done. A lot can happen here in just a single weekend.

In this battle between cherry trees and the NFL, the clear winner was Nashville itself. The draft ended up attracting not 100,000 but *600,000* visitors and brought in $133 million in direct spending, with total economic impact estimated at $224 million.[28] It was such a success that the city hopes to leverage it to secure a 2026 World Cup hosting spot as well as a future Super Bowl. The city undoubtedly came out ahead, with a cherry on top in the form of 200 additional cherry trees for the city.

A big part of Nashville's secret sauce—what makes Nashville *Nashville*—is the "both/and" mentality epitomized by the cherry trees controversy. We aren't willing to take one or the other—NFL draft or cherry trees, economic growth or cultural development, big city or small town. We want it all, and we fight for it.

The result is that the city is transforming not into a metropolis, but a *cosmopolis*. Being cosmopolitan means that we are "citizens of the world." We aren't just a city with a large population and economic opportunity. We are a worldly city—a city founded on culture. Since Nashville's beginnings, the city has been defined by its huge creative class. We're a city of makers. That creative spirit is woven into the fabric of the city and has been a major contributor to the city's recent growth.

Cultural Factors Contributing to Nashville's Growth

A city without culture is a city without identity. People are naturally drawn to cities with strong cultures because culture is what transforms a city from a network of buildings to a home. Nashville has a unique culture founded on music, art, and sports.

Anyone who knows anything about Nashville knows it's a city of music. Nashville's soul and edge is music. It's the undertone that flows through the entire city.

Nashville is known specifically for country music, but our live and recorded music scene extends beyond country, as evidenced by Kings of Leon, Nashville's alternative rock pioneers, and Jack White's Third Man Records, which is a nexus for indie rock and Americana artists. We also have a highly regarded $123.5 million symphony hall that opened in 2006.

Nashville's music scene is a blend of established heavy hitters and up-and-coming artists. In the 1990s, Lower Broadway's honky-tonk strip underwent a revival, and there's now a synergy between the big performance venues like Bridgestone Arena and the honky-tonks. Many artists will perform an arena show and then hop across the street to a place like Tootsie's Orchid Lounge to give a more intimate performance. As a result, you never know who you will see performing in Nashville. You can go to a tiny hole-in-the-wall to see an unknown band, and then Pink or Metallica will come out on stage. It's an incredible experience and far more common than you'd expect. Just about every Nashville native has at least one story like this. (Brandon and Angie, for instance, were both fortunate enough to catch a surprise REM performance at Mercy Lounge, a small venue with a standing room capacity of 500.)

Music is Nashville's soul, but the culture extends beyond music to include festivals, galleries, and museums. Taking advantage of nearly year-round beautiful weather, Nashville is host to outdoor festivals celebrating everything from tomatoes and wine to, of course, music. We have been ranked as having the fifth most vibrant arts community among large cities in the United States.[29] The city has numerous monthly neighborhood art crawls as well as the Frist Museum, a contemporary art museum that opened in 2001, and OZ Arts Nashville, a contemporary art performance center. (For more on Nashville's art scene, see Chapter 12.)

Our most iconic piece of art is the world's only full-scale reproduction of the Parthenon, with a 42-foot-tall golden statue of Athena—the tallest indoor sculpture in the Western world.[30] Another artwork favored by locals and tourists alike is the bronze *Musica* statue on Music Row. The statue's dancing figures are typically nude, but on game days, you will find them adorned with local sports jerseys. In response to COVID-19, they were even bedecked with their own face masks.

Accolades and Awards[31]

- Nashville ranked number 15 on *U.S. News & World Report's* 125 Best Places to Live in the USA (as of April 2019).

- Nashville appeared on *Forbes Travel Guide*'s list of the Top 20 Destinations for 2020.

- Nashville was named *Sports Business Journal*'s Best Sports City in 2019.

- Bridgestone Arena was named Arena of the Year, and Ryman Auditorium was named Theatre of the Year by *Pollstar* in February 2018.

- *Southern Living* named Nashville one of the South's Best Food Cities 2019.

- In June 2018, TripAdvisor named Nashville as one of America's Best Cities for Beer and Brewery Tours and one of the 10 Best Foodie Vacations in America.

- In July 2019, Nashville hit number 6 on Cvent's Top 50 Meeting Destinations in the U.S.

As demonstrated by the way we festoon the *Musica* statue, the city has a vibrant sports culture. We have a trifecta of professional sports teams with the NFL's Tennessee Titans, the NHL's Nashville Predators, and the MLS's Nashville Soccer Club. There's also been talk of MLB expansion, with Nashville mentioned as a potential location. Right now, the city's focus is establishing the new soccer team, but who knows what the future holds? Our trio might become a quartet with a baseball team added to our list of achievements. (For more on all things sports in Nashville, see Chapter 10.)

Nashville's culture provides the city's personality and sets Nashville apart from other cities. A city typically can't run on culture alone, though. Nashville's robust economy has been a key factor driving the city's growth.

Economic Factors Contributing to Nashville's Growth

Nashville economic stability draws many people to the city. This recent growth isn't just about how many more people there are but *who* those people are. The people coming to live in Nashville are ones that help an economy grow. The city's population skews young, with a median age of 36.5—prime working age.[32] The big reason why? Our universities. Nashville has a lot of higher-education students (123,000 in 2016), and a strong majority of them—60

percent—stay in Nashville after graduating.[33] For good reason, too: in 2019, SmartAsset ranked Nashville as the second-best city for college grads, based on a variety of metrics measuring affordability, fun, and jobs.[34] It's a mutually beneficial situation, with the college grads getting a great place to live and the city getting tens of thousands of talented new workers pouring into the labor force. Companies are drawn to Nashville because of the talent here. They provide job opportunities, which then attract more talented young professionals. As long as this dynamic continues, it will feed on itself, making Nashville a hotbed of innovation and business success.

Nashville is a city of opportunity, with one of the lowest unemployment rates in the country at 2.4 percent.[35] All three of us chose Nashville for its career opportunities. The kinds of jobs we wanted weren't available in our hometowns, but were available here. It's true that we could have gone to other cities, but remember that Nashville also has the benefit of a strong culture. It's a great place to work *and* live. (After graduating from Harvard Law School, Brandon actually chose Nashville over such heavy hitters as New York, Boston, and Washington, DC. At the time, his classmates thought he'd lost all sense, but he hasn't regretted it once.)

Nashville's economy is a robust, multidimensional tapestry woven of music, healthcare, tourism and hospitality, manufacturing, technology, publishing, and higher education.

8 ★ *Climbing the Charts: The Ascent of Nashville*

By having a multivariate economic base, Nashville is protected from dips or temporary setbacks in a single industry, and it can attract a wide array of organizations. The city's business environment is discussed further in Chapter 4, with specific chapters dedicated to music (Chapter 6) and healthcare (Chapter 7).

On top of Nashville's strong culture and economy, astute political maneuvers have helped to elevate Nashville to the city we know today.

Political Factors Contributing to Nashville's Growth

Arguably the best political move Nashville has ever made is the consolidation of the city and county governments in 1963, which is discussed further in Chapter 8.

The merger unified Nashville into a single force as a city and exponentially increased Nashville's apparent size as a city. The Nashville Metropolitan Statistical Area (MSA) covers about 530 square miles. For comparison, New York City covers only about 300 square miles. Many of the businesses and developments we will discuss in this book lie outside Nashville's urban core, but because of the government merger, anything that falls within the MSA directly benefits the city. This is part of what has allowed Nashville to keep a small-town feel while being able to compete economically as a large city.

Additionally, the importance of dealing with only one regulatory body can't be overstated, especially for real estate developers. Instead of having to navigate the regulations, taxes, and approval of two different layers of government—both city and state—in Nashville, you only have one governing body to work with. This allows Nashville to be more efficient and aggressive with its decisions.

Since the 1963 merger, Nashville has continued to make smart political decisions. To an outsider, some of the choices might have seemed risky, but Nashville believes in itself enough to invest in itself. Time and time again, Nashville has invested money into large development projects in order to drive the city's growth.

In the late 1990s, Nashville invested in not just one, but two stadiums. The first was the Bridgestone Arena. Like in the movie *Field of Dreams*, Nashville took a "build it, and they will come" approach with the arena, in the hopes of attracting an NBA or NHL team. It was a gutsy move that caused some worry as the arena sat empty, but it ultimately paid off when we snagged the Nashville Predators hockey team. Around the same time, when Bridgestone Arena's future was still uncertain, the city also committed to building a new football stadium in order to secure the Tennessee Titans NFL franchise.

Even during the 2008 downturn, when many cities were tightening their purse strings, Nashville was looking to the future. At the time, Nashville had two convention centers, but we kept losing events to Las Vegas. It seemed a bit audacious to think that we could compete with Las Vegas, but the city planner, Rick Bernhardt, was convinced that if we simply built a large enough convention center, we could pull in more convention business. Construction on the Music City Center began during the economic downturn, which was actually the perfect time to start because construction completed just as the economy entered an upswing. Nashville then had a brand-new convention center ready to go at a time when no one else did. And it came in under budget!

The city planner ended up being 100 percent correct, and Nashville has hosted a number of impressive gatherings since the new downtown convention center was built. Many of the conventions have been particularly noteworthy for developers, like the International Roofing Expo and the Urban Land Institute convention, which attracted leading developers from all over the country. We'll likely see even more conventions in the future, as we recently hosted the Professional Convention Management Association's convention, which brought the country's leading convention planners to the city.[36]

Nashville is willing to step up to the plate when it comes to investing in the city, and the city's faith in itself has paid off handsomely, with home run after home run of new real estate developments, as discussed in Chapter 5.

Underdog Mentality

Nashville has plenty to be proud of, but we tend to operate from an underdog mentality. There are two reasons for this: (1) we *are* an underdog because we're always punching above our weight, and (2) nobody expects the underdog.

In Nashville, we understand that often, not being number one is actually better than being number one. If you're *talking* about being at the top, you're probably not at the top. City leader Butch Spyridon said, "As soon as you start self-proclaiming yourself as the 'it' city, you take your eye off the ball. Fame is fleeting. You have to earn it and re-earn it."[37] As soon as you stop striving to be the best, someone else will overtake you. Nashville would rather be the city doing the overtaking instead of the one getting overtaken. Our underdog mentality helps us to retain this striver energy. It's like the brilliant marketing slogan for Avis, the *second* biggest car rental company: "We Try Harder." We don't waste time congratulating ourselves for being the best; we're too busy trying harder.

When Nashville wants to do something, we look to the best-of-class to set the bar. Wherever they do it best, that's the city we look to. When we wanted to build a new convention center, we didn't look at Austin's convention center; we looked at Las Vegas. When we want to throw a New Year's celebration, we don't look at how Charlotte does it; we look at how they do it in Times Square. We aren't trying to compete with cities on our level in terms of size and GDP; we're striving to compete with the best cities in the world. This approach often makes us the underdog, but being the underdog allows us to hide under the radar. Others come to realize that they've been underestimating us only after it's too late.

Coda

Nashville is a unique city. The secret sauce that makes the city tick is a whiskey-smooth blend of culture, economic fundamentals, and smart politics. To be understood, this secret sauce needs to be described and experienced rather than analyzed through stats because so much of what has driven the city to new heights is intangible—it's the city's personality and attitude.

In the next chapter, we'll provide an overview of the city's history to explain how the city we know and love today was formed.

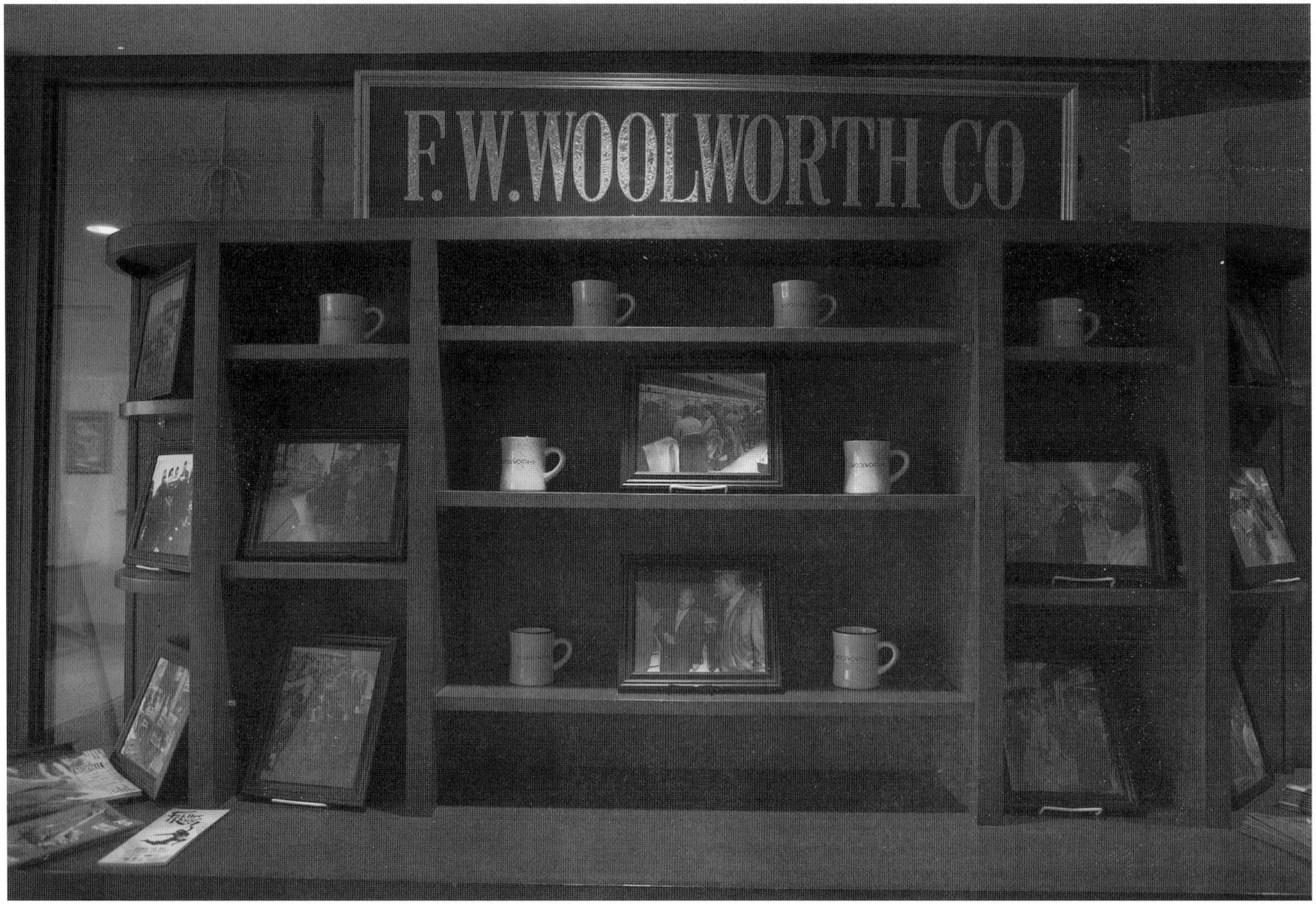
F. W. WOOLWORTH CO

CHAPTER 2

A BIT OF HISTORY

Many seem to think that Nashville's history began with the *Grand Ole Opry*. Indeed, the *Grand Ole Opry* was a critical inflection point in the city's identity.

The *Grand Ole Opry* is the longest-running live radio show in history (with another Nashville show, Ernest Tubb's *Midnite Jamboree*, being credited with the second-place spot, though this may be up to some debate).[38] The *Grand Ole Opry*'s roots trace back to 1925 and the WSM radio station.[39] WSM was (and still is) a clear-channel radio station, which means broadcasting on a frequency that nobody else is broadcasting on. However far WSM's signal could travel, that was how far people could hear their broadcast. Thirty-eight states and even sections of Canada could tune into this little AM radio station out of Nashville.

For many, the *Grand Ole Opry* and the *Midnite Jamboree* were their first and only exposure to Nashville. Since both these shows were known for country music, thus did Nashville's soul become inextricably linked to country music, despite the fact that the city had a vibrant and diverse music scene at the time. While Nashville fostered many genres internally—jazz, R&B, gospel, pop, big bands, and more—it was primarily country music that was exported out of the city.

The *Grand Ole Opry*'s popularity spiked in the 1940s. Until that point, the live performances took place at a variety of venues—whoever would have them—but starting in 1943, the *Grand Ole Opry* found a more permanent home: the Ryman Auditorium on Lower Broadway.[40] The Ryman Auditorium, "the Mother Church of Country Music," would host the *Grand Ole Opry* for the next 30 years, until the program moved to the Grand Ole Opry House in 1974.[41] Without the *Grand Ole Opry*, the Ryman Auditorium fell into decline and disuse, but it has since experienced a revitalization. Today, the *Grand Ole Opry* returns to broadcast from the Ryman Auditorium for part of each winter.

Fun Fact

Today, WSM is synonymous with country music to many people. In fact, it actually stands for "We Shield Millions"—the motto of National Life & Casualty (L&C), the one-time Nashville-based insurance company that established the Grand Ole Opry program.[42] Much like today, even in the 1920s, Nashville culture benefited from corporate sponsorship and philanthropy. In Nashville, commerce and music have always intersected in interesting ways.

Another fun fact: The L&C Tower, completed in 1957, was Nashville's first modern skyscraper and the Southeast's tallest commercial structure, at 409 feet and 31 stories, until the mid-1960s.[43]

---

14 ★ Climbing the Charts: The Ascent of Nashville

History of the Ryman Auditorium

The Ryman Auditorium began with Captain Tom Ryman, who ran riverboats up and down the Cumberland River. There was money to be made hauling freight, but more than freight, liquor was the golden goose. Ryman's true fortune came from taking a cut of liquor sales, both on board his riverboats and in the ports where the boats laid anchor.

As legend goes, in 1885, Ryman attended one of Sam Jones's tent revivals and was so moved by the sermon that he swore to change his ways. He also pledged to build Jones the biggest, grandest church ever.

Ryman raised money and poured much of his own wealth into the church, and after seven long years, the Union Gospel Tabernacle was completed in 1892.[44] It was indeed a very big, very grand church—so big and grand in fact that it could not support itself as a church. In a twist of irony, the church that Ryman had built as a testament to his conversion into a teetotaling, God-fearing man became a venue for honky-tonk music and other "unholy" events.

Throughout Ryman's life, people tried to name the building after him, but he always resisted. Following his death, the people finally got their way, and the Union Gospel Tabernacle became the Ryman Auditorium.

Arguably, the *Grand Ole Opry* put Nashville on the map and on people's radar, but it was a small slice of the whole. Nashville's history as a nationally recognized city may have begun with the *Grand Ole Opry*, but its true history began far earlier.

Nashville's Beginnings

Like most places in America, Nashville was first inhabited by Native Americans. The earliest European settlers arrived in the seventeenth century, establishing a trading post along the Cumberland River in what would become Nashville in 1689. Approximately a century later, in 1779, James Robertson and John Donelson founded Fort Nashborough, named after Francis Nash, a brigadier general in the American Revolutionary War. At that time, the settlement was still part of the state of North Carolina, so it was by an act of the North Carolina legislature that the town was officially created and named Nashville in 1784.[45]

Most early towns developed as a consequence of a strong geographical location, like easy access to a river thoroughfare, an ocean, or a large harbor. In Nashville's case, the town was born out of its location on the Cumberland River, a major tributary of the Ohio River. Musician Ketch Secor, founder of Old Crow Medicine Show, believes the river is still the heart of Nashville. While the city has grown and changed, moving outward and upward, the river has remained the same, always flowing forward. As Ketch said, "If you look at the Cumberland River, nothing's changed."[46]

In Nashville's early history, the city was like the river: slow moving but steady. By 1800, the population of the "city" had climbed to 345 residents.[47] Despite its small size, the city had recently been named the state capital, when Tennessee became its own state in 1796. Several other cities would serve as temporary capitals, but in 1843, Nashville was selected as the permanent capital, beating out nearby Charlotte, Tennessee, by one vote. Today, Charlotte is a small, largely unknown town of around a thousand people, while the Metro Nashville area has grown to nearly two million people. Perhaps the cities' fates would have been reversed if Charlotte had instead been chosen as the capital.

Modern infrastructure has made Nashville into a central trade hub, but in its early years, it was a tiny settlement nestled in a huge wilderness. It originally developed as a cotton center and a river port, and later, a railroad hub. Slowly, it rose to become the commercial center of Tennessee. It was largely Nashville's commercial backbone that defined its role in the Civil War and its rise in the war's aftermath.

Nashville in the Civil War

In the Civil War, Tennessee was last out, first in—it was the last state to secede from the Union, on June 8, 1861, and the first state to rejoin it, on July 24, 1866. The state was fairly evenly split on the decision to leave in the first place. The western part of the state wanted to secede, while the eastern part wanted to stay in the Union. Nashville was caught right in the middle, with a mix of both viewpoints.

Something everyone in Nashville could agree on was that they still wanted to make money, war or not. With the introduction of railroads, Nashville had become a manufacturing center. During the war, many of Nashville's factories were converted into munitions manufacturing plants for the South. The North quickly figured out that taking Nashville would provide a key strategic victory. It would significantly hamper the South's manufacturing capability, and it would help them to control transportation, since Nashville was a railroad hub and shipping port.

Accordingly, the North attacked Nashville in 1862. Within three days, the city had given up, becoming the first large Confederate city captured by the North.[48] Following the occupation, the mayor at the time urged Nashvillians to continue with their normal lives: "I, therefore, request that everybody get back to business."[49] Though the occupation was not without its trials and tribulations, compared to other Southern cities, Nashville suffered little. Throughout its occupation, the North heavily fortified Nashville. Today, if you drive around the city, you can spot historical markers identifying various earthworks and ruins left over from these fortifications.

There were no major attempts by the Confederacy to reclaim Nashville until 1864, with the Battle of Nashville. This two-day battle resulted in one of the Confederacy's most important strategic defeats. The defeat marked the end of large-scale fighting in the Western theater.

While other Southern cities were economically devastated by the war, Nashville escaped relatively unscathed, thanks in large part to its manufacturing capabilities. In the decades following the war, Nashville rebounded quickly, experiencing growth in population and industry.

Civil Rights Era

Like much of the country, especially in the South, Nashville's history contains the black spot of segregation and racial discrimination. However, as the country evolved throughout the civil rights era, Nashville was on the leading edge of the change. Nashville produced important civil rights leaders like John Lewis (a US congressman for Georgia until his death in 2020) and Diane Nash, and notably, several of the city's business and political leaders eventually came out in support of the drive for civil rights.

In general, though there was resistance to integration in Nashville, it was not on the same overwhelming level as seen elsewhere in the country. The city was already progressive, so it did not experience clashes as violent as those in Southern peer cities in Alabama and Mississippi. The large university base, including Vanderbilt, Fisk University, and Tennessee State University (TSU), was pro-integration and played an integral role in pushing the city forward. The students of Fisk and TSU, historically Black universities, were especially critical in the fight for civil rights.

In early February 1960, the first influential sit-ins of the civil rights movement took place in Greensboro, North Carolina, sparking a broader sit-in movement across the country. Sit-ins were a passive, nonviolent form of protest in which Black activists would sit at segregated lunch counters. Though the sit-ins were passive and nonviolent on the side of the protestors, white citizens were decidedly less passive, verbally berating and threatening the Black activists. Thus, planning sit-ins and withstanding that level of abuse required a great deal of planning and training. Civil rights activists in Nashville had begun preparation as early as 1958.[50] When the Greensboro sit-ins occurred, they did not want to wait any longer. They sprang into action, beginning sit-ins just a week and a half following the Greensboro ones.

A major focus of the sit-ins were the lunch counters at local Nashville department stores, like Woolworth and Kress. Black people were allowed to shop at the department stores, but they were prohibited from the lunch counters. Nashville activists had performed early tests at these lunch counters in 1958 to gauge reactions to potential sit-ins. The tests had mixed results. While all activists had been refused service, some of the lunch counters were polite and apologetic about the refusal, while others were derisive.[51]

In 1960, full-scale demonstrations began to take place, with dozens upon dozens of people, largely university students, participating. Over 150 students were arrested, and things reached a boiling point when the home of the lawyer defending many of these people was bombed.[52] The attack triggered a large protest march, with nearly 4,000 participants marching to city hall to confront the mayor, Ben West.[53]

When they reached the courthouse, student leader Diane Nash asked West, "Do you feel it is wrong to discriminate against a person solely on the basis of their race or color?"[54] West agreed in front of all the protestors that yes, it was wrong. Nash pressed on: "Then, mayor, do you recommend that the lunch counters in Nashville be desegregated?"[55] Again, West agreed: yes, they should be desegregated.

The city's political leaders brokered a deal with the city's business leaders, and within three weeks, small groups of Black Nashvillians were eating at the lunch counters.[56]

The achievement marked Nashville as the first major Southern city to desegregate public facilities.[57] Following this victory, Nashville civil rights activists continued to work for greater equality over the years to come. Martin Luther King Jr., who spoke at Fisk University the day after the march, said, "I came to Nashville not to bring inspiration, but to gain inspiration from the great movement that has taken place in this community."[58]

Today, Woolworth, one of the sites of Nashville's first sit-ins, has reopened its lunch counter. It functions as a mini museum, commemorating the efforts of Nashville's Black activists in the civil rights era.

Early Economic Base

As already mentioned, Nashville's early economy was founded largely on manufacturing. Its central location and easy river and railroad access made it a natural hub for shipping and distribution. Then, following World War II, Nashville experienced rapid suburbanization, leading to a boom in schools and other support facilities. Around this same time, the banking and insurance industries grew rapidly.

Interestingly, Nashville established itself early on as a place for innovation and entrepreneurship. The story of Maxwell House coffee is an excellent example of how the city's entrepreneurs were gifted at creating solid products and then crafting compelling marketing messages.

Nashville Innovation: Maxwell House Coffee[59]

Today, in the post-Starbucks era of customizable coffee with a multitude of blends and roasts, *innovative* isn't the word most people would use to describe Maxwell House coffee. However, when John Cheek first crafted the Maxwell House blend in the late nineteenth century, it was indeed innovative.

Cheek was a traveling salesman for a wholesale grocery operation. As the story goes, in 1873, one of his customers asked which of the coffees he sold was best. The question sent Cheek down the path to what would become the Maxwell House blend. He began experimenting with different beans and roasting techniques, in pursuit of the perfect cup of coffee.

Cheek moved to Nashville in 1884, and by 1892, he'd finally succeeded in crafting what he believed to be the perfect coffee blend. Cheek took the new blend to the Maxwell House Hotel, a prestigious hotel in Nashville with such famous guests as Buffalo Bill, Thomas Edison, Henry Ford, Annie Oakley, O. Henry, and seven US presidents.[60] (The hotel is now defunct, having been destroyed by a fire on Christmas night in 1961, but its spirit lives on through the Millennium Maxwell House Hotel, built on a separate site but named after the original hotel.) Cheek gave the hotel 20 pounds of his new blend for free. The hotel happily accepted and used the coffee, but when it ran out a few days later, they switched back to their original supplier. Patrons immediately began complaining. They missed Cheek's smoother, richer blend. The people had spoken, and Maxwell House listened, becoming the exclusive provider for Cheek's new blend.

With partner Maxwell Colbourne, Cheek formed the Nashville Coffee and Manufacturing Company, later renamed the Cheek-Neal Coffee Company. The coffee brand became a well-respected name. At the time, Cheek's blend designed for Maxwell House was known for having highbrow appeal that set it apart from its competition. The company created a variety of blends, though, with lower-cost options as well.

According to legend, in 1907, President Teddy Roosevelt himself had a cup of the Maxwell House blend while in Nashville. Upon finishing the cup, he declared that it was "good to the last drop!" It's uncertain whether he actually uttered these words, but much of good marketing comes down to myth-making. Maxwell House did this skillfully, incorporating this quote in advertising campaigns. Regardless of its origin, the slogan has stood the test of time.

For nearly a hundred years, until the late 1980s, Maxwell House was the highest-selling coffee brand in the United States. (Today, Folgers holds the title.[61]) While Maxwell House got its start in Nashville, it is no longer based here. Maybe if the company had stayed in Nashville, things would have turned out differently.

The Start of "Today's Nashville"

The most important event in shaping the modern economy of Nashville was the founding of Hospital Corporation of America (HCA) in 1968. HCA is now the world's largest operator of hospitals, and it is a big reason Nashville has been called the Silicon Valley of Health Services.

Beyond cementing Nashville as a center of healthcare, HCA also served as the seed for corporate expansion within and into the city. This corporate boom accelerated during Phil Bredesen's terms as mayor, from 1991 to 1999. Bredesen made urban renewal one of his top priorities. Some of his big projects included the Country Music Hall of Fame expansion, the downtown Nashville library, Bridgestone Arena, and Nissan Stadium. Nashville would not be what it is today if not for Bredesen.

Throughout the 1990s and the early 2000s, Nashville was easily the fastest-growing part of the Upland South and was quickly becoming a crossroads of American culture. A key part of Nashville's rise was the revitalization of downtown. In the '70s and '80s, Nashville's downtown, especially the main thoroughfare of Broadway, was a seedy place, filled with drug dealers, drunks, prostitutes, and adult bookstores. In fact, when the original convention center was built downtown in the mid-'80s, they didn't put any windows facing Broadway because they didn't want visitors to witness the gritty honky-tonk strip.

A big contributor to the downtown turnaround was the band BR5-49, featuring Chuck Mead and Jay McDowell. The band was formed in 1993 and began playing at the honky-tonk Robert's Western World. The band had a new sound that was built on the older tradition of rockabilly. In bringing back and updating Nashville's sound from the 1950s, they drew locals back to Broadway, rebuilding the downtown vibe of the '50s. The band gained immediate traction and was soon joined by other young, hip musicians in town. Before long, Broadway left behind its dicey reputation and reverted to its historical status as *the* place to go for music. Today, the honky-tonk strip is a favorite destination for tourists and locals alike. It is at an all-time high in terms of attendance and revenue. Kid Rock recently opened a honky-tonk, and John Rich (of Big & Rich) just paid $19 million for a building he intends to convert into a honky-tonk. In 1985, that building easily could have been bought for under $1 million, despite—or because of—its downtown location.

A number of new civic cornerstones (several of which began during Bredesen's mayoral terms) further encouraged the downtown revival. Nashville welcomed the new millennium with a flurry of completed development projects: in 2001, the Frist Museum opened, the Country Music Hall of Fame underwent a $100 million expansion, and the new downtown library branch opened. In 2006, the Schermerhorn Symphony Center opened, and in 2009, a former parking lot was turned into a green space, and Live on the Green, Nashville's free outdoor music festival, began. These developments elevated Nashville to a new cultural level as a city.

Then, in 2013, Music City Center opened, pumping new streams of revenue into the city's economy. The 2.1-million-square-foot convention center cost $623 million to build. (In comparison, the original downtown convention center, built in the '80s, cost $39.5 million.)[62] The convention center is attached to the Country Music Hall of Fame and included the construction of a $270 million Omni Hotel, with 800 rooms. The whole project was one of the city's largest and most successful investments in itself. It ignited a large convention industry, which in turn sparked a hotel building boom. Just a year after opening, Music City Center catapulted Nashville to the number 3 spot of *USA Today*'s list of top convention cities, as determined by a reader poll.[63] Nashville remains a top choice for conventions, ranking number 6 in Cvent's Top 50 Meeting Destinations in the US in 2019.[64]

Fun Fact

If you're a fan of cotton candy, you have Nashville to thank! Nashvillian candy makers William Morrison and John C. Wharton invented the first electric cotton candy machine in 1897. They premiered it at the 1904 St. Louis World's Fair, where they sold over 68 boxes of their "fairy floss" at the high price of 25 cents apiece, which was approximately half the cost of admission to the fair. "Fairy floss" was eventually renamed "cotton candy," but the machine itself has remained largely the same.[65]

Coda

Though Nashville has changed much as a city, some things have remained the same. Music; strong economic fundamentals, including entrepreneurship; and social progressiveness have always been an integral part of the city. In the next chapter, we'll explore Nashville's open, welcoming community in more detail.

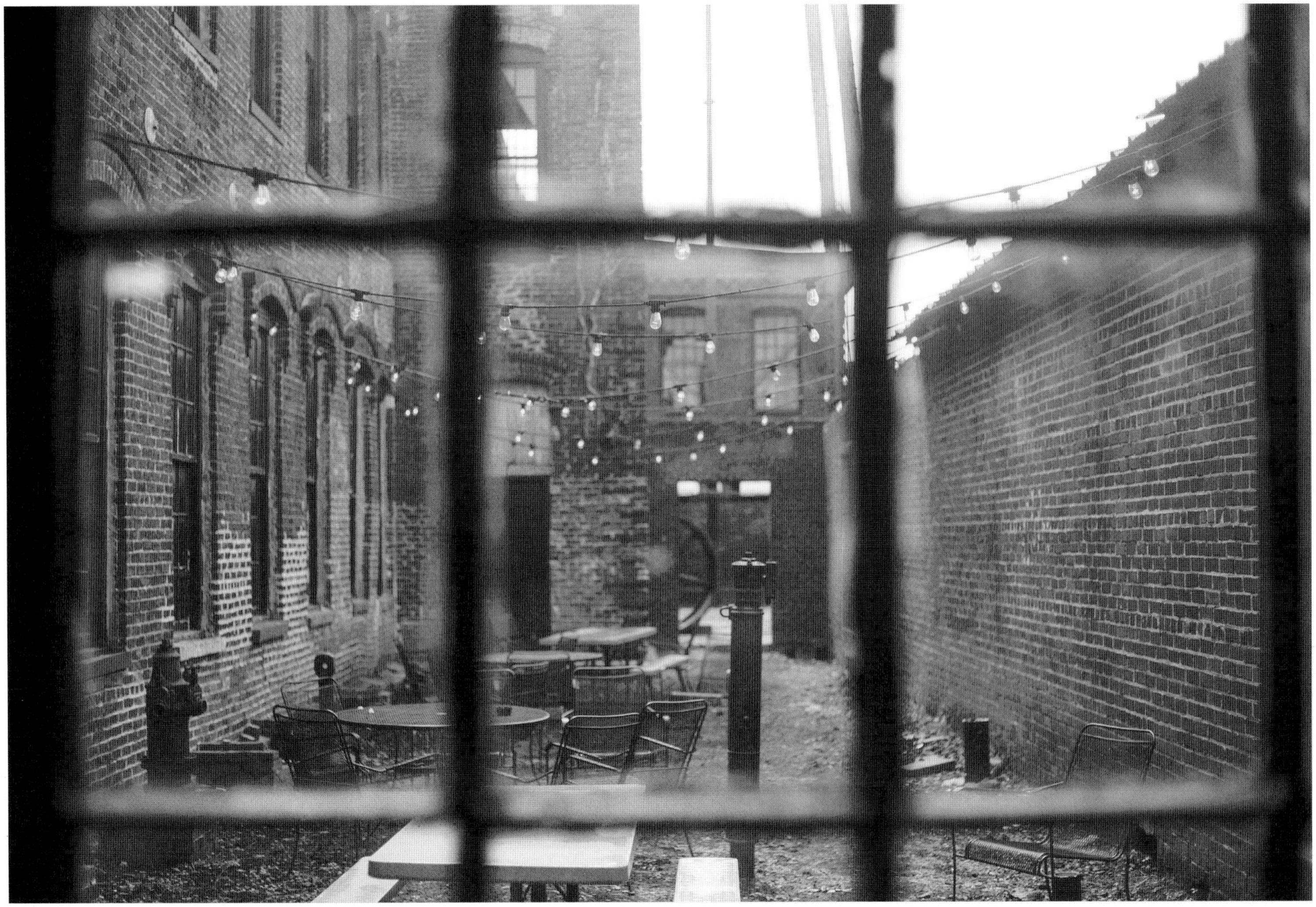

CHAPTER 3

SOUTHERN HOSPITALITY

In 1873–1874, Nashville's Fisk Jubilee Singers traveled to England. At that time, the choir, from the historically Black Fisk University, consisted of nine members, all but two of which were former slaves.[66] The group performed only for integrated audiences. With much of their repertoire revolving around slave spirituals, they were responsible for introducing many to the African American oral music tradition. According to local legend, when they performed for Queen Victoria, she was so impressed by them that she said they must come from the "Music City." (Some say this is the origin of our city nickname, but others argue that the "Music City U.S.A." moniker began with WSM radio announcer Dave Cobb, who popularized the name in the 1950s.[67])

When the Jubilee Singers were formed in 1871, Fisk University was on the brink of bankruptcy. By the end of the group's English tour, they had earned enough to save the university from financial collapse. Today, Fisk University still stands in Nashville, and in 2015, 141 years after their original tour to the queen's country, the group returned to England to perform once more.[68]

Much has changed in Nashville since the chorus's original trip to England, but many things have remained the same. Throughout Nashville's history, music, social progress, and business acumen have been inextricably tied to the city's identity, and these ideals will undoubtedly continue to play a role long in our city's future.

Nashville's Civic and Social Atmosphere

In 2016, Nashville was voted friendliest city in America by a Travel & Leisure poll.[69] *Huff-Post* called the result unsurprising, considering that "Nashville has music to fill your soul, BBQ to fill your belly, a fun nightlife and undeniable Southern charm." We don't take ourselves too seriously, so we tend to be laidback, fun, and approachable.

The South has a reputation for superficial politeness—the "Bless your heart" syndrome—but Nashville's kindness runs deep. People in Nashville are friendly enough to speak to you but also direct enough to say what's actually on their mind. The result is an authentic, open atmosphere.

Nashvillians are proud of their home and eager to share it with visitors and newcomers. Even the people who complain about the occasional disruption progress has brought—like the traffic-dodging pedal taverns—are quick to recommend their favorite restaurants and spots around town.

This friendliness has made Nashville welcoming to outsiders, which is a major reason the city is growing so quickly. It seems that out of every 10 people you meet, only 1 will have grown up in Nashville. Outsiders come to the city and feel so welcomed and comfortable that they make Nashville their home. Once you come to Nashville and put down roots, you're a Nashvillian, no matter where you came from before. Natives and transplants are embraced equally. In fact, since the merger of the city and county governments, roughly half of our mayors have been Nashville natives and half Nashville transplants.

Nashville's social establishment largely consists of native inhabitants of upper-crust neighborhoods like Belle Meade. Belle Meade has long been one of the wealthiest neighborhoods in the United States. There's a connotation and a reputation associated with this blue-blood area, but these "social elite" of Nashville do not make an effort to be exclusive. Rather than trying to control the city, they seek to support it, using their wealth to further the city's arts community, charities, and sports franchises. Because they wish to build the city up, they readily welcome outsiders who will inject new life into the city, especially entrepreneurs and developers. Our unique class of social elite has helped develop Nashville into a cultural center with big-city amenities while letting it remain a livable city whose character is defined not by its wealthiest residents but by its working inhabitants.

Like any city, Nashville has its own culture and atmosphere. Thus, some small measure of culture shock is unavoidable. However, most immigrants and "outsiders" (perhaps better called soon-to-be insiders) find the transition relatively easy, even if they come from a major urban center like Chicago.

Former mayor Megan Barry, whose mayoral term and resignation will be discussed in Chapter 8, summed Nashville up well: "Nashville is a place where people say 'Here's what can I do for you,' instead of asking what you can do for me, and it shows. We are the friendliest, warmest, and most welcoming city in America. We're diverse. We're progressive. But we're also pro-business. We still have that small-town feel with lots of small businesses that are bringing their creativity and passion here, and it creates this unique culture that you don't find anywhere else in America."[70]

Nashville benefits from the steady influx of new, diverse people, but how and why do those people come to Nashville in the first place?

How and Why Do People Come to Nashville?

According to *U.S. News & World Report*, Nashville is number 15 for best places to live, based on the quality of life, job market, value of living there, and people's desire to live there.[71] People have any number of reasons for wanting to make Nashville their home, including the culture, the cheaper cost of living, the job prospects, the central location, and the laidback pace.

A lot of people first come to Nashville as tourists or students and become bewitched by the city. With Nashville embedded in their brains, they decide to move or build second homes here. This is what happened with Angie and Steve. They came to Nashville to attend Vanderbilt University, fell in love with the city, and stayed.

As stated by Courtney Ross, chief economic development officer for the Nashville Area Chamber of Commerce, "Our universities provide a powerful local pipeline of young and seasoned talent, both homegrown and imported from all over the nation and the globe, to continually fuel the business and industry engines already thriving here, and once those college graduates discover the region's energy, dynamic economy, job opportunities, and unique quality of living, 60 percent of them stay." Vanderbilt is a key driver of that talent, and Belmont University is also experiencing increasing prominence in national rankings, recently tying for the number 6 spot for *U.S. News & World Report*'s 2019 Regional Universities South list.[72]

Millennials and Gen Zers are especially attracted to the city. In 2019, SmartAsset ranked Nashville the third-best city for young professionals (tied with Denver),[73] and Nashville boasts a low unemployment rate of 2.4 percent.[74] As such, younger people are confident of finding work here. According to Alex Hughes, Vice President of Talent, Attraction, and Retention for the Nashville Area Chamber of Commerce, "One of the main things that brings young professionals here is the industry diversity."[75] We have strong healthcare, manufacturing, music, entrepreneurship, and tech opportunities in the city.

The economic opportunities of the city also attract businesspeople, developers, and investors. Nashville is a hotbed for development and construction, ranking eighth in the country for greatest number of tower cranes, with twice as many cranes as Boston and Phoenix combined.[76] Investment has also been rising rapidly across the state. In 2016, investors from New York and Boston invested over $420 million in Tennessee-based startups, more than double the amount from five years prior.[77]

Real estate investment in particular is very promising for Nashville. Per the *Emerging Trends in Real Estate 2019* survey, investor demand in Nashville is ranked 4.51 out of 5, one of the highest ratings of the country.[78] Many investors are outsiders buying property to rent out on Airbnb. With an estimated annual profit of $47,228, that's no surprise.[79]

Conexión Américas

Conexión Américas is a prominent nonprofit in Nashville working to help Hispanic Americans transition into life in the city. They help people receive job training and find employment.

Renata Soto, José González, and María Clara Mejía founded Conexión Américas after the 2000 US Census showed a nearly 450 percent increase in Nashville's Hispanic population.[80] As Soto explained it, they saw a need in Nashville for a "broader-voiced" organization that would create opportunities not only "to support families in pursuing dreams, but also to have a direct conversation with Nashville."[81]

Since its founding, Conexión Américas has helped tens of thousands of Nashvillians and later hosted President Obama's visit to the city.

Nashville's traditional tolerance and social progressiveness has led to a surge of international immigration in recent years. In 2000, only 2 percent of Nashville's population was foreign-born; as of 2017, more than 12 percent of the population was foreign-born.[82] Represented ethnicities include Kurdish, Middle Eastern, Hispanic, and Southeast Asian. With this diversity, more than 120 languages are spoken in Nashville MSA schools.[83] This linguistic diversity is important to the city, as proved by the defeat of the English-only referendum in 2009.

Defeat of the English-Only Referendum

In 2009, a ballot measure was proposed in Nashville that would make English the official language and restrict all government communication to English alone. Nashville was the largest city to consider this kind of restrictive legislation, and it brought a national spotlight to the city that was more controversial than the usual positive-spin media coverage.

A bipartisan, diverse coalition—including Mayor Karl Dean, civil rights groups, representatives of the business community, ministers, and leaders of nine Nashville colleges—quickly formed to oppose the measure. These key political, business, and social leaders thus declared that diversity and tolerance were nonnegotiable in Nashville.

When Nashville is faced with an important, difficult choice, it tends to make the wise business choice, like when it chose to focus on manufacturing as opposed to fighting during the Civil War. Throughout its history, Nashville has made many socially progressive decisions. While social progressiveness is an admirable goal in its own right, Nashville has also long realized that diversity and economic success are intertwined. While those making progressive decisions undoubtedly felt a moral responsibility to do so, they likely also understood the positive economic ramifications to be gained.

Businesses large and small were worried that the English-only referendum was a damaging reflection on Nashville. As Ralph Schulz, President of the Nashville Area Chamber of Commerce said regarding the English-only referendum, "Economics is global, and to be competitive you cannot drive away immigrants and the businesses that rely on them. Businesses from outside Nashville have been calling and saying, 'Is Nashville a xenophobic place?'"[84] Business leaders, like Tom Oreck, of Tennessee-based Oreck vacuums, shared these concerns. Oreck worried that if the ballot measure passed, it would send "an isolationist message in a global economy."[85]

Nashville voted, and the amendment was rejected, with 56 percent voting against and 44 percent voting in favor.[86] That might not sound like a huge landslide, but it was. The decisive victory "reaffirm[ed] Nashville's identity as a welcoming, friendly city," in Mayor Karl Dean's words.[87] We sat down with Dean for breakfast, and he told us that the defeat of the English-only referendum was one of his two proudest moments as mayor (the other was the city's response to the 2010 flood, which we'll discuss shortly). Some people felt embarrassed that the referendum took place at all, but Dean wasn't embarrassed. He told us that cities are supposed to vote on big issues, and he was proud that the city came together and defeated this proposal.[88] He emphasized that it was the people of Nashville who made this possible, with a little push from government, business, and community leaders.

Nashville's inclusivity isn't happenstance; it's a result of a series of choices the people of Nashville have made over the years, including the defeat of the English-only referendum. This was a huge win for the city. If the English-only referendum had passed, there's a good chance we would not have the Amazon Operations Center of Excellence or the MLS expansion team, and who knows what other companies and people we could have scared away? Instead, with the defeat of the referendum, the spotlight of bad press that had been focused on Nashville was spun into a positive story of progressiveness, paving the way for companies to relocate headquarters and branches here and ultimately leading us toward the "it" city narrative.

The year following the defeat of the English-only referendum, Nashvillians were faced with another challenge that provided an opportunity to demonstrate their character: the May 2010 flood.

"We're in This Together": The Great Flood of 2010

On May 1, 2010, it began to rain. It rained for two days, hard and steady. It was unusual, but at first, many people gave it no thought, beyond wishing it would end soon. Then I-24, one of Nashville's major interstates, flooded. All sign of asphalt disappeared on sections of the interstate, and Nashville suddenly had two rivers that ran through the city. The news released video of the flooding showing a portable classroom from Lighthouse Christian School floating down the interstate, as if it were a barge on the Cumberland.

Mayor Karl Dean led us through how that weekend unfolded for him. On Friday, the day before the rains started, they knew that there would be two to four inches of rainfall, which would cause stormwater problems. By about noon the next day, while Dean was performing his normal Saturday routine, the deputy mayor contacted him to inform him that major flooding was imminent. The rain was here, and it wasn't going to stop.

Dean went to the emergency communication center to monitor the situation. At first, his job was to tell people to watch the news, stay in, and stay off the roads. Then, that afternoon, the portable classroom was washed away, and Dean and the rest of the city realized just how serious and destructive the flooding was going to be. A record 13.57 inches of rain fell in 36 hours.[89] To put that in context, on average, only 5.51 inches falls for the *entire month of May*.[90]

By the end, nearly 30 people would die across Tennessee and Kentucky, more than 10,000 would be displaced from their homes, and billions of dollars in property damage would occur.[91] Yet the flood would receive relatively limited national media coverage, being overshadowed by other events. The *Deepwater Horizon* BP oil spill in the Gulf of Mexico had just come to light, and the same day the flood began, a terrorist bombing attack was attempted on Times Square. If it weren't for these other disasters, the Nashville flood likely would have garnered more attention. As it was, the focus of relief efforts would have to come from Nashville itself.

Notable Nonprofits

A strong thread of volunteerism runs through Nashville, and we have many fantastic nonprofits. The following are just a handful of the standouts:

- Big Brothers Big Sisters Middle Tennessee—provides children who face adversity a personal one-on-one relationship to create a positive influence in their lives: www.mentorakid.org.

- Community Foundation of Nashville—helps connect people willing to donate funds with various charitable organizations in need in our community: www.cfmt.org.

- Hands On Nashville—organizes volunteers throughout Nashville to maximize their impact: www.hon.org.

- Nashville CARES—seeks to end the HIV/AIDS epidemic through education, advocacy, and support: www.nashvillecares.org.

- Nashville Food Project—works to alleviate hunger: www.thenashvillefoodproject.org.

- Nashville Rescue Mission—seeks to help the hungry, homeless, and hurting: www.nashvillerescuemission.org.

- Pencil Foundation—links community resources to Nashville public schools to help students achieve academic success: www.pencilforschools.org.

- Poverty and the Arts—works with those who are impacted by homelessness, helping them secure employment and income by utilizing their creative talents and establishing social networks/relationships: www.povertyandthearts.org.

- Rebuilding Together Nashville—restores, rebuilds, and repairs homes of low-income residents: www.rtnashville.org.

- Second Harvest—provides food for a number of after-school programs, soup kitchens, senior centers, and other nonprofits dedicated to feeding hungry people in our community: www.secondharvestmidtn.org.

- Soles4Souls—provides sustainable jobs and clothing/shoes for people around the world: www.soles4souls.org.

- Tennessee Disability Coalition—promotes the full and equal participation of people with disabilities in all aspects of life: www.tndisability.org.

- YWCA Nashville & Middle Tennessee—dedicated to eliminating racism, empowering women, and promoting peace, justice, freedom, and dignity for all: www.ywcanashville.com.

As was the case with the English-only referendum, while the government organized and did its part in this time of crisis, it was the people of Nashville who truly carried the city through the flood and its aftermath. In particular, the Hands On Nashville volunteer organization rose to the challenge in a big way. Their efforts were remarkable both in terms of scale—in the weeks following the flood, 19,000 volunteers assisted with relief efforts—and in terms of coordination.[92]

Often, in the wake of disaster, disorganization is a city's greatest enemy. Relief supplies sit unused and become damaged because there's no structure to efficiently distribute them. Volunteers wish to help but don't know what to do. Emergency services are preoccupied, so looting and general lawlessness breaks out. That didn't happen in Nashville. Instead of looting or squandering efforts and supplies, people came together to help one another.

One reason Hands On Nashville succeeded in their skilled coordination of the efforts was their already established place in the community, with existing community outreach and volunteer structures. Brian Williams, Executive Director of Hands On Nashville, said that "at the end of the day for us," the flood relief efforts were "just an extension of what we do."[93] Because of the nonprofit's prior experience in the community, they were able to jump into action to organize people and supplies quickly and effectively. Instead of idling around at a job site, volunteers were given specific tasks that gave them a sense of impact, making more Nashvillians want to come out to help. The nonprofit made great use of preprepared disaster plans but also improvised and adapted.

Floodwaters recede, but their destruction remains. In total, the flood caused $2 billion in private property damage, and Nashville sustained $120 million of public infrastructure damage.[94] Sometimes floods can be blessings in disguise, destroying old, rundown buildings and clearing the way for new construction. In this way, short-term destruction can be leveraged into long-term economic benefit. Unfortunately, in Nashville's case, much of the property damage involved crown jewels of the city, not outdated buildings. Second Avenue, a major tourist district, faced substantial flooding and power outages. The Schermerhorn Symphony Center and the Pinnacle at Symphony Place, the first new skyscraper that had been built in the city in nearly two decades and which had opened only a couple of months prior, both experienced flooding as well. Most of the stores in the Opry Mills outlet mall were under a dozen feet of water, and the mall would not reopen for two years, after an estimated $200 million in repairs.[95] The historic Grand Ole Opry and the Opryland Hotel were also flooded. The flood was a major setback for the city, with the destruction of valuable, historically and culturally significant buildings.

As destructive as the flood was, it truly brought out the best in Nashville. The immediate response was admirable, but recovering from a natural disaster takes longer than a few days, weeks, or even months. One of the things that set Nashville's response apart from other cities was the way the community continued its support in the aftermath, even years later. In the two years following the flood, more than 29,000 volunteers gave 375,000-plus hours of their time to flood-related efforts coordinated by Hands On Nashville.[96] Executive Director Williams said, "The response to the 2010 flood was a remarkable demonstration of the power of volunteerism, and that service and enthusiasm continue today. These long-term flood recovery programs give volunteers the opportunity to address critical issues facing our community, from improving the energy efficiency of homes to restoring our waterways."[97]

As a personal example, one of our employees was hit particularly hard by the flood. She lost nearly everything—her home, her possessions. She had to be rescued by boat. With her entire life uprooted, she then learned that her insurance would cover only half of what was needed to fix her house. Though her home was unlivable, she still had to pay the mortgage on it, making it difficult for her to afford a place to live. Two of our developer clients—Zac Thomas and Brett Diaz of Woodland Street Partners and Paragon Group—went above and beyond to help her. They had a couple of houses for sale at the time, and they let her live in one rent-free for a year. In addition, they extended an interest-free loan to her to cover what her insurance would not. Others from the community stepped up as well. Nearly 30 people from her church helped her start the repairs on her home, ripping out waterlogged carpet and ruined drywall.

This is what Nashville is. It's a community of good-hearted people you can rely on when it counts.

Coda

As the city has grown, our population has become increasingly diverse. We are welcoming of outsiders, perhaps because so many of us, like we three, are not natives but transplants. In Nashville, whether you were born here or moved from someplace else, you are a Nashvillian.

Part of the reason so many people choose to move here and become Nashvillians is our strong business environment, which leads us to our next chapter.

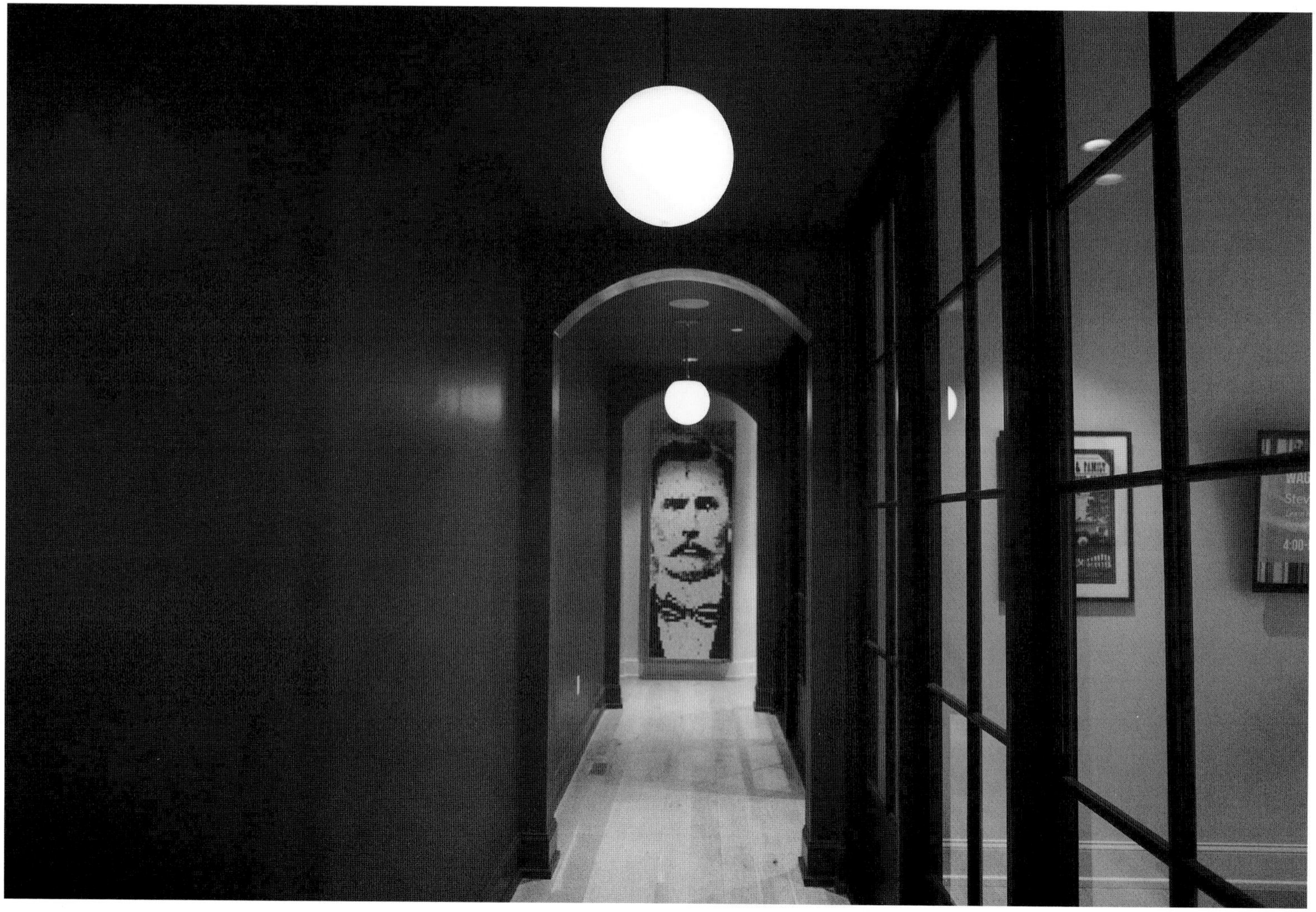

CHAPTER 4

★

BUSINESS ENVIRONMENT AND ENTREPRENEURSHIP

Nashville has long had a reputation for strong economic policy, and the statistics are compelling:

- As ranked by POLICOM in 2018, Nashville has the fourth-strongest economy in America.[98]

- Over the past decade, the Nashville MSA has experienced job growth of 25 percent, making it the second fastest growing economy in the country since the Great Recession, behind only Austin, Texas.[99]

- As of 2015, there are more than 41,609 businesses in the city.[100]

- In 2019, Nashville was ranked as having the lowest unemployment rate of any top 50 metropolitan statistical area, at 2.4 percent, which is effectively no unemployment.[101]

Statistics tell only part of the story, though. What makes our business community so vibrant cannot be measured. It is a unique culture of collaboration, innovation, entrepreneurial spirit, and philanthropy.

The Spirit of Nashville's Business Community

In 2019, *Inc.* ranked Nashville as the fourth-best city in which to start a business.[102] Most articles that rave about Nashville as a business city focus on our low taxes and light government regulation. Those traits undoubtedly contribute to the health and success of a business, but they are not enough on their own to earn a place as one of the top five cities to start a business. It is the business culture that takes a city over the edge.

For developers, entrepreneurs, and business owners, the culture shock of Nashville's business environment is refreshing and appreciated. In Nashville, we always give people the first interview or meeting. You might not get the second, but you will be given a chance to prove yourself. Matthew Wiltshire, as the former Director of the Mayor's Office of Economic and Community Development, played a key role in cementing this culture and translating it to businesses that moved to town. The Nashville business community's openness and willingness to help others succeed allows newcomers to more quickly break into and integrate into the business community. In other cities, old boys' clubs and high barriers to entry build communities of exclusivity instead of inclusivity. A significant portion of Nashvillians are nonnative transplants, so we don't hold the same insider-vs.-outsider mentality as some other cities, where who you know can be more important than what you know. We don't care where you were born; we only care about how good your ideas are.

With our pervasive musical roots, Nashville has always been a city that emphasizes and encourages creativity. Our open-mindedness further amplifies our tendency toward innovation. As *U.S. News & World Report* states it, "Music City is home to a community fiercely driven by a desire to create… This innovation positively influences the lives of residents in nearly every respect."[103] In the business sphere, the innovative spirit of the city has led to a wealth of entrepreneurs and creators.

Nashville is one of the leading incubators of entrepreneurship. The Entrepreneurs' Organization (EO) in Nashville, of which Angie is a member, is one of the most active chapters in the world, with 220 members with median sales of $2 million and 9,101 employees.[104] The organization is a hotbed of collaboration, with community business owners working together to raise the bar for not just their individual companies but for the city as a whole. In addition to the EO peer network, we have the Nashville Entrepreneur Center, which provides many resources to aspiring businesses, from mentorship to help finding angel investors. The center is one of nine tech hubs in North America partnered with Google for Startups.[105]

With organizations like these, Nashville has a robust ecosystem of support for business endeavors, especially budding entrepreneurs and startups. They make building relationships and networking easy and provide a guide through the somewhat murky waters of opening and growing a business. With a spirit of innovation, collaboration, and openness, Nashville is the ideal city to start and own a business.

Recent Business History

Like the rest of the country, Nashville was hurt by the Great Recession and housing bubble crash of 2008. The local economy stalled for about four years, but then it bounced back with a vengeance. Nashville's post-recession recovery was one of the quickest in the country. In 2012, with the shadow of the downturn still looming over the United States, a Gallup poll ranked the city as one of the top five regions in the nation for job growth, and the following year, in 2013, the *New York Times* declared Nashville the new "it" city.[106] In 2016, Freddie Mac named Nashville the hottest housing market in the country,[107] and by 2017, Nashville had overtaken Memphis as the most populous city in Tennessee.[108]

Former mayor Megan Barry summarized our economic resiliency well: "We have always been a city that can weather downturns in the economy. We're steady. We have a lot of different businesses here, but this current meteoric rise is because of the entrepreneurs who are bringing restaurants and other start-ups into Nashville which help us to accelerate our cultural cred. That means people want to move here, they want to live here, they want to start a business here."[109]

Historically, Nashville's economy has relied heavily on healthcare and music. Those industries continue to thrive in the city, but there has been a recent surge of economic diversification. Charlie Brock, CEO of Launch Tennessee, a Nashville-based public-private partnership supporting entrepreneurship across the state, is in a unique position to observe these changes. "Healthcare has always been Nashville's mainstay but that's changing quickly," he says. "There's more homegrown venture capital coming into Tennessee and Nashville right now than we've ever seen before, and that's having ripple effects through the economy as our early stage companies start to mature."[110]

In addition to a proliferation of homegrown entrepreneurship and innovation, powerhouse companies across the nation have been drawn to Nashville in recent years. Large businesses find the city's business-friendly environment conducive to establishing branch offices and relocating home offices. It seems as if every month there is a new announcement about a business moving to Nashville.

For more than a decade, the city has provided a stable, advantageous home for businesses, and in return, Nashville business leaders have fostered a culture of gratitude and reciprocity.

The City's Key Industries

Nashville's top two industries, measured by annual economic impact, are healthcare and music, which will each be discussed in depth later in the book, in Chapter 6, "Music: Country and Beyond," and Chapter 7, "Healthcare: The Number One Industry." Aside from these, the city's most important commerce sectors are tourism and hospitality, technology, manufacturing, and logistics and transportation.

Tourism and Hospitality

In 1978, 7.7 million people visited Nashville; in 2018, we had *15.2 million visitors*.[111] A Department of Public Works study discovered that foot traffic in downtown on a typical Thursday and Saturday was comparable to the foot traffic of Times Square.[112] A significant portion of that foot traffic is bachelorettes, as Nashville is now the bachelorette party capital of the world.[113] Nashville is becoming a top spring break destination as well and made *Condé Nast Traveler*'s list of the 20 best places to go in the world in 2020, alongside popular destinations like Dubai and the Canary Islands.[114] All these tourists bring a nice chunk of change with them: an annual $6.5 billion in revenue, to be specific.[115]

Q&A with Butch Spyridon, CEO of the Nashville Convention and Visitors Corporation

Q: Since 1991 you've been well known as the President and CEO of the Nashville Convention & Visitors Corporation, but you didn't always have that job. What made you want to take on that challenge?

A: I had always said Nashville was the only "inland" city I would ever live in. Something about this town! I was working in Baton Rouge and had an awesome gig. However, we had been extremely successful, and I felt like the opportunity to grow there was limited. Fortunately, Nashville called, and I had to answer. I needed the challenge to grow professionally.

Q: How have you seen your role grow and change over the years? What are some advantages you have now that weren't yet on the horizon in 1991?

A: When I started, we were an Opryland (hotel, theme park, and TV networks) dominated town. The Nashville Convention and Visitors Corporation didn't influence much of the direction for the city's hospitality industry, and we weren't adding the value that we should. After the Opryland theme park closed and the Nashville Convention and Visitors Corporation separated from the Chamber, we began to grow and had the opportunity to engage more on the direction of the industry. I think/hope it's been a good thing. The opportunities now surround sustaining this incredible success story and managing the growth itself. The biggest advantage now is that we don't have to explain or defend Nashville to our clients. They have seen it and experienced all the good.

Q: What's your big, hairy, audacious goal for Nashville?

A: Nashville has proven it can do whatever it sets out to accomplish. We need to keep dreaming big and being true to ourselves. I think hosting the Grammys, the World Cup, and one day the Super Bowl are pretty big, audacious goals!

Why Businesses Love Nashville

- Competitive business costs—Class A office space is typically two or three times more expensive in San Francisco and New York compared to Nashville. And it's not just office space—almost everything is cheaper here.

- Supportive, nonrestrictive government—Many Nashville and Tennessee political leaders are businesspeople. They understand what it takes to run a business, and they understand how businesses benefit a city. The result is a pro-business government that encourages business growth, including giving incentives for businesses to relocate.

- Large, well-educated talent pool—Especially with all our area universities, Nashville's population skews young and educated, providing a large talent pool for businesses.

- Capacity for growth—Nashville's real estate market is booming, but there is significantly more room for expansion here than in compact cities like Chicago, New York, and Seattle, where space is at a premium.

- Strategic location—Nashville's central location makes it a logistics and distribution hub.

- Quality of life—If given the choice between two essentially equal cities, it only makes sense to choose whichever one is more fun. With our music scene and active sports culture, Nashville is a great place to live.

The financial impact of tourism extends into many industries, including restaurants and hospitality. Nashville's tourism boom has triggered a corresponding hotel boom. Right now, dozens of hotels are under construction, with more than 6,000 rooms soon to be added to the city's current count of roughly 45,000 hotel rooms.[116]

Luxury hotels are a particular focus for development. When we first moved to the city, if you wanted to stay in a luxury hotel, your only options were Opryland, the Hermitage, or the Loews. With low supply and increasingly high demand, for a few years, Nashville hotel prices were on par with the most expensive hotels in America. Staying at the Marriott in Times Square would have been cheaper than staying at the one in Nashville. New luxury hotels—like Omni, Virgin, Westin, Four Seasons, and J.W. Marriott—have begun sprouting up, with several featuring Las Vegas-class rooftop pools, but there is still room for more development.

Technology

The technology industry in Nashville is midsize but vibrant, and it's growing every year. From 2012–2017, Nashville had the third fastest-growing technology workforce in North America, after Charlotte and Toronto.[117] Nashville is an ideal city for tech companies, especially startups, because it has a growing talented pool of young workers while being significantly less expensive than traditional tech centers like Seattle and San Francisco.

There's a surprising amount of venture capital moving in the city, but more is always welcome. In 2016, investors from New York and Boston poured more than $420 million into Tennessee-based startups, more than double the amount from five years prior.[118] The health tech and music tech sectors are especially innovative here thanks to the strong foundation provided by our music and healthcare industries.

The most exciting recent development in our tech scene is the Amazon Operations Center of Excellence, which will create 5,000 new jobs, with a focus on management and tech roles, with an average predicted salary of $150,000.[119]

Manufacturing

Nashville's early economy was built on manufacturing, and this sector has continued to be an important piece of the city's economic pie. The story today is that we don't make things in America anymore. While much of our country's manufacturing has been outsourced overseas, Nashville has made itself an exception. Manufacturing provides more than 82,000 jobs and has a $9.5 billion economic impact.[120]

The bulk of our manufacturing is automobiles. We have an enormous Nissan plant, which was the largest car plant in North America at the time it was built, even bigger than the car plants in Detroit. Nissan is actually the second-largest employer in the area, with more than 10,000 employees.[121] There is also a large GM plant in nearby Spring Hill and a Volkswagen plant in Chattanooga.

Logistics and Transportation

Nashville's central location makes it an ideal hub for logistics and transportation. About 50 percent of the US population lives within 650 miles of the city, with 12 million people living within a two-hour drive.[122] When you increase that to a 10-hour drive or a 2-hour plane ride, you can reach 75 percent of the US population.[123] Nashville is also one of just six places in the country where three interstates converge.[124] While locals love to complain about potholes, there's no denying that our interstates provide easy access to surrounding areas. If you're a transportation or logistics company, Nashville's easy, quick access to large swaths of the country can translate to outsized economic advantage.

Being a logistics center is one of Nashville's greatest competitive advantages in attracting companies. In 2015, the French company Geodis—which distributes for Apple and is one of the largest distribution companies in the world—bought Nashville-based Ozburn-Hessey Logistics. So now, Geodis's US headquarters is in Middle Tennessee. When we interviewed former mayor David Briley, he told us, "A lot of people in Nashville don't even know what [Geodis] is, but I'm sure the resources that make Geodis a success were factors when Amazon was evaluating the city."[125] Amazon, in many ways, is a logistics company, so when they were choosing a city for their Operations Center of Excellence, our world-class logistics infrastructure must have been appealing.

Home Sweet Home: Headquarters Hub

Because Nashville is such a business-friendly city, many companies have chosen to open or relocate their headquarters or back offices here, bringing jobs and money with them.

- Amazon is opening the Operations Center of Excellence here, bringing a $230 million investment to the city, as well as 5,000 jobs.[126]

- Lyft opened a national customer service center in Nashville in 2015. Their goal was to hire 400 local employees, but they now employ nearly twice that many, more than 750.[127]

- EY (formerly Ernst & Young), one of the Big Four accounting firms, opened a 600-person office in the city, bringing a $22 million investment to the city.[128] EY picked Nashville as a top-three contender out of 18 cities. Nashville reached that stage of the process on its merits alone, and only after that did negotiations and incentive packages come into play.

- Gibson, which employs 500 people in Nashville, recently relocated its Memphis factory here and is moving its headquarters to downtown.[129]

- About 10 years ago, Bridgestone was considering moving its North American headquarters to Chicago, but after the city and state offered a competitive incentive package, they decided to stay. They just built a new 30-story downtown headquarters building, bringing 1,700 workers to downtown.[130]

- Nissan moved its headquarters to the city in 2005 and currently employs more than 10,000 people locally.[131]

- AllianceBernstein is moving its headquarters here, which is expected to bring 1,050 jobs and a $70 million investment.[132]

- Oracle is currently scouting for 800,000 square feet of office space in downtown and could bring up to 3,000 jobs.[133]

The Importance of Giving Back

The soul of the Nashville business community is locally owned enterprises. When people establish businesses in Nashville, whether they are Nashville natives or transplants, they tend to stay put. When you live in the same city where you do business, it's in your best interest to help that city thrive. As a result, one of the defining traits of Nashville's business community is that when people make it to the top, they don't take their chips off the table and cash out; rather, they give back to the community. The Frist family (of HCA), Cal Turner (of Dollar General), and the Ingram family (of Ingram Industries) are model examples of giving back in the Nashville way.

HCA was established here in 1968 and has remained even as it has grown into one of the largest companies in the nation, ranking number 63 on the 2017 Fortune 500 list.[134] Simply by nature of its presence in Nashville, HCA has helped the community, as it is the third-leading employer of the area, with more than 10,000 local employees.[135] In addition to this indirect impact, HCA gives back directly through the Frist Foundation. The foundation, established in 1982, is "dedicated to sustaining and improving the quality of life in Nashville, Tennessee," and has contributed generously to the Frist Art Museum, the Nashville Zoo, and many other local nonprofits.[136]

Dollar General was founded in Kentucky, but in 1989, Cal Turner Jr., son of founder Cal Turner, moved the headquarters to Nashville.[137] The company has remained in the Nashville area ever since. Among the company's contributions to the community is the Dollar General Learning Center, established in 1993 to provide economically disadvantaged people with training, education, and jobs.[138] Cal Turner Jr. has donated millions to Vanderbilt, including $6.9 million to the Vanderbilt Divinity School and $2 million to Vanderbilt Law School in 2017.[139] Siblings Cal Turner Jr., Steve Turner, and Laura Turner also gifted $15 million to the Schermerhorn Symphony Center, among other charitable donations.[140]

The Ingram family's impact has been woven into the fabric of the city such that, if you look for it, you will see the Ingrams' all-permeating fingerprints everywhere: from the Nashville Symphony to Vanderbilt University to the Nashville Soccer Club. Sometimes it seems that every street you walk down, every building you pass, every arts initiative you hear about, you see the Ingram name.

Ingram Industries started as a barge business on the Cumberland River. E. Bronson Ingram II inherited this medium-size oil and barge company and transformed it into one of the largest wholesale distributors in the world, becoming one of the wealthiest men to live in Nashville in the process. Headquartered in Nashville, Ingram now has more than 5,000 employees.[141] While subsidiary Ingram Marine still operates barges, Ingram Industries has expanded to other fields and is perhaps now best known for its leading role as a distributor and service provider in the publishing industry.

Just about every new book purchased in the United States passes through Ingram's distribution channels.[142]

Beyond providing employment for Nashville residents, the Ingrams—Martha Ingram, in particular—have been integral to the city's cultural development. Arguably, one of the best things to happen to Nashville was E. Bronson Ingram II snagging Martha as a wife and turning her into a Nashvillian. Following her husband's death in 1995, Martha took over the business and has been the poster child for charitable giving ever since. Martha, born in South Carolina, has embraced Nashville as her home and has invested millions of dollars into the city to support the arts and education.

Barge Barons: E. Bronson Ingram II and Tom Ryman

Two of Nashville's most influential characters earned their fortunes through barges: E. Bronson Ingram II and Tom Ryman. Both men used their barge earnings to give back to the city, Ingram through charitable giving and Ryman through the Ryman Auditorium.

---

44 ★ *Climbing the Charts: The Ascent of Nashville*

In 1972, Martha was appointed to the President's Advisory Committee on the Arts for the John F. Kennedy Center, and that experience gave her a template for what Nashville could be. "I thought we needed something like the Kennedy Center in Nashville because there was no place to have opera, ballet or professional theater," she said. "I wanted my children to have exposure to the arts, which was something I had too little of as a child."[143]

Thanks in large part to Martha's tireless efforts, that dream has become a reality. Nashville has a strong arts community today, with opera, ballet, and theater offerings. The Ingrams have offered financial support for the Tennessee Repertory Theatre, the Nashville Ballet, and the Nashville Opera.[144] Martha was also the driving force behind the Schermerhorn Symphony Center, donating $30 million for the project.[145]

In addition to supporting the arts community, the Ingrams have donated generously to Vanderbilt University. In 1989, Martha's husband, Bronson, was named chair of the Campaign for Vanderbilt, which ended up raising $560 million for the university and medical center.[146] Then, approximately a decade later, in 1998, Martha gifted $300 million worth of stock to Vanderbilt University—at the time, the largest donation ever to a private university.[147]

Martha isn't the only Ingram to have an impact on the city. The three Ingram sons—Orrin, John, and David—play a critical role in the Ingram business ventures. While there is some overlap in the brothers' duties, each is largely responsible for one major branch of Ingram. Orrin is CEO of Ingram Industries, David is chairman and president of Ingram Entertainment, and John runs the Ingram Content Group.[148] As well as helping to strengthen the city's economy, each is involved in philanthropic efforts, following in their mother's footsteps.

John Ingram in particular has made a great impact via his contribution in securing an MLS expansion team. If he had not agreed to be the team's lead investor, we would not have the team today. In speaking about the team, John said, "I wanted to do something 'In Nashville, for Nashville, with Nashville.'"[149] For his role, he was selected Tennessean Sports Person of the Year for 2017, but he tried to shift focus away from himself, saying, "This is not a John Ingram story. This is a Nashville story."[150] Like many Nashville business leaders, he is not interested in personal attention or praise; he is interested in developing our community into a first-tier cosmopolitan center.

Coda

With a history of economic stability, Nashville is known as a business city and for good reason. Our business community is welcoming and founded on innovation and collaboration, and business ventures in the city span a wide range of industries: music, healthcare, tourism, manufacturing, technology, and logistics and transportation. In the past decade, a slew of companies have relocated or opened headquarters here, and the city continues to attract more businesses, thanks to our strategic location, competitive business costs, supportive government, quality of life, capacity for growth, and quality talent pool.

In conjunction with the business growth, Nashville has seen a boom of development and real estate, as will be discussed in the following chapter.

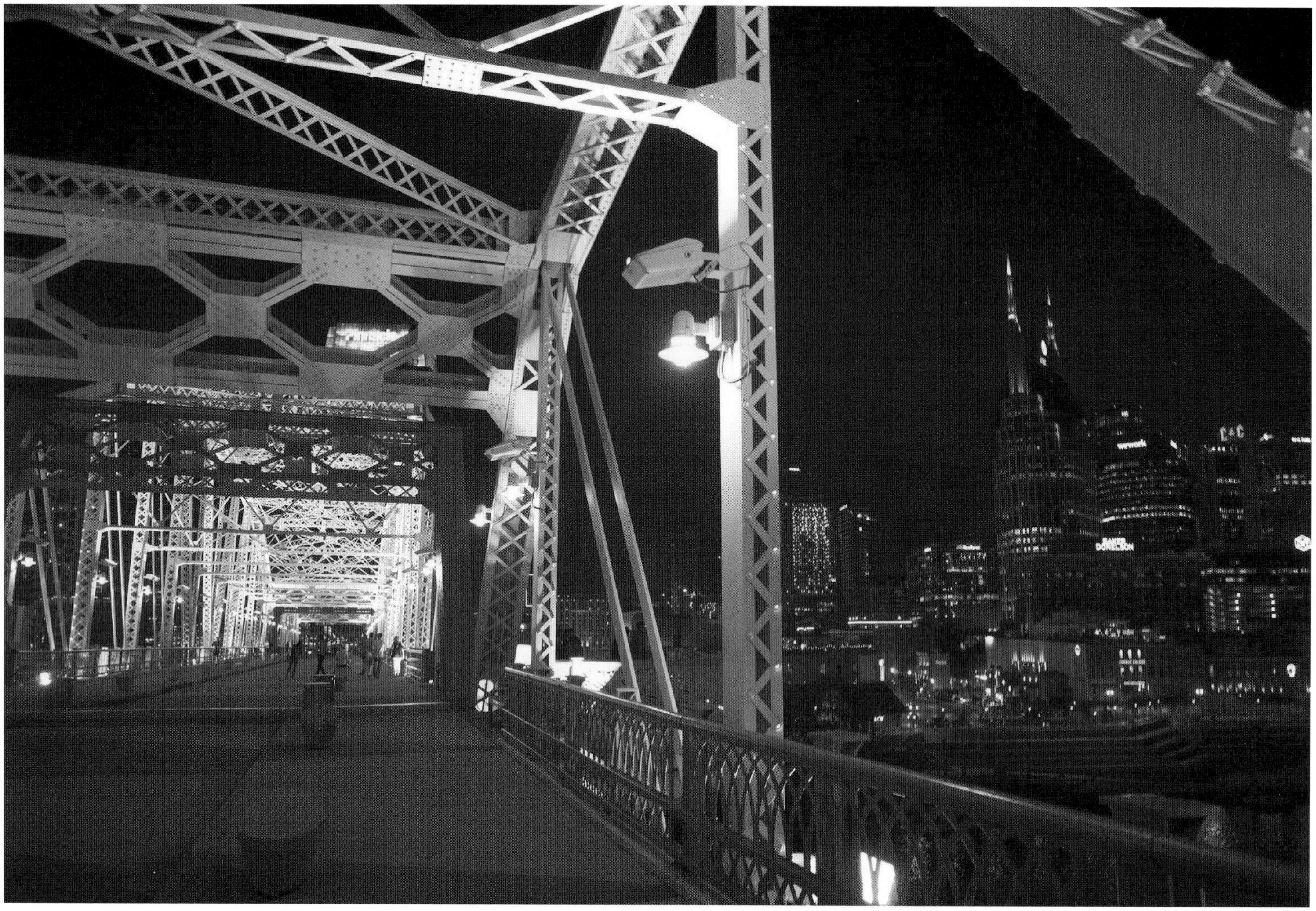
BAKER
DONELSON

CHAPTER 5

DEVELOPMENT AND REAL ESTATE

In 2018, when Redfin CEO Glenn Kelman, one of the most brilliant minds in real estate, was asked on CNBC what one city he would personally invest in with his own money, he said, without hesitation, "Nashville or San Antonio." When pressed to choose just one, his answer? "Nashville."[151] Kelman is not alone in recognizing Nashville as an ideal place to invest. A PricewaterhouseCoopers (PwC) and Urban Land Institute national study ranked Nashville as the second-best place among US metro areas for development opportunities and third-best place for overall real estate prospects in 2020.[152] In the past two decades, real estate projects have sprung up across Nashville, and the pace of development shows no signs of abating.

The Downtown Urban Housing Turnaround

Real estate development tends to come in boom-and-bust cycles, and Nashville is no exception. The city has been growing in sporadic bursts since it began with just a handful of settlers in the late 1700s. The urban housing boom of today is the largest the city has ever seen.

In the 1950s, Nashville's downtown was a thriving center of activity, but by the 1980s, few spent time downtown for anything except their jobs, let alone lived there.

Part of the reason was a city ordinance, in place since 1963, that prohibited the construction of apartment buildings downtown.[153] The only downtown residential development possible was the conversion of spaces in older buildings' upper floors for personal residences. With the restrictions in place, by the mid-'90s, "there were only 10 people living in downtown's central business district, and fewer than a thousand in the broader downtown area."[154]

Then in 1993, the zoning laws were changed, planting the seeds for Nashville's downtown urban housing turnaround. Two of the first pioneers of the urban development push were Tony Giarratana and Mark Deutschmann.

Giarratana's first downtown residential project was the Cumberland, a high-rise apartment complex. Just three years after the zoning changes, which Giarratana had helped push for, he broke ground for the Cumberland. Shortly after, an article appeared in the *Tennessean* with the headline "Today Begins Quest for Downtown-Dwellers."[155] The 24-story Cumberland functioned as an early test of whether anybody would want to live downtown. The Cumberland opened in 1998, and though it wasn't fully leased until late 2000, it got people thinking about living in downtown.[156]

Giarratana went on to develop several more influential condo and apartment towers, including the Viridian in 2006, the Encore in 2008, SoBro in 2016, and 505 in 2017.

Deutschmann and Core Development, which he founded in 2003, took a different tack to downtown development. While Giarratana focused on constructing brand-new buildings, Core Development focused on breathing new life into vacant or semi vacant buildings, converting them into mixed-use residential living spaces. This repurposing of the existing infrastructure enhanced the value of our urban core. One of these projects was the Exchange Lofts, which is where Angie and Brandon bought their first loft condos. The building was originally constructed in the 1890s, with significant additions in the 1950s. It had been the home of the *Nashville Banner* newspaper, which gave it historic charm as well as unique building features, like three-foot-thick concrete floors designed to support the weight of the printing presses.

What Core Development and Deutschmann's Village Real Estate team did particularly well was market the vision of downtown living. Though revitalization had begun, downtown was still nothing like the vibrant area it is today. There were no grocery stores (until the H.G. Hill Urban Market in Giarratana's Viridian in 2006), few restaurants that were open late, and a general lack of amenities that people had grown used to in suburban Nashville living. Deutschmann and his team were selling a new lifestyle of downtown living in a city where no one had ever really lived downtown. They launched a grassroots marketing program, hosting downtown bus tours to showcase the emerging neighborhoods and highlight the walkable features. Their hard work paid off, and the 47 condominium lofts quickly sold out.

The Cumberland and the Exchange Lofts were the first major projects to test the viability of the downtown market. Once they established proof of concept for downtown living, other developments quickly followed.

The Exchange Lofts were fully completed in 2006, and residents, including Angie and Brandon, began moving in in 2005. At the time, there were only about 600 people living downtown. As of 2018, over 11,000 people lived downtown, in a total of 7,622 units, with eight in-construction projects to create an additional 1,664 units.[157] Even with this increasing supply, more is needed. According to Matthew Wiltshire, former Director of the Mayor's Office of Economic and Community Development and now Chief Strategy and Intergovernmental Affairs Officer in the Metropolitan Development and Housing Authority (MDHA), "Nashville probably has half of the residential [housing units] that we should have downtown compared to other peer cities like Austin, Texas."[158]

Affordable housing is in high demand in Nashville, but surprisingly, luxury condos are also very much in demand. When the downtown turnaround first began, there was essentially nothing available over $400,000. Anything more expensive than that was viewed as too risky. This mindset has shifted in recent years, thanks in part to the Adelicia, developed by Ray Hensler, who went on to also build the Twelve Twelve luxury condominium tower.

The Adelicia raised the bar for what luxury means in Nashville. When it was first built, people scoffed. "Those are New York condo prices," they said. "That will never work in Nashville." While locals were cynical about the $350 per square foot price tag, out-of-state buyers couldn't believe what a steal the units were. While it took about four years for the condos to sell out, the price points, per square foot, were the highest that had ever sold in the state of Tennessee. Taylor Swift as well as Caleb Followill (of Kings of Leon) and Lily Aldridge purchased condos there, and Kelly Clarkson rented one. The Adelicia proved that Nashville does have a market for luxury condos. Today, some of the easiest-to-sell condos in Nashville are in the seven-figure range.

The story of Nashville's downtown is one of continuous growth. Now is the perfect time for developers to invest in the city. The "risky" first experiments in downtown living have already been completed, successfully proving the demand, yet the market is still far from saturated. As of February 2020, close to 200 projects are currently under construction or in the pipeline, with 30-plus tower cranes dotting Nashville skies.[159]

In 20 short years, downtown Nashville has become a very desirable place to live, and condo towers continue to creep upward across the Nashville skyline. Outside of downtown, distinct neighborhoods throughout Nashville have experienced their own development, creating unique identities.

Nashville Neighborhoods

Nashville has several different kinds of neighborhoods. Some areas have always been highly desirable; others have had ups and downs. And in recent years, certain districts have exploded with growth, including some brand-new neighborhoods.

Nashville has been called America's biggest small town, and our vibrant neighborhoods are a big reason why. Each district is like its own town within the larger city, allowing Nashville to retain a small-town feel even while providing big-city amenities. In this section, we will highlight a few of the neighborhoods we find notable.

Streetcar Suburbs: Richland–West End

As Nashville expanded and urbanized, streetcars provided the map. People wanted all the conveniences of downtown, but they didn't want to actually *live* there. So neighborhoods grew up along the streetcar routes. These streetcar suburbs offered the perfect compromise: a taste of country living with all the modern conveniences of the day just a streetcar ride away.

The streetcars are now gone, but you can still catch glimpses of the old streetcar tracks when potholes crack open the pavement. Even without streetcars, the neighborhoods remain and continue to prosper. The Richland–West End neighborhood is a good example. In 1905, when the neighborhood was created, medians were constructed, and the streets were lined with trees. This historic neighborhood is close enough to downtown to make for an easy commute but far enough away to have larger houses with reasonably sized yards, great trees, and plenty of sidewalks. It's a nice balance, and many people agree, making the area expensive.

Revitalized Districts: East Nashville and Germantown

Everyone loves a good comeback story, and Nashville has its share. Both East Nashville and Germantown were highly desirable neighborhoods that fell on hard times but later rose once more to prominence after extensive revitalization.

EAST NASHVILLE

East Nashville is right next to downtown, to the east. At the time of the Civil War, the East Nashville neighborhood was where the stateliest houses were and where many prominent people lived. It was also the center of the Civil War action in Nashville. When people invaded Nashville, they marched through East Nashville before crossing the river to the state capitol. Compared to other parts of the city, East Nashville was hit especially hard by the Civil War. Then in the early 1900s, much of the housing stock burned down, and the district entered a period of decline that lasted decades, up through the mid-1990s.

In recent years, East Nashville has undergone a Brooklyn-ification. The neighborhood supports a growing hipster culture. East Nashville is the epicenter of our craft cocktail scene and is home to some of the city's trendiest artisanal coffee shops, restaurants, shopping, and bars. The neighborhood offers everything you would want in Brooklyn at a much cheaper price while also having the added benefit of Nashville's unique cultural blend of southern hospitality and world-class music.

GERMANTOWN

Germantown is north of downtown, within walking distance, and it experienced a downturn similar to East Nashville's. In Nashville's early days, Germantown was a desirable neighborhood, with lots of big, nice houses and brick sidewalks. The area was a hub for industry, with a slaughterhouse and several factories. Then the industry left, and the people with money left with it. Thus began a downward spiral, until revitalization began in the mid-1990s.

Like East Nashville, Germantown was known as a low-income area of high crime, but starting a few decades ago, it has become highly desirable. In a relatively short amount of time, it has transformed from an area people really didn't want to live in to a place people wish they could afford to live in. This rise is likely to be reinforced by New City Properties' forthcoming Neuhoff redevelopment, a 14-acre project along the Cumberland River in Germantown. New City Properties, the Atlanta developer responsible for the Ponce City Market, plans to transform these 14 acres into a mixed-use development, with office space, apartments, and retail shops.

Dark Horse Neighborhoods: Wedgewood-Houston and 12 South

Some neighborhoods, like Wedgewood-Houston and 12 South, managed to fly under the radar for a long time before blowing up in popularity. People have always lived in these areas, but historically, the neighborhoods lacked a distinct, coherent identity. Now, they've become branded places that everybody knows.

WEDGEWOOD-HOUSTON

Wedgewood-Houston (also called WeHo) used to be referred to simply as the Fairgrounds, due to its proximity to—you guessed it—the fairgrounds. Despite its prime location a 10-minute drive or 20-minute scooter ride south of downtown, there were a few houses and not a lot else. Then, a few medium-size condo buildings were built, and a couple of warehouses were repurposed into fancy restaurants. One building was turned into a "maker space"—a place for artisans to build and create. Mark Deutschmann has been a key player in the vitalization of this area, doing the same for WeHo as he did to downtown.

Now, WeHo is emerging as a trendy, artistic neighborhood, and it's poised to grow in popularity even more, as the new soccer stadium is set to be built at the fairgrounds.

12 SOUTH

The 12 South neighborhood used to be a four-lane commuter road leading to downtown. In the past, you drove down Twelfth Avenue South as fast as you could and didn't bother looking to see what was on either side of the road. Then the city came up with a genius, widely ridiculed plan to narrow the street.

At first, people were greatly opposed to the plan. Traffic was already heavy on the road with all the downtown commuters, and now the city wanted to turn the four-lane thoroughfare into just two lanes, with dozens of crosswalks? It seemed like a terrible idea. The city had a vision, though, and did it anyway.

The transformation was striking. Almost immediately, a bunch of new restaurants and shops opened. Foot traffic exploded, with pedestrians filling the sidewalks and the bus stop getting more use than it ever had before. Simply by narrowing the road and slowing the traffic down, the city had turned 12 South into a destination. It was a counterintuitive but brilliant city-planning decision.

New, Designed Neighborhoods

The Gulch, SoBro, and Westhaven are three communities that essentially did not exist 30 years ago and were built from the ground up. These are interesting neighborhoods because they have been designed with modern living in mind. There are neat things that you can do when a neighborhood is planned and not cobbled together from past decades.

THE GULCH

When the three of us first moved to Nashville, the Gulch was a wasteland. It had the Station Inn, a great music venue still open today that will be discussed in Chapter 6, "Music: Country and Beyond," and a plumbing company, and that was about it. The only traffic through the area was people whipping past on Twelfth Avenue South on their commute to and from work.

Then the city announced that they would be closing Twelfth Avenue South through the Gulch so that a condominium tower could be built.

In 2008, the Icon tower was completed, and the neighborhood blew up. It developed in a fascinating way, according to a master plan. The Turner family, mentioned in the previous chapter, played a key role in backing a $400 million plan to redevelop the Gulch.[160] What made the Gulch unique was that it was the nation's first LEED (Leadership and Energy Environmental Design)-certified neighborhood. This means that it is one of the greenest, most environmentally friendly neighborhoods in the United States. Part of what earned it LEED certification was its high walkability score. You can easily live in the Gulch without needing a car because there's a good mix of residential and commercial amenities. You can walk or bike to work, the grocery store, restaurants, and more.

If we had to pick one neighborhood that has the most development in the last 10 years, it would be the Gulch. It has quickly become one of the most desirable spots in town, especially for tourists and VRBO/Airbnb enthusiasts.

SOBRO (SOUTH OF BROADWAY)

When we first started hearing talk of developments south of Broadway, there was a lot of skepticism. Broadway itself was a hot area, with its row of honky-tonks and proximity to Bridgestone Arena, but abruptly, as you moved south of Broadway, anything of interest disappeared.

54 ★ *Climbing the Charts: The Ascent of Nashville*

The first residential tower that went up in the area, Giarratana's Encore in 2008, was 20 stories tall. When it was first erected, it was a giant in the area, towering over all else. Fast-forward 10 years, and the Nashville skyline has been altered by a smattering of newer, taller towers that soar above the Encore, making it look Lilliputian in comparison.

One of those taller towers is the Pinnacle at Symphony Place, a 29-story office and retail skyscraper completed in 2010. Keith Simmons, as managing member of Bass, Berry & Sims, served as a major catalyst in ensuring the tower's success by committing the firm to be the anchor tenant.

As the neighborhood sprouted, it shed its traditional South of Broadway descriptor in favor of the trendier SoBro appellation. Perhaps the old name has been eschewed simply because of the way SoBro rolls off the tongue, or perhaps it is because the neighborhood has grown into a distinct identity, no longer defined by its proximity to Broadway. Whatever the case, SoBro has become the center of downtown development in a way that few could have foreseen 20 years ago.

WESTHAVEN[161]

The master-planned Westhaven community is located south of Nashville, in the burgeoning Franklin suburbs. While it is not in Nashville proper, it is worth mentioning for its uniqueness. With 3,500 homes and a commercial center, the development is an interesting case showing how Metro Nashville's businesses have successfully leveraged their local knowledge and faith in the market to make strong gains, at a time when outsiders were less confident.

Before Southern Land Company began developing the immense residential, golf, and commercial project, founder and CEO Tim Downey commissioned several consulting firms to analyze the housing market and growth projections for the area. The firms were concerned whether sleepy West Franklin was actually in the growth path for the area. The planned site was two miles from downtown Franklin and about eight miles from the heart of the thriving Cool Springs retail and office district. Some wondered about sustained job growth in the Nashville metro area and the real demand for premium homes at prices high enough to support the massive amenity program envisioned by Downey.

But Downey felt the data showed real strength for the Franklin jobs corridor and the regional base of healthcare, entertainment, and automotive industries. There was population inflow to the metro region, low taxes, and good schools. With two successful projects in Franklin and Brentwood already under his belt, he had the confidence to proceed.

A master-planned community of this scale had never been tried in Middle Tennessee, and the unique traditional neighborhood design concepts were also new to the region. The new urbanism concept of higher-density town centers, traditional streets, sidewalks, parks, a school, and alley-loaded garages was catching on across the nation, but not yet in Tennessee. Downey had seen several examples of great traditional neighborhood development projects and believed that Nashville and Franklin would embrace the return to the traditional elements and lifestyle, but the execution had to be exceptional.

Southern Land Company engaged Duany Plater-Zyberk (DPZ), the Miami-based architectural firm that designed the award-winning Seaside project near Destin, Florida, which was made famous as the set for the movie *The Truman Show*, to lead the initial visioning planning and design effort.

The Westhaven plan is consistent with DPZ's belief that master-planned communities of this scale function best as small towns within a town. This includes providing a variety of home sizes and prices with a mix of townhomes, condominiums, and "age-in-place" options (homes for older adults to remain in as they age). All homes feature strong architectural details, have no repetition, and are immersed in verdant horticulture, tall trees, and stunning public spaces. The community includes a golf course and a 300,000-square-foot town center complete with restaurants, shops, a salon, grocery store, health center, bank, and solutions for all daily needs and services. At its launch, it was one of the grandest undertakings in the vein of new urbanism nationally.

© *Zach Goodyear*

The original plan called for up to 3,500 houses and completion in 20 years. When the financial collapse led to the recession and housing crisis, about 600 homes were occupied. New home sales slowed dramatically, but the project was well funded and remained profitable during the recession, returning to brisk sales in a few years. The community now has over 2,000 occupied homes with about 1,500 to go.

Downey believed in the region's future growth and leaped. Projects of this scale carry great risk, but by creating something special and filling both unmet and projected needs in the market, Southern Land Company has prospered. Westhaven, like Nashville and Franklin, has drawn people from across the country. In the end, it paid to bet on Nashville.

Neighborhoods to Watch

In Nashville, you can throw a dart at a map, and chances are, you'll hit a neighborhood that's worth investing in. The city on the whole is experiencing an enormous development boom. However, there are a few standouts among the tightly packed field.

East Nashville is certainly one neighborhood to keep an eye on. While there has been much development there in recent years, the first plans for high-rise development have only recently been announced. It is such a desirable neighborhood that there's potential for many more high-rises.

Downtown is a great area still on the upswing. Specifically, the West End corridor is a place to watch. For unknown reasons, there has not been a lot of high-rise development there for several years.

Finally, the Cumberland River area in downtown should be on every developer's radar. The fact that so much prime waterfront land, right in the heart of downtown, has gone undeveloped is mind-boggling. This is sure to be an area of large development in the coming years, especially with the River North project, which will be discussed in the next section.

Commercial Real Estate Development

Commercial real estate development is experiencing just as large of a boom as residential development. In the '80s, just three office towers were built in downtown Nashville, and in the '90s, just two.[162] Today, you can find that many projects in a month, and demand is still high. Downtown office vacancy rates are a low 5.4 percent.[163] As reported by *Urban Land*, "There is enough demand from companies to fill an additional 4 million square feet (372,000 sq m) of new, class A office space in downtown Nashville, according to a 2018 market analysis."[164]

Fortunately, numerous developers are investing in the city in order to help meet the demand. (For more information on commercial developments, the Nashville Downtown Partnership provides an excellent interactive map of downtown business development: www.nashvilledowntown.com/business/development-map.) It's interesting to note that in the early days of Nashville's development, the majority of developers were Nashville natives, but today, that trend has reversed itself. Out-of-town developers have poured massive amounts into the city, allowing it to transform in remarkable ways that local money alone could not accomplish. Some of the biggest developments in Nashville right now are funded by firms outside of the city, including Nashville Yards, River North, Fifth + Broadway, OneCity, Broadwest, and Four Seasons.

Nashville Yards

Nashville Yards is the brainchild of Southwest Value Partners, a San Diego real estate firm. The master-planned development will lie on a 14-acre site in downtown Nashville that used to be the home of the Christian publishing company LifeWay. (LifeWay is still in business and simply relocated, not needing 14 acres.)

As a fun side note, to make way for the new development, the 15-story LifeWay building, made of a pinkish-tan granite with a huge cross on the side, had to be demolished. It was a very recognizable building in town, so on the day of the demolition, Nashvillians (including Angie and her family) gathered to watch it be imploded. In saying goodbye to the iconic building, we can now greet a massive development that matches the growing scale of our city.

With more than 3.5 million square feet of Class A and creative office space, 400,000 square feet of retail and entertainment space,

1,000 residential units, and 1,100 hotel rooms, Nashville Yards will have a little bit of everything.[165] Tourists, residents, and office workers will all find something to draw them to Nashville Yards. There will be a Grand Hyatt hotel, a concert venue, a movie theater, and a 1.3-acre park, and the development will be home to Amazon's new Operations Center of Excellence.[166]

River North[167]

Since 2000, Monroe Investment Partners has been assembling land on the East Bank of the Cumberland River to create what is now known as River North. The 125-acre River North Development District is ideally situated between historic Germantown and East Nashville and is becoming Nashville's premier riverfront mixed-use community.

In June 2019, more than 12 acres were sold, inaugurating a project that will ultimately include 1,136 apartments, 138,000 square feet of retail space, and 48,000 square feet of office space. With its mile-long riverfront park and pedestrian bridge over the Cumberland River connecting to Germantown, River North will provide an incredibly special environment in which to live, work, and play.

Fifth + Broadway

Another of the big developments right now is Fifth + Broadway, which is being built on the lot where the old convention center was. The project will include a 34-story apartment tower and a 25-story office tower, most of which has been leased by AllianceBernstein for their massive corporate relocation of their global headquarters from New York to Nashville. The building will also house the 56,000-square-foot National Museum of African American Music, which will include a 200-seat theater.[168]

OneCity

OneCity is a 19-acre development near Centennial Park. It's home to a Microsoft regional office and the Center for Medical Interoperability, a revolutionary healthcare nonprofit that will be discussed more in Chapter 7, "Healthcare: The Number One Industry."

Like the other mentioned developments, OneCity is focused on creating a place not just to conduct business but to live. To this end, lifestyle features are interwoven into the project, including a lot of green spaces, sand courts for volleyball, a vegetarian restaurant, and an indoor cycling studio. Ryan Doyle, General Manager of OneCity, said, "If you sacrifice some space for really great urban design and connections with nature, we think it will pay back tenfold in real-estate values."[109] It's a win-win: Nashville gets beautiful developments on the forefront of urban design, and developers make more money.

Broadwest

Among the large developments mentioned in this chapter, Broadwest is noteworthy in that it includes a 21-story office tower, a

34-story skyscraper containing 196 high-end condominiums and a 234-room luxury Conrad hotel, and a three-story building with retail and creative office space.[170] The three buildings will be connected by a 1.5-acre plaza. The $550 million, 1.2-million-square-foot mixed-use project is being developed by Huntsville, Alabama-based Propst Development. Occupying a full city block located right outside downtown, Broadwest will connect downtown to Midtown through the West End corridor.

Said Chris Brown, Principal, "Propst Development is excited and honored to have a part in expanding Downtown Nashville's vibrant core. The unprecedented growth that Nashville is experiencing is a reflection of all that the city has to offer, and we feel that Broadwest is a key component of that growth."

Four Seasons

Broadwest is not the only development to combine a luxury hotel with private residences. A 40-story luxury tower developed by Dean Stratouly's Congress Group is currently rising in SoBro and will feature a Four Seasons hotel and private residences.

Residents will enjoy all hotel amenities, with room service and 24-hour valet parking, and will have access to Four Seasons' worldwide network of properties.

The City's Role in Development

Nashville's development boom was not a fluke of chance but a calculated expansion encouraged by the city's leaders. New developments benefit the city, both directly with property taxes and indirectly through boosts to the local economy. For instance, Wiltshire, former Director of the Mayor's Office of Economic and Community Development and now Chief Strategy and Intergovernmental Affairs Officer in the MDHA, estimates that Nashville Yards "will generate $429 million in property taxes plus an uncounted amount of sales tax income over the next 30 years."[171]

With the economic benefits to be gained, the city understands that it has an important role to play in encouraging development. A key way the city supports developers is through investment in infrastructure. If you want to build in a city, you can either convert or tear down current structures, or you can build somewhere nothing has been built before. The challenge of building on new land is that the needed infrastructure of roads and utility lines is typically absent. In Nashville, developers can rely on the city's partnership in creating this infrastructure base. For Nashville Yards, the city has committed $15.2 million for road, sewer, and other infrastructure work.[172] The city is also working on transit improvements to accommodate Nashville's recent expansion; several of these initiatives are discussed in Chapter 8.

While the city is quick to support developers, it is strategic in guiding development to reflect Nashville's identity as a livable city with small-town feel. Nashville does not encourage development for development's sake; rather, it invests in the projects that enhance the city. A great example of this is when the city shot down a proposal for a six-lane interstate through downtown, recognizing that you don't build a neighborhood by putting a freeway through it. An interstate could have killed Nashville's downtown. Fortunately, instead of an interstate, the city reached an agreement for the four-lane Korean Veterans Boulevard, which injected new life into the area, expanding the footprint of downtown and becoming an epicenter for development. Along these same lines, Nashville has adopted a parks and greenways master plan—Plan to Play—that encourages new developments to incorporate green spaces. This ensures that as Nashville develops, it will not turn into a concrete jungle.

Ultimately, developments in Nashville are increasingly a mutually beneficial partnership between the city and developers.

Coda

Nashville is experiencing a boom of both residential and commercial real estate. Downtown in particular has seen an explosion of growth in the past 20 years, but neighborhoods across the city have seen development. Some of the most exciting dimensions of Nashville real estate right now are luxury hotels, multiuse condo towers, and other large development projects.

In the next part of the book, we will explore the characteristics of Nashville that have served as catalyst for this great rise in development.

PART II

★

WHAT MAKES NASHVILLE SPECIAL

NEAL FRANCIS
BUDDY & JULIE MILLER
BIG CROWN
BIG CROWN
BUDDY & JULIE MILLER
BIG CROWN
Peter Stringer-Hye
MOTOWN
DOUBLE-HIT SERIES
JOHNNY CASH
LOCAL
RSD RELEASES
NUTTY

CHAPTER 6

---★---

MUSIC
Country and Beyond

When you land at the airport in Las Vegas, you are immediately greeted by brightly lit slot machines. In Hawaii, your welcome comes in the form of leis. In Nashville, it's live music. In the airport terminal and on the streets downtown, the music of Nashville lets you know exactly where you are.

Nashville is justly proud of being the capital of country music. We've earned our moniker "Music City." Nashville's music industry provides 56,000 jobs and has an approximately $10 billion economic impact on the region each year.[173] Nashville's music business is the most concentrated of any city in the country. There are about 7.8 music industry jobs for every 1,000 working-age residents in Nashville; in comparison, New York has just 2.0, Los Angeles has 2.8, and Austin has 2.6.[174]

Being the capital of country music has been a double-edged sword. It has brought us deserved recognition, but it has also led to the so-called "curse" of Nashville that says country music and country music alone can succeed in Nashville.

Breaking the Curse of Nashville: Music Diversity

For many years, country music was a rural entertainment, limited mostly to the South. It has since become more mainstream across the country and even the world. This internationalization of the art led to a surreal moment for Brandon when he was in Dublin for New Year's and every bar was playing country music; it felt like he was back home in Nashville.

Though today country music is a global phenomenon among consumers, its production is still concentrated in the South, specifically Nashville. As Nashville was increasingly aligned with country music, it became pigeonholed. As soon as people heard an artist was from Nashville, they immediately thought country. This made it difficult for Nashville artists from other genres to succeed in Nashville, much less on a national scale.

The Jack White–Black Keys Feud

Perhaps the greatest modern rock feud involved two Nashville transplants: Jack White and the Black Keys.

The details of the feud are rife with clickbait potential—with White barring Black Keys frontman Dan Auerbach from entering his Nashville studio; complaining about his kids going to the same school as Auerbach's kids, saying, "He gets yet another free reign to follow me around and copy me and push himself into my world"; and allegedly trying to pick a fight with drummer Patrick Carney.[175]

They say there's no such thing as bad publicity, and Jack White and the Black Keys received quite a lot of publicity for the feud. They appear to have since mended fences, and they're both influential figures in the Nashville music scene.

White moved his Third Man Records from Detroit to Nashville in 2009, despite having no previous connection with the city or its music scene. He's made a name for himself as a producer and has become an impresario and an impressive mentor to new artists, as proven by his protégée Margo Price's rise to international superstardom and Grammy-winning sound. He did the score for *Cold Mountain*, produced

64 ★ *Climbing the Charts: The Ascent of Nashville*

the critically acclaimed Loretta Lynn album *Van Lear Rose*, and with the use of a high-altitude balloon, played the first vinyl record in space.

In addition to the enormous success of Dan Auerbach and Patrick Carney's band the Black Keys (four Grammys and millions of albums sold), Dan Auerbach has also become a successful producer. He has his own record label in Nashville, Easy Eye Sound, with a promising roster of up-and-coming artists.

Ultimately, the feud seems to have worked in White's and the Black Keys' favor. Nashville has certainly come out on top, as the two's rivalry and competition has led to a new generation of rock and Americana Nashville artists cultivated by some of the best in the industry.

Thus was the curse of Nashville born: if you were an artist that did anything but country in Nashville, you typically had no chance of making it in or out of Nashville. Indeed, the first few non-country bands who were signed out of Nashville on major contracts ended up being flops commercially.[176] The curse rose to such prominence that many rock bands and artists became superstitious, bordering on paranoid. They went to incredible lengths to disguise that they had any connection with Nashville. Under no circumstances would they admit to the treason of living or recording here.

While the curse had some basis in reality, as the *Nashville Scene* reported, Nashville has never been "the exclusive haven of hillbilly singers many historians make it out to be."[177] Nashville has a long tradition of a diverse music ecosystem, with thriving blues, gospel, pop, and R&B scenes. Today, more than ever, a wide variety of genres flourish in the city, thanks in part to key players who broke the Nashville curse.

The curse was definitively broken about a decade ago with the rise of Kings of Leon, who formed in Nashville. Jack White (best known for being in the White Stripes, the Raconteurs, and The Dead Weather as well as his successful solo career) and the Black Keys further debunked the curse when they chose to move to Nashville. Now, thanks to these heavy hitters clearing the way and proving that it's possible to not just survive but to flourish in Nashville as a rock band, the city is a much more appealing prospect to artists.

Today, as declared by Lonely Planet, "Music City's live scene is as rip-roaring and diverse as a city three times its size. Rock, jazz, soul, hip hop, blues, indie and electronica are all on tap in Nashville."[178] The city is still an incubator for country music, but it has also built thriving niches for rock, hip-hop, indie, and more. In particular, singer-songwriters are drawn to Nashville. Up-and-coming indie and Americana artists, who are typically known for songwriting skills, are flocking to the city.

The Third Coast of American Music: The Importance of Infrastructure

LA and New York—representing the West Coast and the East Coast—are epicenters of the American music industry. However, Nashville has become a music hub (and not just a country music hub) in its own right, becoming the "third coast" from its landlocked position in America's heartland. As Seth Riddle, former talent scout and now Nashville real estate agent, says, "Beginning with the *Grand Ole Opry* and WSM radio broadcasts in the first part of the twentieth century, artists and fans have come to Nashville to create and observe."[179]

Nashville has succeeded as a music hub because we have the infrastructure to support every part of the process. If you want to become a musician, you need a lot more than a place to play on the weekend. Nashville is a one-stop shop for all artist needs, with performance venues, recording studios, places to rent equipment, and more—complete vertical integration. As former mayor Karl Dean said, "What we do differently than a city that just does live music is that we do it all. We do the writing, the production, the creation of the tours. It is all here. The lawyers, the business side, the PR. It is a big, complex industry and Nashville thrives."[180] To give you an idea of the full scale and intricacy of the infrastructure working behind the scenes to support the music industry, we even have a Celebrity Bus Drivers Academy. According to the founder of that academy, Chip Huffman, "Nashville is the entertainer bus capital of the world,"[181] and that's largely because of musician touring.

Important players in the music industry have begun to take notice. As Keith Shackleford, an agent with Paradigm Talent Agency, explains, "Recently, the major agencies have shifted some of their agents and resources from New York and LA to Nashville. With Nashville becoming such an important home base for artist, labels, producers, songwriters, etc., it's important to have the city 'covered' just as they do in New York and LA. It also makes more sense to have back-end resources, such as contract departments, accounting, tour marketing, digital departments, etc., in a city like Nashville, which is relatively affordable but still has access to the industry and creative talent."

All the big talent agencies are here, including Paradigm, CAA, and William Morris. *Rolling Stone* has opened a bureau here, signaling that Nashville has arrived as a rock city and also indicating that country is an important genre that can't be ignored. Apple Music just signed a lease in Wedgewood-Houston to set up a content-creation office. They will no doubt focus on country music, which forms a vital portion of their streaming ("Pure Country" is the second-most popular radio channel on Apple Music, and "A-List Country" is the third-most popular playlist), but they've also indicated a desire to build relationships with pop, hip-hop, and rock artists who operate out of Nashville.[182] This office will be Apple's first real presence in the city and marks Nashville as a streaming music hub.

Nashville Artists

The following artists have all called the Nashville area home at some point. We've included their hometowns, to show how many of them moved from across the country and world to reach this music mecca:

- Dolly Parton—Sevierville, TN
- Justin Timberlake—Memphis, TN
- Taylor Swift—Reading, PA
- Jack White—Detroit, MI
- Kid Rock—Romeo, MI
- Carrie Underwood—Muskogee, OK
- Kesha—Los Angeles, CA
- Nathan, Caleb, Jared, and Matthew Followill of Kings of Leon—Oklahoma; Memphis, TN; and Mississippi
- Peter Frampton—Bromley, England
- Robert Plant—West Bromwich, England
- Keith Urban—Whangarei, New Zealand

- Luke Bryan—Leesburg, GA
- Blake Shelton—Ada, OK
- Michael McDonald—St. Louis, MO
- Tim McGraw—Delhi, LA
- Sheryl Crow—Kennett, MO
- Faith Hill—Ridgeland, MS
- Jason Aldean—Macon, GA
- Hayley Williams, Taylor York, and Zac Farro of Paramore—Meridian, MS; Nashville, TN; and Voorhees Township, NJ
- Gillian Welch—Manhattan, NY
- Alan Jackson—Newnan, GA
- Billy Ray Cyrus—Flatwoods, KY
- Steve Winwood—Handsworth, England
- Patrick Carney and Dan Auerbach of the Black Keys—Akron, OH
- Hillary Scott of Lady A—Nashville, TN
- Martina McBride—Sharon, KS
- Joy Williams and John Paul White, formerly of The Civil Wars—Nashville, TN, and Muscle Shoals, AL
- Vanessa Carlton—Milford, PA

TMZ also recently opened a bureau here. Our personal opinions of the paparazzi aside, the gossip media is an undeniable part of celebrity culture, so having TMZ in town is a sign that Nashville is now recognized as a city of celebrities, primarily musicians, but increasingly, also of actors and professional athletes. More and more artists from outside of Nashville are choosing to relocate here. Some move here at the start of their career, and others come after already achieving a measure of success.

While our infrastructure can rival that of New York and Los Angeles, Nashville's small-town vibe and deeply ingrained music culture offers unique benefits that the East Coast and West Coast hubs can't provide.

What Sets Nashville Apart from New York and Los Angeles

In the trio of Nashville, New York, and Los Angeles, Nashville may seem like the clear underdog, but remember: don't underestimate the underdog. Nashville has a lot to offer that Los Angeles and New York can't.

The number one advantage Nashville has over New York and Los Angeles is that everything is cheaper here. Nashville is more expensive than a small town in the middle of Kentucky, but if you're a starving artist just starting out, it will certainly be much easier to make ends meet in Nashville than in New York or LA. As *Forbes* writer Danny Ross reported, "As of February 2017, the average

Chapter 6: Music ★ 67

apartment in New York rents for $3,073 a month. In Nashville, you can rent two entire houses for that amount (the rent average is $1,420), often with a backyard shed to function as a home recording studio and office."[183] (The rent average has gone up since 2017, but Nashville remains far more affordable than New York or LA.)

The fact that the "third coast" is not on a coast at all and instead in the middle of "flyover country" is another benefit. If you're on one coast or the other, it's incredibly difficult to physically reach the population on the opposite coast. In contrast, from Nashville's central location, you can reach half of the country's population with a day's drive.[184] From a logistical standpoint, Nashville is the perfect place from which to start tours and ship records. Touring has quickly outpaced album sales as the primary revenue source for musicians, so Nashville's ideal geographic location is a strategic advantage.

While Nashville is smaller than New York and LA, we have the music infrastructure of a much larger city. "World-class studios filled with amazing gear are peppered all over town," says Seth Riddle. "You don't need to go anywhere to work when you're not on the road."[185] We have many great recording studios—more than 190,[186] some famous, some obscure—so artists can find one that fits their needs and style. With Nashville being a smaller city but still having so many recording studios, it's easier to get noticed here than in bigger cities like New York and Los Angeles. Sometimes it pays to be a big fish in a smaller, more concentrated pond. In the big cities, even incredible talent can be overlooked.

Nashville has many quantifiable advantages, but one of the greatest can't be summed up with facts and figures; it's the music community itself and its deep roots of collaboration and support. There's relatively little backstabbing in the Nashville music community, with artists seeking to support one another instead of competing with each other. As the *Washington Post* described it, "The country music songwriting community is competitive but uniquely close; a tightknit, supportive, fiercely loyal family."[187]

The sheer quantity of working musicians—more than 5,000[188]—in the city guarantees that artists will be able to make and develop important professional and networking relationships. In our opinion, we have the most talented session players and backing musicians in the world. Nashville is such a great, desirable place to live in that many of these free agents have chosen the city as their home. That means if you need a bass player last minute, you'll be able to find one nearby who is available. You also never know when you'll run into a fellow musician. Your Uber driver could be a drummer, who invites you to a house party, where you meet yet more musicians, who introduce you to more industry contacts. Before long, you could be in touch with a publishing company.

Nashville's small-town feel and prevalence of talent have combined to create an environment that demands respectful working relationships. There's enough talent in

Nashville that people can be easily replaced if they exhibit poor behavior, and the tight-knit community ensures that word of that poor behavior will soon travel to others. As such, people are thoughtful and considerate in how they treat others. Luke Laird of Creative Nation, a Nashville-based music company, said, "If you have a poor attitude about stuff or you start trying to be shady, it doesn't matter how talented you are. There are just too many talented people in this town. If you do something unethical, people just quit working with you."[189] We've found that this attitude is true within the real estate community in Nashville as well; throughout nearly every industry in Nashville, disreputable characters are discovered and quickly held accountable.

Cowriting and collaboration are the standard in Nashville. Nashville even has a local musical language, the Nashville Number System, that makes it easier for artists to collaborate. With this simplified notation system, as long as you know a few basic chord progressions, you can jam with others. It's only natural that collaboration should be so important here, as country music and related genres are not "learned" but passed from one generation to another. That tradition continues today, even as the music changes and evolves.

Since music is woven into the fiber of the city, the general community is also very supportive of artists. It may seem like a small thing, but it makes a huge difference. People respect music as a career choice here and won't scoff at artists. Having people treat your career choices as legitimate goes a long way in keeping you encouraged in your path. Plus, people are more accommodating of artists here than elsewhere. Employers will work around music schedules in a way that wouldn't happen in a lot of other places. They often give significant time off for a tour with the promise of a job still waiting when the musician returns. Even something like getting a bank loan is easier here, where people understand the unique challenges that come with being an artist.

In addition to these location, infrastructure, and community benefits, Nashville as a city is supportive of artists.

How the City Supports the Music Scene

Nashville has worked hard to position itself as a place that is hospitable to artists and supportive in their endeavors. There are several programs and organizations designed specifically to assist artists.

The Music City Music Council, an association of business leaders working to develop Nashville into *the* place to be for musicians, has been a great ally for artists. One project they helped bring to life was the Ryman Lofts, a 60-unit downtown apartment complex of subsidized housing specifically for people pursuing a career in the arts.[190]

The National Entrepreneur Center has also provided unique opportunities to those involved in the arts, with their music business accelerator, Project Music, created in conjunction with the Country Music Association (CMA). It's like a mini *Shark Tank* specifically for music-related startups. The accelerator will provide six to eight startups with a $20,000 investment and mentorship to help get their idea off the ground.[191]

Another way the city supports artists is through rebates. It's a little-known fact, but an increasing number of Hollywood films and video games are being scored right here in Nashville. Electronic Arts, one of the largest video game companies in the world, now does the majority of its scoring in Nashville because, in the words of Steve Schnur, the worldwide executive for music and music marketing for EA, "[Nashville] musicianship is as good as it gets."[192] This segment of the music business greatly contributes to the economic viability of the music scene. As such, the state is working on financial incentives—like a 25 percent rebate for producers—to encourage more of this business.[193]

With all the state-of-the-art amenities of a big-city music scene but the tight-knit, supportive community of a small town, Nashville is the best of both worlds. It's no wonder it has been so attractive to artists, both new and established. While Nashville has a place for nearly all genres, one is particularly special to the city: Americana.

Nashville Music Associations[194]

Nashville is home to several music associations that provide resources and offer networking opportunities for artists:

- Americana Music Association
- Academy of Country Music
- Country Music Association
- Gospel Music Association
- International Bluegrass Music Association
- National Museum of African American Music
- Barbershop Harmony Society Quartet (which sponsors various competitions)
- Nashville Songwriters Association International

The Americana Tradition: Song Is King

Americana is a newer term, first entering the Merriam-Webster dictionary in 2011, where it is defined as "a genre of American music having roots in early folk and country music."[195] Americana is a unique blend of history and modernity. The music is rooted in long, wide-ranging traditions of country, gospel, folk, bluegrass, R&B, and blues music, but the Americana artists of today instill their own modern fingerprints on the music. The result is a distinctive sound that feels simultaneously old and new.

Though the label "Americana" is new, the genre itself represents a decades-old tradition of country music. What we call Americana today used to be called alternative country, which was the blanket term for all the country music that didn't fit into the sanitized, cookie-cutter music designed for the radio. Alternative country boasted a "rebel outlaw" sound and lyricism, as epitomized by Hank Williams, one of country music's first rebels. Williams has been described as "Americana 70 years before the word gained popular usage."[196] Americana has also claimed artists like Johnny Cash, Waylon Jennings, Willie Nelson, George Jones, Townes Van Zandt, Woody Guthrie, Patsy Cline, John Prine, Mavis Staples, and even modern rockers like Beck and Keith Richards. Though Americana is particularly suited to single artists, it is home to bands as well, like the Flying Burrito Brothers, the Band, and the Highwaymen.

One of the most well-recognized examples of Americana is the soundtrack for *O Brother, Where Art Thou?*, which has strong bluegrass roots and helped propel Americana into popular culture.

The very act of giving this genre its own label has allowed it to refine and develop its identity. It has also made it easier for fans to access and enjoy this kind of music. Joni Mitchell said, "I used to be monastic, almost. Now I'm like a Tibetan that has discovered hamburgers and television. I'm catching up on Americana."[197] The label of "Americana" has allowed many to discover, appreciate, and binge-consume a whole new genre of music.

Americana has an anti-commercialism streak, but though it operates outside of the traditional music complex, it has a strong grassroots following. PEN/Faulkner award-winning novelist Ann Patchett, who grew up in Nashville and wrote *Bel Canto*, has said, "Americana is the coolest music today."[198] Americana is actually one of the hottest-selling genres not only in Nashville but the country as a whole. In 2016, according to Billboard, Americana albums actually outsold R&B, hip-hop, and dance.[199] Americana artist Chris Stapleton's record *Traveller* sold nearly one and a half million copies, making it the seventh-bestselling album of 2016, just behind records by pop megastars such as Adele, Beyoncé, and Rihanna.[200]

Perhaps more than anything else, what separates Americana from commercial music is that it is rooted in the songwriter tradition. In other areas of the country, when hearing a new song, people may not think much about who wrote it, but in Nashville, we give a lot of credit to the writer behind the song. To us, music is about telling a story, so we understand that the writing is as important as the singing. As Caleb Chatman, of the band Colony House, said, "Song is king."[201]

The result is that Americana music is often far more personal and true to life. One of the reasons Williams has been claimed by Americana is because of his lyricism. He was one of the first "to express, in direct and elegiac lyrics, the intense personal emotions, the dreams and heartaches, of the common people."[202] Americana artists Chris Stapleton, Jason Isbell, and Sturgill Simpson—the trinity of the Americana music revival—have also been celebrated for their lyricism, being called "literary-level songwriters."[203] They don't shy away from difficult, painful emotions or experiences. Simpson said, "I want all that dirt and grime and life-sauce."[204] With this vulnerability and realism, Americana music packs a stiff emotional punch and attains an authenticity missing from some establishment music.

Americana started out in small venues, like Tuesday night performances at American Legion Post 82. It has since blossomed into a genre with mainstream appeal. Isbell's 2015 album, *Something More Than Free*, hit number one on the rock, country, and folk charts and was nominated for two Grammys, winning the Grammy for Best Americana Album.[205] Stapleton has performed with Justin Timberlake and won multiple awards, including multiple Grammys and CMA Awards, and Simpson has attained similar critical acclaim, including a Grammy for Best Country Album for his *A Sailor's Guide to Earth*.

For anyone interested in Americana—listening to it or producing it—Nashville is the place to be. While Americana has reached mainstream status, Americana artists are some of the few who can support themselves and have a successful career with just a local following. Nashville has exactly that kind of dedicated local audience.

Live Music Mecca

Austin, Texas, has styled itself as the Live Music Capital of the World, but Nashville doesn't see it that way. No matter what day of the week it is, you can find live music in Nashville. We have more than 120 performance venues, ranging in size from intimate honky-tonks no bigger than a living room (and sometimes *actual* living rooms) to the 20,000-seat Bridgestone Arena and 69,143-seat Nissan Stadium.[206] *Travel + Leisure*, *Nylon*, *SPIN*, and *Rolling Stone* have all praised Nashville's live music scene,[207] and Bridgestone Arena was *Pollstar*'s 2017 Arena of the Year.[208] In 2018, Bridgestone was ranked sixth in the United States for ticket sales, with 728,629 ticket sales across 61 performances.[209]

Nashville's live music scene is built on a robust mix of traditional honky-tonks and historic venues, alternative music venues, and small, boutique venues.

Holding on to Tradition: United Record

Twenty-four hours a day, six days a week, Nashville-based United Record churns out vinyl records, pressing 30,000 to 40,000 records a day.[210] They are responsible for one-third of all vinyl records sold in stores today and are planning to open a second plant to double their production capabilities.[211]

With the increasing prevalence of on-demand digital music and music streaming services, it can be hard to believe that vinyl records sell so well. But just like some people prefer physical books to e-books, some audiophiles are drawn to records. There has recently been a big uptick in sales of "real" books, and "real" records are experiencing a similar revival.

Many argue that a fresh vinyl record on a state-of-the-art record player provides the best fidelity sound you can create. The sound quality degrades over time with heavy use, but that doesn't deter record lovers. There is something special and alluring about physical, palpable items from a bygone era. People are drawn to the idea of being able to hold music in your hands and even the idea that each listen to the record will be slightly different due to scratches and wear, just as no two live performances are alike.

Traditional Honky-Tonks and Historic Venues

The honky-tonks along Broadway form the neon-lit foundation for Nashville's live music scene. Like Disney World during the day and Las Vegas at night, the Broadway strip is a must-visit spot. If you only have the chance to visit two of Broadway's honky-tonks, we recommend you go to Robert's Western World and Tootsie's Orchid Lounge.

Robert's Western World is one of Nashville's most historically significant honky-tonks. This is where BR5-49 began playing during the 1990s, serving as the catalyst for downtown's meteoric revitalization.

Tootsie's Orchid Lounge, with its iconic purple brick, is one of Nashville's most famous honky-tonks. Tootsie's was first established in 1960. It rose in popularity due to its proximity to the Ryman Auditorium, the exclusive home to the *Grand Ole Opry* at the time. In between acts, artists would pop out the back door and go across the alley to hang out at the Broadway honky-tonks. Tootsie's in particular became a favorite among musicians.

Like the rest of Lower Broadway, the honky-tonk began to struggle as the downtown strip corroded. It received an injection of new life when owner Steve Smith purchased it in 1992, at the seedy nadir of the downtown music scene, when "Lower Broadway was a sea of pornography shops, peep shows and handsome old buildings sitting vacant."[212] When the honky-tonk first opened, they were lucky to make $500 in a day; today, $100,000 is a good day.[213]

Smith describes the honky-tonk as "a museum for, really, music in general, not just country music."[214] Like Robert's Western World, the bar helped to revitalize downtown, and it has become a rite of passage for Nashville stars, with famous faces like Taylor Swift, Kris Kristofferson, Jason Aldean, and many others passing into this electrifying music haven clad in purple.[215]

Lower Broadway is the hub of all things honky-tonk, but it is well worth wandering off the main strip to visit the Station Inn. The Station Inn is a bar in the Gulch that offers up traditional bluegrass. Vince Gill, among others, is a frequent face at the Station Inn and may pop in on any random night to treat the crowd to a set.

Honky-tonks offer intimate performances, often heightened by energy-infused crowds. For a more traditional concert experience, the Ryman Auditorium, with seating for more than 2,000, is a good option. The Ryman is a true slice of Nashville's history and is well worth a visit for its historical value alone. From a technical standpoint, the Ryman also offers some of the best acoustics in the world. With its now iconic status, the venue can draw big names, and each winter, it hosts the *Grand Ole Opry*. The bar for entry at the Ryman is high, essentially guaranteeing that you won't see a bad show there.

Alternative Music Scene

Those looking for a more alternative music scene in Nashville will not be disappointed.

For outlaw country, Dee's Country Cocktail Lounge, which has no cover, is a great choice. For 1950s-vibe Americana, check out the American Legion Post 82, and for more modern Americana, try 12th & Porter.

For punk, Drkmtter is a popular venue. Much of Nashville's music takes place in bars, meaning it's a 21-and-older scene, but Drkmttr offers a much-appreciated safe space for teenager punk shows, with crowds mostly composed of fifteen-to-twenty-five-year-olds. It's a place for cutting-edge, experimental indie and punk music. Coffee shops are another great place for the under-21 crowd to experience live music.

For rock and indie music, the Basement, the Basement East (known locally as the "Beast"), the 5 Spot, 3rd & Lindsley, Cannery Row (the trifecta of the High Watt, the Cannery Ballroom, and Mercy Lounge), and Jack White's Blue Room are solid bets, as is the East Room in East Nashville.

While some places are better than others when it comes to alternative music, don't discount a venue simply for having a country music reputation. Nashville's music scene is becoming increasingly diverse, and that is reflected in the kinds of artists being featured by traditionally country music venues. For instance, the Wu Tang Clan recently played a show at the Ryman, as did Lizzo.

Country Music Hall of Fame

A music tour of Nashville would not be complete without a visit to the Country Music Hall of Fame.

In its early days, the Country Music Hall of Fame was not particularly impressive. It was one of those tourist attractions that your granddad might go to but that you would probably skip. Then, in 2001, the museum was moved to a 130,000-square-foot facility downtown. It is *enormous*. It is also a beautiful, architecturally significant building, designed to look like a piano with windows set in twos and threes to represent a piano's black keys. It installed a ton of new exhibits, and visitor numbers skyrocketed.

Within a few years, the city realized that the museum was still completely undersized. With $100 million in private donations, the museum expanded to 350,000 square feet. The designer and team leader behind the museum's updates was the supremely talented David Baird, of Nashville-based Building Ideas. It's safe to say that Baird is one of our favorite Nashville architects, as he designed our Wagon Wheel office, Angie's house, and Brandon's house, and he is now working on Steve's house as well.

In 2018, TripAdvisor ranked the Country Music Hall of Fame number 12 of top US museums to visit.[216] The general public agreed, with more than 1.2 million people visiting the museum in 2018[217]—and it doesn't even have any dinosaur bones!

Small, Random Venues

It is the small venues that make Nashville's live music scene so distinctive. In these venues, artists can not only play but *get noticed*.

Many of these venues are random one-offs. One of our favorites is the Commodore Grille, which is in the Holiday Inn lobby. When you walk in, you'd think you were in a Wendy's without the counter. There's no stage, just a small platform with some stools. On the surface, there's nothing to suggest it's special, but then the artists get up to perform. The informal environment makes for intimate performances. The venue is a favorite among songwriters and is frequently used as a place to premiere and test brand-new songs.

Local vinyl stores also offer intimate performance spaces. Grimey's New and Pre-Loved Music is one such space that pulls in surprisingly big names. The late John Prine did a Q&A there in 2018, and Mumford & Sons gave a concert there on the same day that they broke the attendance record at the Bridgestone Arena.[218]

The Groove, which is right up the street from our Wagon Wheel office, was the first record store in East Nashville and an important part of Nashville's "it" city designation. Alabama Shakes played there before they even had a record recorded. Seth Riddle, now a real estate agent but previously a talent scout who helped sign Arcade Fire, saw Alabama Shakes perform at the Groove for Record Store Day. "I should've signed them right then," he told us. By the time the Kings of Leon independent label, which Riddle was managing, was up and running, the *Aquarium Drunkard* blog posted an MP3 of Alabama Shakes' "Hold On," and the band was being courted by every label in the US and the UK.

Finally, when it comes to small, unique venues, we would be remiss to not mention Sofar Sounds (Instagram: @sofarnash). Sofar transforms everyday spaces—everything from climbing gyms to clothing boutiques to locals' living rooms—into music venues for secret live shows. If you're fortunate enough to win the ticket lottery, a Sofar performance is an experience not to be missed.

The Music Scene's Connection to the Larger Community

Nashville's music scene is an integrated part of the city. Even if you are not directly involved in the music scene—for instance, if you're a real estate developer—it's important to have an understanding of Nashville's music culture. There are lots of different, objective ways to measure what the best place to live is, but what ultimately draws people to a city is intangible: it's the culture. For Nashville, that's music.

The more vibrant the music scene becomes, the more people want to visit and live in Nashville. When the three of us were considering where we wanted to live, Nashville's music scene certainly played a role in our decision. Atlanta and Charlotte had arguably better job prospects for the careers we wished to pursue, but you can't beat the thrill of live music on a hot summer night. In the words of Ed Hardy, co-chair of the city's music council, "The businesses we are now attracting are not only music businesses, but they want to be here as a place to do business. They may not all be related to music, but music is part of what makes people want to be here."[219]

Besides attracting people and businesses to the city, Nashville's music community has formed strong bonds with the larger community. In general, Nashvillians are respectful of musicians' privacy, and in return, our artists demonstrate great loyalty, giving back to the community through public service and business ventures that benefit the city. For instance, Ketch Secor co-founded the Episcopal School of Nashville, and Kix Brooks co-founded Arrington Vineyards, a world-class vineyard in Arrington, Tennessee.

Two fantastic music-sponsored projects are The Store and Musicians on Call. The Store is Brad Paisley's partnership with Belmont University to provide a "free" grocery store for families in need. Families who are referred by nonprofits and government agencies can shop free of charge at the grocery store, which stocks healthy food and is run by Belmont students. Musicians on Call is an organization that works to bring live and recorded music to patients in healthcare facilities who are unable to leave their beds. As co-founder Michael Solomon says, "Music is this wonderful tool that can change and shape your day, your mood, your memories. Because of those reasons, there was no choice but to bring music to people that need it most."[220]

Another interesting way musicians have begun to interact with the community is by encouraging people to get out and vote. In 2018, Sheryl Crow and Jason Isbell were just two of the musicians who performed a free concert for a Party at the Polls voting rally in Nashville.[221]

Nashville's music scene and the larger community have formed a mutually beneficial relationship, one supporting the other.

Coda

You can't beat our music scene because it encapsulates that "both-and" attitude so common in Nashville. It is richly steeped in history and tradition, yet there is always something new going on. This blend of the familiar and the new is what makes Nashville music so unique. It's a constant reinvention.

Music is inextricably entwined with the city's identity. As such, Nashville, both as a community and as a city, is deeply supportive of its artists. Our music community, which is known for collaboration and the caliber of its songwriting, is a respected, valued part of the city.

When people think of Nashville, music is the first thing to come to mind, but healthcare is actually our largest industry and well worth a deeper discussion.

Mike "Grimey" Grimes[222]

Mike Grimes, a.k.a. "Grimey," represents so much of what makes our music scene so special. He has launched numerous grassroots music venues and hangouts and is an icon in the community.

Grimey grew up in Owensboro, Kentucky, and from about eleven years old, he knew that music was all he ever wanted to do. Indeed, for his entire life, except for a stretch of about eight months, his job has been related to music.

He attended Western Kentucky University and played in a band there. At his girlfriend's urging, he moved to Nashville in 1989. He told us that within the first 10 years that he lived in the city, he hoped he could make a contribution to Nashville and help put the city on the map in some way beyond pop country music. That has been a personal mission statement for him. "Music City is called Music City, but people thought about it as country," he said. He wanted to help change that perception.

One of his first steps in that mission was the record store Grimey's New and Pre-Loved Music. In the 1990s, Grimey played with Bobby Bare Jr. in the band Bare Jr. They toured some pretty big stadiums—5,000 to 10,000 seaters—but their record never quite took off. Grimey had worked with several record companies, including a three-to-four-year stint with Sony Music Distribution, and after quitting Bare Jr., he initially thought he'd get another gig. That didn't work out. He'd amassed around 6,000 records due to his work for Sony and his general passion for music, and he decided to put them all in a little house and open a record store. He put his name on the outside in the hopes that people might see it and come inside to hang out with him. Thus was Grimey's born. The year was 1999, just in time for Grimey to achieve his goal of making a contribution to Nashville within 10 years of first moving here.

Grimey's contributions were far from over. Grimey's had low overhead, and he had a rent-free living space with a friend for a year, so he had some flexibility with his finances. One day, he was doing a session with Josh Rouse, and the drummer happened to be a friend who wanted to start a bar. After the session, they walked out of Woodland Studios and into the dive bar Shirley's. Shirley herself was there, and they got to talking. Shirley had leased the bar for 17 years. She was ready to get out and was considering handing the reins over to a woman who wanted to turn it into a Titans bar. "What if I take over the lease and write you a check for all the contents?" Grimey asked her. She said she'd leave right away if he did that, so he wrote her a check for $10,000—his entire savings.

Shirley's had a going-away party the following Monday, and five weeks later, on November 17, 2000, just 10 months after the opening of the record store, Grimey and his friend opened Slow Bar. It was never meant to be a live music venue, but friends of Grimey would record across the street and come play at the Slow Bar after. The bar made more money on nights music was played, so Grimey started inviting more artists to play. As the bar transitioned to a live music venue, it lost its initial clientele, who didn't want to pay covers. So Grimey buckled down and started booking more gigs, so that the bar had live music almost every night and could build a new customer base. Among the acts that played the Slow Bar were the Shins, Kings of Leon (the Slow Bar was actually their first show ever), Postal Service, and the Black Keys. Most of the bands played just for the money earned through cover charges, but he did pay $1,000 for the Shins. The Black Keys asked for just $100, which he gave them. The next day, he tried to book them again, but they'd gotten a spot opening for Beck on his tour and didn't return to Nashville for a while.

Unfortunately, despite being well loved, the Slow Bar ended up closing down after three years. Grimey was new to running a business, and the lease was unattractive. The bar simply became unsustainable. "It was my school of hard knocks lessons," he said. Despite its short tenure, many—including us—credit the Slow Bar with igniting the spark for a new music vibe in Nashville. It also helped revitalize the East

78 ★ *Climbing the Charts: The Ascent of Nashville*

Nashville neighborhood. The bar is still missed today. In the song "East Nashville Skyline," singer-songwriter Todd Snider says, "I'm still mad about the Slow Bar. I guess that's just the way things are. Something good comes along. Then it's gone."

After the Slow Bar closed, Grimey's next venture was as co-owner of the Basement, a 200-cap room in the basement of the record store, and then later, the Basement East (the "Beast"), with a cap of 600. Both are popular venues in town that have featured big-name talent and propelled Grimey to tastemaker status. Metallica played the Basement the night before Bonnaroo, and Cage the Elephant played there when they were called Perfect Confusion. Grimey books artists from a wide variety of acts, with no genre discrimination. What excites him the most about Nashville is that there's a constant influx of new people, so you're never bored. There's always something new to see and hear.

One of Grimey's strongest skills is recognizing new talent before they make it big. He wants the Basement to be the place where people get their first chance to be heard in Nashville. To this end, he hosts New Faces Night, an open mic for up-and-coming artists. No matter how many things he has booked, he always tries to make it to New Faces Night. "I love nothing more than nurturing new talent," Grimey told us. "Some are going to make it, some aren't, but all of them need to be treated equally. Too many places, too many clubs, too many cities herd them in like cattle. They don't treat them like humans, don't act like they're important. I come from the other side and know that I wouldn't be making a penny if they weren't here. So every band should be treated like you're in your living room."[223]

Grimey has undoubtedly succeeded in making a contribution to Nashville and helping put the city on the map in a way beyond pop country music. His venues and record store maintain funky, authentic vibes and feature a diverse array of music beyond pop country.

He said that he loves that what he's doing is resonating with Nashville, but at the end of the day, he's just focused on doing what he loves. That's part of what makes the Nashville music scene so special. There's a place for everyone and everything. If you do what you love, you can find a community that resonates with it.

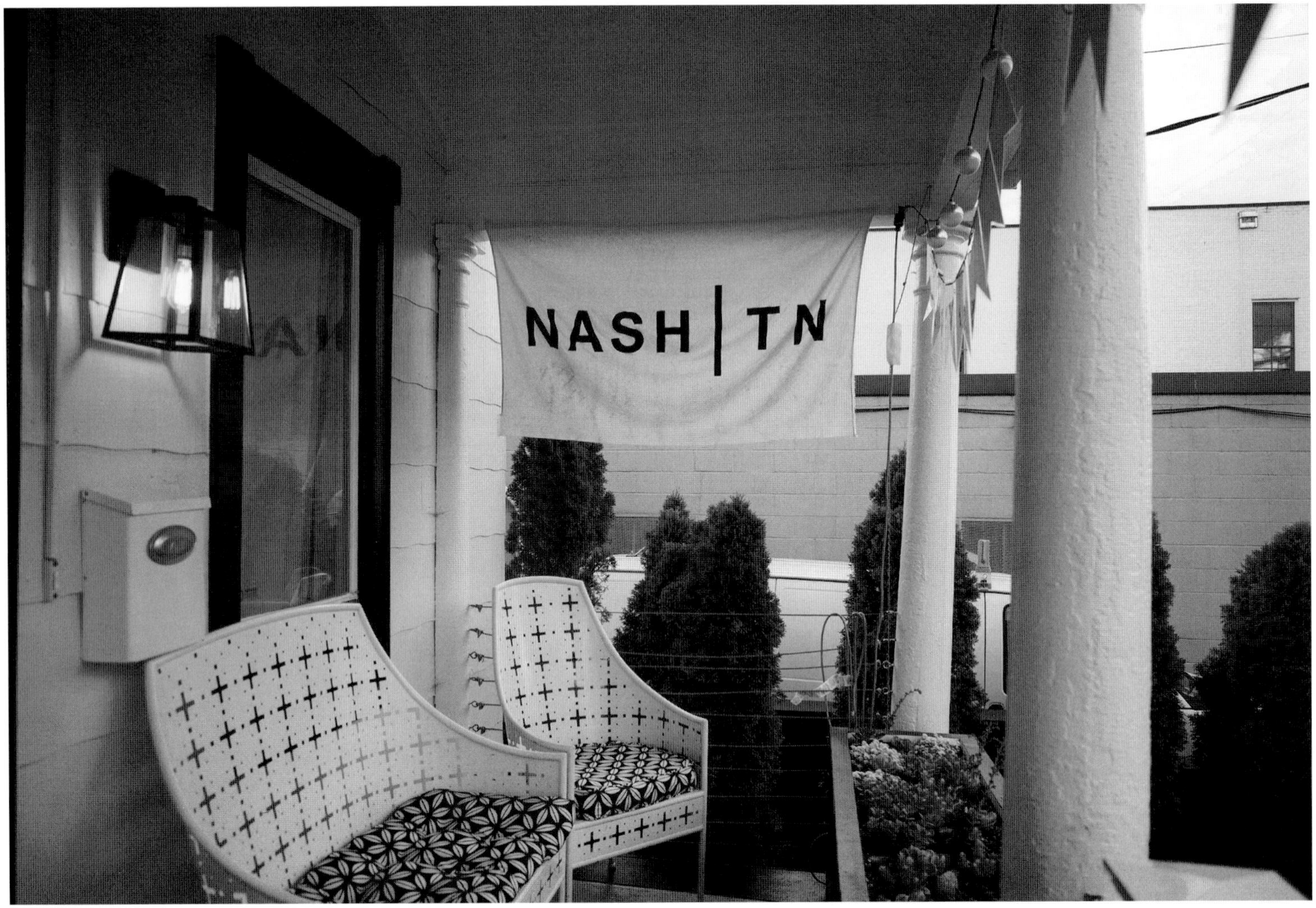
NASH | TN

CHAPTER 7

HEALTHCARE
The Number One Industry

When people think of Nashville, Music City, they assume music is our number one industry. Music is integral to the city's identity and culture, but in terms of economic benefit—dollars brought in and number of people employed—healthcare is the winner. Take a look at the numbers:

- Nashville has 500 healthcare companies and an additional 400 professional service companies—from legal practices to accounting firms—designed to support the healthcare industry.[224]

- The Nashville healthcare industry generates $92 billion in annual revenue, with $46.7 billion yearly economic impact on Nashville.[225] That's more than four times what the music industry generates.

- Nashville healthcare companies provide a total of 570,000 jobs, 273,000 of which are local.[226] In a metro area of 1.6 million, that's a significant number. By 2022, 1 in every 11 new jobs in Tennessee will be in healthcare.[227]

Nashville has been called the "Silicon Valley of Health Services." Simply put, Nashville has become the place to be when it comes to healthcare.

Nashville's Healthcare Roots: The Hospital Corporation of America

Five of the eight largest for-profit hospitals in the United States are based in the Nashville MSA.[228] Of these, the Hospital Corporation of America (HCA) is the largest, with 185 hospitals and 119 freestanding surgery centers across 21 states and the United Kingdom as of 2018.[229] HCA employs approximately 38,000 doctors, 87,000 nurses, and 250,000 overall employees.[230] To help put the size of HCA in context, 1 in every 20 babies born in the United States is born in an HCA hospital.[231] It's not just quantity where HCA excels. In the 2019 IBM Watson Health study of top-performing hospitals in the country, HCA had 10 of the top 100.[232]

HCA is a titan of not only the Nashville economy but also of the Nashville community. HCA was founded in 1968 by Tommy Frist Jr. and his father, Dr. Thomas Frist Sr. A year before the founding, in 1967, Tommy was in the army working as a surgeon and considering what to do following his service. With a father as a doctor, medicine had always seemed a clear path, and it was the one he had followed until this point. However, he was also drawn to the world of business. His career decisions were further complicated when his father's friend Jack Massey, who had bought Kentucky Fried Chicken and transformed it into a large chain, offered him a job leading Kentucky Roast Beef, a new division intended to compete with Arby's.[233]

So Tommy had a choice. As scribbled by Massey on a Kentucky Roast Beef brochure, "Chicken, beef or medicine. Make your decision soon."[234] In characteristic Nashvillian fashion, Tommy rejected the supposedly either/or decision and instead chose both/and. He wanted to be both a doctor and a businessman. He began by buying, with other investors, a single small, local hospital. After transforming that hospital into a moneymaker, he moved on to expansion. He was inspired by chains like KFC and Holiday Inn, which had successfully expanded across the country while maintaining consistent levels of quality. With both KFC and Holiday Inn, you knew exactly what you would get, no matter

Q&A with Hayley Hovious, President of the Nashville Health Care Council

Q: If an individual or company is moving to town and wants to get into healthcare, where should their first stop be and why?

A: The Nashville Health Care Council should, without question, be a company's or individual's first stop in Nashville. It's what we are here to do—welcome and connect healthcare interests to Nashville.

The council has programs for the needs of both individuals and companies. For individuals, our Leadership Health Care program nurtures the talent of leading young professionals in Nashville's healthcare community. Through the program, emerging leaders are able to increase their knowledge of the industry and meaningfully expand the size of their network. Another program for individuals is our Council Fellows program. It's a unique educational initiative that brings together highly select industry executives, from around the country, to explore solutions to challenges facing the US healthcare system.

From the larger perspective, the Nashville Health Care Council has an impressive corporate network. As the connector here, our role is to make sure new interests have a good sense of what the healthcare industry here looks like.

The beauty of the council for companies is that it immediately plugs them into a network of executives in healthcare, which are some of the richest and deepest industry networks you'll find in the country. Our event programming gives companies amazing exposure to insights from top-notch thought leaders on a range of timely healthcare topics.

The council's efforts and the Nashville healthcare community are very relationship based. So, if you're a service or auxiliary company that works with healthcare companies, we provide a forum for you to get to know people in a way that's very Nashville.

Q: Is there a particular type of healthcare business or affiliated business that Nashville could really use or needs more of?

A: Nashville is, by far, the healthcare services capital of the nation. Where we have specific opportunities to build our ecosystem are on the forefront of health tech and in increasing the number of medical device and pharmaceutical companies located here. With strong medical and academic centers of excellence, like Vanderbilt University and Vanderbilt University Medical Center, which are located right here in Nashville, there is a huge opportunity for us to make an impact in these key areas.

Q: What are you the most excited about regarding Nashville healthcare over the span of the next two to three years?

A: I'm excited about what's ahead. In the next two to three years, the Nashville healthcare industry has a huge opportunity. That opportunity focuses around our ability to promote innovation. Nashville is where the rubber meets the road. This makes us incredibly valuable when it comes to creating the next generation of healthcare service delivery companies and health tech companies who will truly benefit patients and benefit them on a large scale.

which location you went to. Tommy sought to apply that same principle to the hospital world, with many hospitals under a single corporate umbrella. Thus were the seeds for HCA sown.

HCA's influence extends beyond its own corporate walls. In the same way that the Nashville music community thrives on collaboration and support of fellow artists, HCA has encouraged the development of new healthcare companies. More than 160 national healthcare-related companies have sprung from roots in HCA, including LifePoint Health, the fourth-largest for-profit hospital as of 2018.[235] Hayley Hovious, President of the Nashville Health Care Council and former Executive Director of the Council Fellows, gives the executives of HCA credit for being supportive of people reinventing themselves and reinvesting in the industry. Instead of getting upset when people went off to start new companies, HCA supported them actively.

That mindset of giving back and supporting the community is a big part of Nashville culture, and it is a key part of what has helped the Nashville healthcare ecosystem become the Silicon Valley of Health Services.

The Power Players of Healthcare in Nashville

It's not just happenstance that so many healthcare companies have clustered in Nashville. In a survey of Nashville Health Care Council member CEOs, 95 percent said that being headquartered in Nashville was "important to their company's positive performance."[236] If you want to be a major player in the tech industry, you go to Silicon Valley, and if you want to be a major player in the healthcare industry, you go to Nashville.

HCA is king of the Nashville healthcare industry, but there are multiple other for-profit health systems based here that, if they were in another city, could easily secure the king position for themselves. Community Health Systems, based in Franklin (which lies in the Nashville MSA), is the second-largest for-profit health system in the United States, with 158 hospitals.[237] As already mentioned, the Nashville MSA is also home to the fourth-largest for-profit health system, LifePoint Hospitals, which is a spinoff of HCA and has 72 hospitals.[238]

Of nonprofit hospitals, Vanderbilt University Medical Center is the largest in Nashville and is a bastion of the community. In 2016, it had more than two million clinic and inpatient visits, and it "provided $513 million in uncompensated care, community benefits, and other unrecovered costs."[239]

Vanderbilt University Medical Center—which includes Vanderbilt University Hospital, Vanderbilt Children's Hospital, and more—is highly respected and appreciated in the community, but Vanderbilt's impact on healthcare is not just in its hospitals but also its outstanding research programs. The medical center is a leader in genome and personalized medicine research. In 2016, Vanderbilt received a nearly $72 million grant from the federal government to establish a data research center, with a focus on genome mapping, as part of the national Precision Medicine Initiative, which seeks to move away from a one-size-fits-all approach to healthcare, instead tailoring healthcare treatment to the individual patient.[240] The award was the largest federal grant in the university's history, but the university has received even larger private donations, like the previously mentioned $300 million gift from Martha Ingram.

Like any industry, healthcare is constantly changing. Companies merge, consolidate, and go out of business, and new companies spring up. Yet Nashville has held an enduring dominance over the sector for decades and remains at the forefront of innovative healthcare.

Q&A with Senator Bill Frist, MD

Q: What makes Nashville's healthcare sector so special?

A: The Nashville healthcare ecosystem is globally recognized as the "Silicon Valley of Health Services." Nashville by far has greater reach and touches more patients through health service delivery than any other city in the US. For example, one Nashville company has 25,000 emergency room visits *every day.*

There are several other examples. HCA, the brainchild of my brother, Thomas F. Frist Jr., had over 31.2 million patient encounters last year, more than any facility or system anywhere in America. Nashville-based Change Healthcare processed over $1 trillion in health claims last year—that's almost one of every three dollars spent on health in the US each year. Another Nashville health organization, HealthStream, founded by my nephew, Robert A. Frist Jr., virtually educates a quarter of a million unique healthcare professionals *every* 24 hours.

The ambitions of Nashville's healthcare ecosystem are not limited to the United States. For example, one Nashville company accounts for a third of all hospital admissions in Greater London

84 ★ *Climbing the Charts: The Ascent of Nashville*

and 40 percent of the healthcare revenue, working with 3,000 consulting doctors.

And all this just barely touches the surface.

Q: Has Nashville always been such a healthcare hub?

A: The modern healthcare ecosystem in Nashville began just over 50 years ago with the founding of HCA. Nashville demonstrated entrepreneurial spirit and was rapidly growing—which is still true today. Deep health management expertise attracted others, initially mainly in the hospital sector. Many healthcare-related, multi-facility chains across the country subsequently either started or moved their hub and corporate headquarters here.

Indeed, Nashville companies today own or manage 15 percent of all hospital beds in the country and 40 percent of all investor-owned beds. HCA today is ranked as the third-largest healthcare company in the world, behind medical device maker Medtronic and laboratory device manufacturer Thermo Fisher Scientific, according to *Forbes*.[241]

Q. When most people think "healthcare," they first think of doctors and hospitals. Tell us a little bit more about what makes Nashville's healthcare ecosystem so diverse.

A: Nashville is much more than hospitals. It shines from the beginning of one's life through one's final years. HCA delivers 1 out of every 20 babies in the country (200,000 babies a year), and at the other end of the life spectrum, Brookdale (based just outside Nashville) is by far the largest assisted living company in the US, with over 103,000 residents living in 1,100 locations across the country. It's over 30 percent larger than its nearest competitor. Yet another company, Aspire, started by Brad Smith and me, is the largest community-based palliative healthcare company in the nation.

Nashville also leads in the outpatient arena. It is home to Envision, which owns and operates 278 surgery centers that serve 33 million patient visits a year, our nation's second largest ambulatory surgery system.

Nashville today is much more than hospitals, doctors, nurses, and outpatient clinics. We are data and analytics and information technology.

Change Healthcare is a full-service healthcare information technology services company that, through 5,500 hospitals and 900,000 physicians, touches over 14 billion transactions each year. That's a lot of data passing through the Nashville ecosystem.

Q: Nashville has also been called the "Athens of the South." How does education tie into the healthcare sector?

A: The investor-owned and for-profit sector works hand in hand with academics, education, and research. Nashville is home to two medical schools, Vanderbilt and Meharry.

The Vanderbilt genomics database BioVU is the largest single-site DNA bank linked to electronic health records in the US. It has roughly 250,000 DNA samples. Moreover, Vanderbilt is the nation's research leader in biomedical informatics with over 100 informatics faculty, the largest geographically centered bioinformatics department in the US.

And building for the future, Vanderbilt is the largest clinical training center in the southeastern portion of the US, with over 1,200 medical residents and clinical fellows training in over 150 specialties.

The transplant center at Vanderbilt that I started 35 years ago today does more heart transplants than any other in the country. On the topic of transplants, there is a Nashville company that systemwide does more bone marrow transplants than any other nationwide, including MD Anderson and the Cleveland Clinic.

Meharry is the nation's largest private, historically Black academic health sciences center and the only medical school whose stated purpose is to train physicians and dentists to treat the underserved ("Dedicated to eliminating health disparities through education, research and patient care").

Healthcare Diversity

Part of what makes Nashville's healthcare industry special is the diversity. We have everything from ambulatory and outpatient surgery to hospital management to academic research to health information technology.[242] As explained to us by leading Nashville healthcare attorney and executive Andy Smith, of all the services offered, five broad categories are especially important to our healthcare ecosystem: for-profit hospital systems, post-acute and long-term care, ambulatory surgery, hospice care, and support companies.

Among the largest for-profit hospital systems are HCA, Community Health Systems, and LifePoint Hospitals. These hospital systems are critical to the foundation of Nashville's healthcare industry because they have spawned many other companies. If you're curious, the Nashville Health Care Council has published a "family tree" of healthcare in Nashville that shows these branching connections. The diagram is easily accessible via a search of their website, www.healthcare-council.com, or you can find a direct URL in the endnotes.[243]

Post-acute and long-term care is composed of skilled nursing facilities and home care. It includes assisting in rehabilitation and recovery following surgery as well as more long-term care. Brookdale, Amedisys, Diversicare, and Compassus are four of the largest organizations in this field in Nashville.

Ambulatory surgery is surgery that does not require overnight hospital stays. We have several walk-in, walk-out surgery centers in Nashville that function as mini hospitals. They can perform ambulatory surgeries in a skilled, sterile environment, but because of their specialization in outpatient surgery, they can offer the services for lower cost than a full-service hospital. Examples of surgery centers in Nashville are Envision and its subsidiary AMSURG, as well as Surgery Partners.

Hospice care, also known as end-of-life care, is focused on palliation of pain for chronically and terminally ill patients. Today, people are living longer, causing a demographic shift to a larger aging population. As such, hospice care across the country is poised for huge expansion. In Nashville, Compassus and Amedisys are hospice care facilities likely to see expansion in the coming years.

Support companies offer ancillary services that help healthcare organizations function. Like the music industry, part of what allows healthcare to thrive here is the support structure. These ancillary services include billing, revenue cycle management, legal services, and more. Three key support companies are Parallon, one of the country's largest revenue cycle partners in the healthcare field; HealthTrust, a business management consulting firm specializing in improving performance of healthcare providers; and Change Healthcare, a leading independent healthcare technology company. As another example of the kinds of support services available, the law firm the three of us previously worked at had a significant healthcare regulatory practice, with dozens of lawyers dedicated solely to that segment of business at all times. Private-equity and venture capital firms are also key to the support system, as they provide the capital needed to build influential healthcare companies.

These five categories only scratch the surface of the Nashville healthcare ecosystem. There are a myriad of healthcare services firms providing essential care, including organizations that specialize in addiction treatment, behavioral health, dialysis, population health management, pharmacy, wellness, and more. Essentially, no matter what area of healthcare someone is interested in, they can find it in Nashville.

Economic Advantages of Healthcare: A Recession-Proof Industry

Obviously, with the 273,000 jobs the industry provides in Nashville, healthcare is a major factor in Nashville's high level of employment overall. However, the concentration of healthcare sector jobs is an especially important economic advantage because of the reliability of the healthcare industry. People don't stop getting sick or injured simply because the economy is stagnating. People always need healthcare, so it is essentially a recession-proof industry.

The stability of the healthcare industry has given Nashville great economic resilience through challenging times. Specifically, the healthcare industry was a critical factor in Nashville's rapid recovery from the 2008 downturn. From 2008–2010, the manufacturing, professional services, construction, retail, and hospitality industries in Nashville all took a heavy hit, losing tens of thousands of jobs.[244] In contrast, the healthcare industry managed to *add* 15,600 jobs.[245]

The job outlook continues to be promising for the healthcare sector, especially because of the aging population, which increases the demand for healthcare. The US Bureau of Labor Statistics projects that healthcare occupations will grow 18 percent from 2016 to 2026 (much faster than the average growth rate of all occupations—7 percent), adding approximately 2.4 million new jobs (more than any other occupational group).[246]

With such promising job outlooks and many entry-level positions available—both in healthcare organizations and ancillary services—the healthcare industry makes Nashville especially attractive to millennials and Gen Zers. It is one of the reasons Nashville consistently ranks as one of best cities for millennials.

The future is often uncertain, but if you have to bet on the long-term success and stability of an industry, healthcare is like betting on the house in Vegas.

Future of the Healthcare Industry in Nashville

With healthcare set to grow exponentially in the coming years, it's a great time to be in Nashville. The city is already firmly established as a hub for all things healthcare, and it is poised to become an even greater leader in the industry.

From 2005 to 2015, Nashville healthcare companies received more than $940 million in venture capital investments—nearly 60 percent of Nashville's total $1.6 billion in capital investments.[247] The healthcare IT sector is growing particularly quickly. In 2009, healthcare IT investments in Nashville totaled $2 million, and just five years later, in 2014, they had skyrocketed to $62.5 million.[248]

There are numerous promising healthcare startups and nonprofits in Nashville doing innovative, cutting-edge work with the potential to revolutionize healthcare as we know it. The Center for Medical Interoperability is one such nonprofit.

The Center for Medical Interoperability's two-part mission is to ensure that all medical devices speak the same language and to streamline the seamless exchange of information. In an emergency room, you can have 14 different devices running 14 different programs, which makes it difficult for the devices to work together. The result is that humans are often in charge of recording and translating data between devices, creating far more opportunities for inadvertent errors. With interoperability, medical devices can directly communicate with each other, reducing the potential for human-introduced errors.

Tommy Ragsdale, the center's Director of Strategy and Business Development, told us that every day, we kill hundreds of people in hospitals across the country due to the lack of interoperable medical devices and systems at the point of care.[249] By striving to make all medical devices work together, many of those deaths could be prevented. Interoperability could save not only lives but money. Wrongful deaths cost hospitals $38 billion; with interoperability, 75 percent of that cost could potentially be eliminated.[250] Additionally, caregivers' workloads and fatigue would be lessened.

Increasing interoperability also allows for the collection of a holistic set of medical data. This data can help hospitals identify and correct issues, and it can also increase the personalization of a patient's medical care. Data is the key to innovation, so interoperability is the holy grail of healthcare.

The Center for Medical Interoperability has the potential to improve the quality of healthcare across the globe. The center's membership comprises some of the largest hospital systems in the country, including HCA, Community Health Systems, Ascension, and LifePoint. Its board of directors is made up of the CEOs of these organizations.[251] Normally, these healthcare systems wouldn't be allowed to work together, due to anti-trust laws, but due to the center's unique structure as a nonprofit, centralized research and development lab, it acts as a buffer to allow innovative collaboration led by healthcare providers.

It's interesting to note that, though the center's mission is global, the majority of their funding is local. The lab requires $6.5 to $7 million each year to operate, and 85 percent of that funding comes from within a 16-mile radius of Nashville.[252] It goes to show how vital Nashville is in the healthcare field.

Another Nashville startup with the potential for positive disruption in healthcare is MDsave. Launched in 2012, MDsave is increasing transparency in healthcare by allowing patients to easily research and compare healthcare services online. The costs of various procedures can vary wildly from provider to provider, and as a consumer, those costs are often unclear. In addition to increasing transparency, MDsave partners with different providers to offer affordable healthcare. Patients can actually purchase their healthcare services online through MDsave and pay for the procedures upfront, eliminating surprise bills after the fact.

Another Nashville-based disruptor is Contessa, co-founded by Charlie Martin, who used to work at HCA. Physical hospitals are massive cost drivers. Contessa's mission is to try to move recovery and even procedures out of hospitals and into people's homes. This move would not only reduce costs but also have positive impacts on recovery outcomes. Hospitals suffer from high infection rates due to the concentration of ill people. If we can create sterile environments in-home in order to perform simple procedures, hospitals can free up beds for patients who really need them, and costs will drop for everybody—patients, insurers, and hospitals.

Healthcare is on the cusp of many innovative developments, and Nashville is at the center. These coming advancements are sure to benefit not just the healthcare industry, but the city as a whole.

Coda

Nashville is the place to be when it comes to healthcare. We have the greatest concentration of healthcare companies in the country, and with our culture of innovation, we have become an incubator for healthcare startups. Because healthcare is a recession-proof industry, it forms the backbone of Nashville's resilient economy. It will continue to play an important role in the future, with many exciting developments on the horizon.

Though healthcare lends security to our local economy, a great deal of our historic stability is due to a tradition of smart politics, as will be covered in the next chapter.

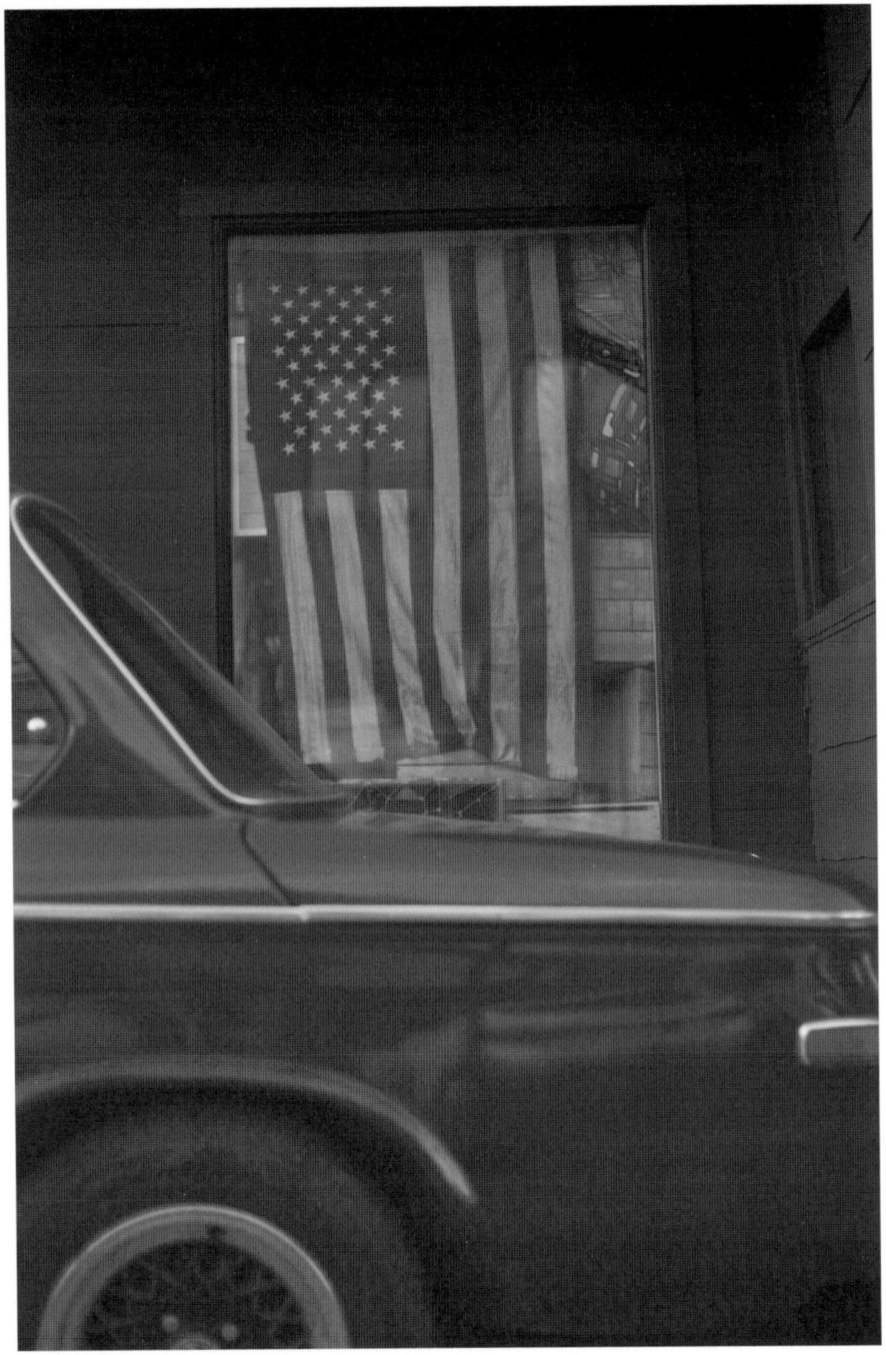

CHAPTER 8

PUBLIC SECTOR AND POLITICS

Nashville Takes Care of Its Own

As the capital of Tennessee and the seat of Davidson County, Nashville is an important political player. Being a state capital may seem inconsequential, but if Tennessee were its own country, its economy would be greater than that of Denmark and would be right behind South Africa, Ireland, and Israel.[253]

In the public sector, the consolidation of the city and county governments has been the most pivotal, defining event of the city's recent history. Though we discussed the merger in brief earlier, it deserves a more detailed analysis.

Consolidation of City and County Government

Leading up to the merger of the city and county governments in 1963, more and more people were moving to the suburbs. The tax base of the city was dropping, and at the same time, the county, which was largely rural, didn't have the tax base or resources to support all the new residents. The rural residents would travel into the city and utilize its amenities and services. In effect, Nashville was supporting the bulk of the county's population while only receiving taxes from within the city limits. This structural imbalance spelled trouble.

Talk of a merger began in the 1950s, with the citizens of Davidson County and the City of Nashville understanding that "the higher cost and inefficiency involved in keeping two separate forms of local government in place and funding them."[254]

To address these issues, Mayor Ben West and Beverly Briley, county judge at the time and soon-to-be mayor, championed a plan to consolidate the city and county governments. It was a novel strategy that had not yet been attempted by any municipality in America. West and Briley first campaigned for the merger in 1958, but it did not pass. The city still desperately needed more funding, so under West's mayorship, the city annexed much of the county surrounding the city. The move outraged those being annexed, but it provided a temporary solution to the city's budget issues.

Five years later, talk of consolidation began anew. This time, West and Briley found themselves on opposite sides of the debate. Briley represented the county, which was still struggling from underfunding. West, on the city's side, no longer had funding issues thanks to the annexations, so he now opposed the merger. The two faced off in the election of 1963, and ultimately consolidation passed and Briley was elected the first mayor of the combined government.

It was the first consolidated metropolitan government in the country. (Still today, there are only 38 other places in the country with a consolidated government.[255]) In general, the consolidation made taxes lower because there was no longer duplication of services. There was one body providing utilities, garbage pickup, emergency services, and so on. However, while some communities outside of the city benefitted from full city services—trash pickup, sewer, water, and so on—others did not. In order to increase political support for the merger, a two-tier system of taxation was adopted, with a lower tax rate for those communities without full services.

Another compromise made to increase political support for the consolidation was an expanded city council. Some local political leaders outside the city were resistant to the merger because they did not want to lose their political power. By increasing the number of city council seats, the city ensured that the local political players could still have a seat at the table. Still today, Nashville has one of the largest city councils in America, with 41 members.

In the merger, six communities negotiated to maintain their town charters: Berry Hill, Belle Meade, Oak Hill, Forest Hills, Goodlettsville, and Lakewood (Lakewood later gave up its charter). These towns are still part of Metro Nashville, but they retain a level of independence, having their own mayors, zoning rules, police forces, and the like.

The consolidation made the region's politics immoderately moderate. With the merger, Nashville chose to remove party affiliations from ballots, helping to move elections, including both mayoral and Metro Council races, toward a nonpartisan ideal. Providing services is not a partisan issue, so it makes little sense to elect officials based on political positions that are irrelevant to the running of a city. The removal of labels has made it more likely that people from different parties will work together for the city. The emphasis is on practical solutions to issues, not ideological labels. Accordingly, the city has shifted from divisive political maneuvering to good, effective governance. In addition to unifying the city from a political perspective, the consolidation has also united the city as an economic force. Having a metropolitan government means that the towns aren't competing against each other in going after grants and economic opportunities. The city and county now demonstrate coordination and cooperation, not competition.

Another consequence of the Metro Nashville consolidation is that Nashville's mayor is in a particularly unique position of power typically not seen elsewhere in the country. Nashville's mayors have wielded much influence over the direction of the city.

Nashville's Mayors: A Legacy of Impact

Nashville has benefited from a long history of stable executive leadership, with the vast majority of modern mayors serving two or three terms. (In recent years, we've experienced more turnover, with four mayors in five years and three different mayors during the two years we've spent writing this book.) As Steve Cavendish, the former longtime editor of the *Nashville Scene*, describes the city's mayoral legacy, "Nashville has kind of been blessed with good managers. Almost all of them have been these slightly progressive, good government sorts of leaders who have gotten business buy-in for what they wanted to do."[256] Not every mayor has been a perfect poster child of the city, but through success, failure, or controversy, each of Nashville's mayors has left an indelible mark on the city, though some have left more fingerprints than others.

Ben West: 1951–1963

The group we term the "modern mayors" of Nashville begins with Ben West. West is a key figure because he was the last mayor before the Metro Nashville consolidation. The end of his mayoral term thus marks a pivotal moment in Nashville's history. Beyond that, West focused his attentions on two areas that have come to define Nashville as a city: civil rights and urban development.

West served three terms in a time that could be difficult to navigate: the civil rights era. By supporting civil rights activists, West was integral in establishing Nashville as a relative bastion of forward-thinking social liberalism among its southern peers. He also helped the business community and the people of Nashville come together. While that transition was not without roadblocks and problems, he sought to make it as peaceful as it could be.

The spirit of West's terms has continued today, with Nashville being an open, welcoming city focused on fostering its business community.

Beverly Briley: 1963–1975

Beverly Briley's great contribution to the city was his championing of the city-county consolidation. In addition to bringing the measure to fruition, he was the first mayor of the combined government—a tricky role. He navigated this strange new territory with skill and set the city on a course of smooth sailing. He served a total of three terms, the maximum allowed, and remained active in Nashville politics after his mayorship.

Richard Fulton: 1975–1987

During his tenure, Richard Fulton helped to begin transforming Nashville's downtown, including driving the development of Riverfront Park, the construction of Interstate 440, and the addition of 485 acres of parks.[257] Prior to becoming mayor, Fulton served seven terms as a US congressman for Nashville. He was the last of Nashville's mayors to serve three terms. After his tenure, a change in the law limited mayors to only two terms.

Bill Boner: 1987–1991

Bill Boner served only one term as mayor and was the catalyst for a fundamental shift in the direction of Nashville leadership.

Boner ran against Phil Bredesen, who would go on to become mayor after him. Bredesen was not a Nashville native, but Boner was. This fact was the main thrust of Boner's campaign: "I'm from here. I've lived in this community my whole life. I know Nashville, and I know you. That other guy just moved here from New Jersey, and he grew up in New York. He's not a true Nashvillian. He's not the kind of person we want to be our mayor."

The strategy worked, and Boner was elected. Once in office, he did not succeed in achieving much of note. What he did do was have an affair with a local singer. He then went on the nationally broadcasted *Phil Donahue Show* and told the world about it. Following this scandal, he did not run for reelection.

The embarrassment this episode caused Nashville cannot be overstated. At this time, Nashville was still relatively unknown on a national level. For many in the country, all they knew about Nashville was that it was home to country music, and now, that the mayor had had an affair. Boner—and, by association, Nashville—had become something of a laughingstock, and it was not something Nashvillians wanted to be known for.

Nashville had been given the choice between Bredesen, an outsider technocrat who promised to run the city like a business, and Boner, a Nashvillian native they thought they knew. After Boner's scandal, many felt they had made the wrong choice. You can see the aftershocks of this realization in the voting records. When given another chance, Nashvillians chose Bredesen. In fact, the next *four* mayors following Boner were Nashville transplants, not Nashville natives. Boner made people realize that being born in Nashville was not the most important trait for a successful mayor.

Bill Boner still lives in the Nashville area. (His former home is close to where Steve plays softball. If you hit the ball into Bill Boner's yard, it's an automatic home run.) To Boner's credit, he is upfront about his past and owns his mistakes, with an attitude of "Yeah, I was mayor. I totally blew it." With time, the controversy has not been forgotten but has faded into good-natured ribbing, like with the *Nashville Scene*'s eponymous Boner Awards, which are granted for the biggest, most high-profile blunders each year.

Following his mayoral term, Boner has contributed to the community in other ways, like teaching social studies and driver's ed. He has also engaged in charitable giving, most notably his facetiously named "Boner

Bears," in which, following Valentine's Day, he made a circuit of local Walgreens to buy up all the discounted stuffed bears in order to donate them to the Nashville Rescue Mission for women and children, the Fannie Battle Day Home, the Martha O'Bryan Center, and Holly Street Day Care.[258]

In a roundabout way, Nashville should thank Boner for his controversial mayor term, as it liberated Nashville from the limiting idea that Nashville's mayor should be a native Nashvillian. Thus was the stage set for the first Nashville-transplant mayor, Phil Bredesen.

Phil Bredesen: 1991–1999

If we had to choose a single most important figure in the rise of modern Nashville since the 1990s, it would have to be Phil Bredesen. In making urban renewal one of his top priorities, Bredesen set the city's trajectory toward "it" city status.

Bredesen was the first nonnative mayor of Nashville. He grew up in Upstate New York, earned a physics degree from Harvard, and relocated to Nashville for his wife's job at HCA. He started and sold a couple of different healthcare companies, amassing a small fortune and demonstrating himself as a resolute businessman and technocrat.

Bredesen won the 1991 election in a landslide, earning 70 percent of the vote.[259] By the time of his reelection, he had become even more popular, winning nearly 76 percent of the vote.[260] His popularity was due in part to his new approach to governance. He was not a lifelong politician and had a business career to fall back on, so he was not as bound to traditional political maneuverings. In his words, he tried "to figure out what the city needed to grow as opposed to managing one group or another, or working for your re-election."[261]

Bredesen focused on education, infrastructure, and business development. He built many new schools, renovated even more existing ones, and was key in the creation of civic cornerstones. During his terms, the city saw many tangible accomplishments:

An NFL team, the Tennessee Titans, and the correlated construction of Nissan Stadium

- The construction of Bridgestone Arena and subsequent recruitment of the NHL Predators

- A new downtown library, which has become a landmark

- Two new parks, Beaman Park and Shelby Bottoms

- The recruitment of Dell Computer

- The Country Music Hall of Fame expansion (the expansion was set in motion during Bredesen's tenure, though it was not completed until after he left office)

With his concrete achievements and intangible influence in redirecting the city's mindset toward development, Bredesen helped to elevate Nashville to a new tier as a city. After his mayoral terms, he went on to become Tennessee governor, continuing his legacy of socially liberal, fiscally conservative governance.

Bill Purcell: 1999–2007

Phil Bredesen focused on big-picture developments, and on his heels, Bill Purcell focused on the small picture, allowing Nashville to retain that delicate balance between big city and small town.

Like Bredesen, Purcell was a Nashville transplant. He was born in Pennsylvania, went to college in New York, and then came to Nashville to attend Vanderbilt Law School. Purcell previously served in the state senate before his mayoral election. He was also a very popular mayor, securing more than 84 percent of the vote in his reelection.[262]

Purcell ran on a campaign of being a "neighborhood mayor." He had one commercial where he sat at a desk in his front yard talking about the concrete neighborhood improvements he would make, like fixing sidewalks. When you look for Purcell's impact on the town, you can't point to major legacy items like Bredesen's stadiums—in fact, one of his greatest contributions to the city is not in the presence but the *absence* of an interstate through downtown, which could have irreparably changed the picture of Nashville's downtown. Though Purcell's influence is quieter, it is still ever-present. He focused on the development of greenways and community centers—small improvements that increased quality of life and moved the city toward new urbanism.

Purcell's other great legacy is in simplifying the government by uniting all the different Metro departments into one campus, housing everything that makes our government run smoothly. In addition, a new courthouse was built during his tenure, so that we now have two courthouses side by side.

Though Purcell is not thought of as a "business mayor" like Bredesen before him and Karl Dean after him, the Nashville economy continued to thrive through his years in office. *Expansion Management* magazine designated Nashville America's hottest city for business expansion and relocation two years in a row during his terms.[263]

Karl Dean: 2007–2015

Alongside Bredesen, Karl Dean was our other "business mayor." He was another nonnative, born in South Dakota and spending his formative years in Massachusetts. He went to Columbia University in New York, and then, like Purcell, came to Nashville to attend law school at Vanderbilt.

As mentioned previously, Dean's two proudest moments as mayor were the defeat of the English-only referendum and the community's response to the 2010 flood. Another signature achievement was a partnership between Nashville and Teach For America, which has attracted many young, motivated teachers to the city. His major infrastructure achievement was the Music City Center. He also was responsible for the Ascend Amphitheater and First Tennessee Park, which is the Minor League baseball stadium.

Part of Dean's mission was to build Nashville's brand around music, culture, and artistry. However, he also pushed a strong business agenda and is credited with incentivizing businesses to relocate or expand in Nashville, including Bridgestone and HCA. "It goes beyond just culture," he said in an interview with the *Nashville Scene*. "Part of Nashville's attraction is that we are a city that is, I think, pro-business. I mean, I think of myself as being pro-business. We are a city and state that is low-taxed, it's easy to do business here, and people want to do business here. And so you get that combination where you're friendly to universities, and arts, and creative folks, and technology, plus you're a friendly place for business—that's the sweet spot."[264]

Megan Barry: 2015–2018

Megan Barry was our first female mayor and yet another nonnative, hailing from California. Like Purcell and Dean, she also came to Nashville for school, to pursue an MBA at Vanderbilt University's Owen Graduate School of Management.

Initially, Barry was well liked and respected. She had the highest approval rating of any mayor in the city's history. Development had continued to explode across the city, and major companies were relocating here. In addition to being an effective technocrat, she was also a widely recognized personality thanks to her strategic use of social media. During her term, she won the Athena Leadership Award, joining the ranks of powerhouse women like Ruth Bader Ginsburg and Sally Ride. She had begun work on key issues in the city, including affordable housing and a multibillion-dollar transit plan.

Then she became cloaked in scandal. She had an affair with a bodyguard, and there were issues of misspent taxpayer dollars related to paying him overtime. Within weeks of the scandal breaking, she resigned. To perhaps no one's surprise, she garnered the *Nashville Scene*'s most infamous recognition: the Boner Award.

There were mixed feelings through the city, ranging from disappointment to feelings of betrayal. The referendum for her transit plan ended up failing, and some blamed Barry, either directly or indirectly. Barry had been the main driver behind the plan, using her political capital to increase support, and after the scandal broke, support for the plan plummeted. In general, many people had placed a lot of hope and faith in Barry. She had been vocal about her love for Nashville and her vision for the city, and people had been excited by what she could accomplish. People felt let down and less trusting of Metro government as the scandal unfolded.

Often, in scandals, the *modus operandi* is to shrink into anonymity and lay low for a while. Barry did not do that. She resigned with as much grace as was possible given the situation. The closing statement of her resignation was "I love you, Nashville."[265] That love seems to have continued to propel her, and she has remained a visible part of the community.

David Briley: 2018–2019

David Briley was vice mayor at the time of Barry's scandal, and he was sworn in as mayor following her resignation. A couple of months later, a special election was held to determine the mayor for the remainder of Barry's term, and Briley won, becoming the first native Nashvillian to occupy the mayor's office since Bill Boner.

Briley, who is the grandson of Beverly Briley (the first mayor of the consolidated Metro government), was well liked by many in the business community, but he inherited much of Barry's agenda, which some believe contributed to his defeat in the 2019 election.

John Cooper: 2019–present

In the 2019 election, native Nashvillian John Cooper won in a landslide, gaining nearly 70 percent of the vote. The Cooper name is well known in Nashville because John Cooper's father, Prentice Cooper, previously served as governor of Tennessee, and his brother, Jim Cooper, serves as the US representative for Tennessee's Fifth Congressional District, which includes Nashville.

Cooper was previously a real estate developer and campaigned on a platform of strong fiscal responsibility. With a recent Metro government budget shortfall, the platform resonated with voters. Popular opinion is that Cooper is who we need as mayor to help guide Nashville's growth.

Mayor Cooper appears likely to focus on highlighting Nashville's business-friendly tax and regulatory environment and ready workforce, and less on economic incentives. "We are an ambitious town, and we want to make the most of our moment," Cooper says. "We've got a generation of economic development narrative here that we are a welcoming, affirming place to move. But you've got to be super careful what you give away, because you're already giving [companies] a major deal in our low tax rate."[266]

Economic Analysis of the Public Sector

Per *U.S. News & World Report*, Tennessee is "the top state for fiscal stability."[267] Tennessee has the highest bond ratings possible: triple triple-A, from all three major credit-rating agencies.[268] The ratings reflect a strong confidence, not just from the leaders of the state but also from independent rating agencies, that Tennessee has the highest capacity to meet its financial commitments. This is great for business and development. The state has also added substantially to its rainy-day fund in recent years, bringing the total up to $1.1 billion, as cited by Governor Bill Lee.[269] This is a hefty chunk of change that could be used to see the state through a financial crisis or to attract businesses.

In addition to strong bond ratings, Tennessee has exceptionally low taxes. Tennessee has no income tax on wage and salary income, no capital gains tax, no intangibles tax, no personal property tax, and no inheritance/estate tax.[270] Combining property tax, income tax, and sales and excise tax, Tennessee has the third-lowest tax burden of any state in 2019, at 6.28 percent of total personal income.[271] A median income family in Tennessee pays the least in state and local taxes compared to other states, with the average Tennessean paying $3,667 in state and local taxes in 2017—more than a third less than the US average.[272] (Other states had lower overall tax rates, but because of higher median incomes, home values, or vehicle holdings in those states, their average taxpayers paid more than an average Tennessean taxpayer.[273])

These low taxes are appealing, both to individuals and to businesses. There's been a recent trend of "half-back" retirees, who initially retired to states like Florida but then decided to double back toward home, settling halfway in between in the Mid-South. Tennessee, with its low taxes, has been especially popular with these half-back retirees. The tax-friendliness also helps the state recruit companies, who are confident that they can attract workers to the area. As Chris Edwards, Director of Tax Policy Studies at the Libertarian Cato Institute, said, "High marginal tax rates reduce productive behavior (working, investing, starting businesses) and increase unproductive behaviors (avoidance and evasion)."[274] Low taxes do the opposite, making Tennessee a hub for business opportunity and wealth creation.

Like Tennessee, Nashville in particular also has strong bond ratings: Aa2 from Moody's and AA from S&P, with Moody's saying, "The stable outlook reflects the expectation that Metro's regional tax base will continue to grow and provide the necessary revenues to support ongoing capital needs and government operations.[275] Former mayor David Briley said of the bond ratings, "This underscores my frequent assertion that the city's financial health is strong."[276]

On top of the strong bond ratings, Nashville has the lowest property taxes of any of the top 50 MSAs, at 0.79 percent, which is the lowest it has been in the history of Davidson County.[277] A $500,000 house in Nashville will cost you about $4,000 in property tax, whereas in Chicago, that same house would cost closer to $15,000 to $18,000 in property tax. The low property tax is appreciated by homeowners as well as those investing in rental properties. Renters also benefit, since rents tend to be lower when property taxes are lower.

Many cities and states with low taxes run terrible budget deficits, but this is not the case with Nashville and Tennessee. Tennessee borrows relatively little money compared to other states. As of 2018, the state's per capita debt is $913, the lowest of any state.[278] Nashville and Tennessee have managed to achieve the seemingly impossible: high bond ratings, *plus* low taxes, *plus* low debt. It indicates a strong economy and strong fiscal management.

Public-Sector Initiatives

Nashville has accomplished much in recent history, but there's always room for improvement. Right now, there are several exciting public-sector initiatives in the works that focus on affordable housing, transportation improvements, and public health.

Affordable Housing

Affordable housing might be the hottest issue in Nashville right now. The city's real estate boom in the past few decades has put a lot of pressure on workforce housing. Lower-priced houses have been disappearing as developers acquire properties, demolish, and then rebuild, with the new homes costing as much as four times as much as the original ones. Such development has brought a lot of good to the city, but it also brings a unique set of challenges.

According to a "Housing Nashville" report issued by Mayor Megan Barry's office in 2017, nearly 25 percent of homeowners and 44 percent of renters in Nashville are considered cost-burdened, meaning they're paying more than 35 percent of their monthly income for housing.[279] Low-income residents have been especially hard hit, with more than 60 percent of low-income homeowners and 70 percent of low-income renters falling into the cost-burdened category.[280]

This lack of affordable housing has become an issue relatively recently. In 2000, Nashville had an estimated surplus of 2,000 units of affordable rental housing; by 2015, that surplus had turned into a deficit of 18,000 units.[281] According to predictions, that deficit will only continue to grow without action by the city. It is estimated that an additional 30,000 affordable housing units will be needed by 2025 to accommodate growing housing needs.[282]

These statistics are daunting, but Nashville is not the first city to face affordable housing issues, nor will it be the last. Having identified the housing issue, Nashville is taking a proactive, multipronged approach to face the affordable housing puzzle head on. One of Nashville's key strategies is tax incentives to encourage affordable housing development. These incentives provide a great opportunity for both in-state and out-of-state developers that specialize in affordable housing.

Rebuilding Together Nashville[283]

Rebuilding Together Nashville (RTN) has a special place in our hearts because Brandon serves on the board, currently as the Board President.

RTN has been serving the Nashville community for over 20 years. The nonprofit provides critical housing repairs to remove health and safety hazards so that homeowners can continue to safely live in their homes. The most common repairs include floor repairs, accessibility modifications for seniors, plumbing work, electrical work, and exterior wheelchair ramps.

Executive Director Kaitlin Dastugue explains:

> Daily cost of living increases and stagnant incomes leave very little room for many Nashvillians to keep their homes in good condition and make critical repairs themselves. With Rebuilding Together Nashville's help, low-income homeowners can choose to remain in their homes and focus their fixed incomes on other basic amenities and living expenses. It is our mission to help our neighbors remain in their communities, age in place, and live in safe and healthy environments. Our work is significantly preserving the supply of Nashville's

single-family, affordable housing stock at a time when these housing opportunities are rapidly disappearing.[284]

Each year, RTN serves approximately 30 homeowners, with a focus on three core populations: seniors, veterans, and individuals with disabilities. Over its lifetime, it has provided meaningful repairs and improvements for more than 500 Nashville-area homes.

For more information on Rebuilding Together Nashville, Executive Director Kaitlin Dastugue wrote a fantastic op-ed for the *Tennessean* titled "Private-Public Partnerships Can Solve Nashville's Affordable Housing Crisis."[285]

In addition to offering tax incentives, the city has also become involved in a much more direct, active way. One such example is former mayor David Briley's Under One Roof 2029 plan, which "seeks to create at least 10,000 units over the next decade, mainly by funding the Metropolitan Development and Housing Agency and the city's Barnes Fund for Affordable Housing, which provides grants to affordable housing developers."[286] A total of $500 million has been earmarked for the plan, with $350 million designated to MDHA to help pay for 5,000 low- and middle-income homes and $150 million promised to the Barnes Housing Trust Fund.[287] This program will address a portion of the demand for affordable housing, but there is still a need and opportunity for private developers and private capital.

In addition to the Barnes Fund, which has constructed more than 1,300 housing units since its inception in 2013, the city has multiple nonprofit organizations focused on affordable housing: Woodbine Community Organization, Renewal House, Affordable Housing Resources, Habitat for Humanity of Greater Nashville, Urban Housing Solutions, Cross-Bridge, and Rebuilding Together Nashville.[288] Affordable housing requires solutions from many different directions. These nonprofits approach the problem from a wide spectrum, with Habitat for Humanity building new houses on one end of the spectrum, and Rebuilding Together Nashville repairing existing homes on the other end of the spectrum.

Another key affordable housing initiative in the city is Envision Cayce, a $600 million redevelopment project.[289] The high-profile project has received a lot of media attention, including the award-winning podcast "The Promise" from Nashville Public Radio—so named because the city has made a promise to not displace current residents in the redevelopment efforts. The project is focused on Cayce Homes, a 63-acre tract of public housing—the largest in Nashville.[290] The housing is in a desirable location in East Nashville, right by Nissan Stadium, but the area has become rundown and dangerous, thus the need for a redevelopment project.

The goal is to have a wide economic mix of tenants represented, so that higher-income renters can generate revenue that will help subsidize the development. The rent prices will be tiered, dependent on renter income, with some residents paying market rate and others paying subsidized rates. For low-income residents, their rent will not exceed 30 percent of their income, and renters in the "workforce housing" category—people who don't fall into the low-income bracket but can't afford market-rate prices—will also qualify for reduced rent.[291]

The experimental Envision Cayce takes a novel approach to what affordable housing should look like. The project extends beyond the idea of building housing to building a *community*, complete with restaurants, businesses, and a diverse mix of tenants. With projects like this, the Under One Roof 2029 plan, and our numerous nonprofits, Nashville could become the model for affordable housing projects across the country.

Transportation Improvements

Anytime a city undergoes rapid expansion, transportation becomes a critical issue. Nashville has three different interstates that form a solid driving infrastructure, but as the population climbs, Nashville's roads are becoming increasingly crowded, marking a need for better public transit.

To address this need, Nashville has redone its bus system. There's a new bus terminal downtown, and our old, dirty buses, typically wrapped with ads for personal injury and bankruptcy lawyers, have been replaced with nice, new, clean WeGo buses. This rebranding has elevated the bus system and made it a more pleasant experience. The city is also working on new transportation management technology, like a smartphone app that shows where buses are in real time. The downtown bus system in particular is widely used, especially for park-and-ride commuters.

The city also has a commuter train, the Music City Star. It does not operate on weekends, which can be inconvenient, but it provides transportation from suburban communities into Nashville. It's mostly commuters who use it, but it also gets a fair amount of game day traffic from Titans fans and is always packed solid for Fourth of July fireworks.

Though we do have this train, it is not sufficient for the city's needs, and the city is interested in establishing light rail. Building new train tracks is too cost-prohibitive, but Nashville has plenty of train tracks in place already. The hope is that Nashville will be able to lay light rail over existing tracks. One pipe dream has been for the city to relocate CSX's Radnor Yard, an enormous freight train depot, and convert the site into the city's transportation hub. For now, this seems unlikely. Estimates place the conversion cost at $767 million, and CSX is unlikely to leave, considering the train yard is one of its largest in the country.[292]

One of the biggest major transportation improvements is a $1.2 billion expansion[293] to the Nashville International Airport, which saw 17 million passengers from July 2018 through June 2019.[294] The plan, which is set to be completed by 2023, is to add six additional gates and expand essentially every aspect of the airport, including adding more international flights.[295] The airport has already secured direct international flights to London.[296] The expansion is the latest development in the airport's longstanding history of looking toward the future.

Beyond traditional transit systems, Nashville has seen the rise of new solutions as well, including ride-sharing and bicycle and scooter rental programs. Like most midsize cities, Nashville suffered from a terrible taxi system. It could sometimes take up to two hours for a taxi to arrive. Ride-sharing services like Uber and Lyft have blown up in Nashville, addressing this need. While other cities initially resisted ride-sharing services in favor of taxis, Nashville embraced them quickly, with our airport being the first to feature a special pickup/drop-off area just for Uber and Lyft.[297]

Bicycle and scooter programs have also been well received in the city. There are scooters everywhere, and they are especially popular with tourists. Scooters and bicycles are appealing because they allow you to travel directly from point A to point B without multiple stops or a circuitous route like on a bus or train. It is also easy to adjust scooter and bicycle numbers to account for demand. For example, during the NFL draft, Lyft provided a special fleet of scooters to accommodate the spike in visitors. Scooters bring a unique set of challenges, though. Following the first scooter-related death in the city in 2019, Nashville leaders are working to develop a plan and regulations that will increase the safety of this transportation method.

Bright red bicycles can be found throughout Nashville as part of the check-in, check-out bike-sharing program BCycle. The program includes 268 bikes at 36 automated kiosks. In 2018, the bikes were checked out 63,935 times and ridden 400,487 miles.[298] Biking in the city has become easier and easier with the city's push for healthy and green initiatives, which will be discussed in the next section.

Though Nashville has many transportation options, both traditional and non-traditional, transit is one area that can use more work. In 2018, the city voted down a $5.2 billion transportation plan that included measures for five light-rail lines, a downtown tunnel, four rapid-transit bus lines, four new crosstown buses, and more than a dozen transit centers around the city.[299] Though the referendum failed, it's a clear sign that transportation is on Nashville's radar as a key issue moving into the future.

A More Livable City: Healthy Nashville and Green Initiatives

Healthy Nashville is a Metro Public Health Department initiative to improve the health and well-being of Nashville residents. A big push of the initiative is to change how people move, encouraging them to walk and bike more than drive, as these habits are associated with better health and longevity.

Walk Bike Nashville, a collaboration between the city and the private sector, has helped create more sidewalks and bikeways. New bicycle lanes have been popping up all over the city, and existing ones have been painted green to mark them more clearly. In addition to shared car-bike roads, there's also a robust system of greenways that allow you to walk or bike from place to place without ever setting foot or wheel on roads.

Healthy Nashville and green initiatives have been interconnected in the city because making places greener tends to result in better walkability, which leads to better health. Among its green initiatives, the city has plans to plant 500,000 trees by 2050, which will increase air quality and help manage heat.[300] Nearly all the major new developments in the city include green spaces of some kind, from small parks to green roofs. Nashville also has "downtown ambassadors" who pick up trash, down to the last cigarette butt, to make downtown a clean, pleasant area where people want to walk and bike.

There are so many noteworthy focal points for Nashville, but a final one to mention here is Healthy Nashville. The Nashville Bicycle and Pedestrian Advisory Committee is constructing greenways all over the city in an effort to encourage people to bike and walk more. The mayor's office has also pushed green building initiatives to make public buildings LEED (Leadership in Energy and Environmental Design)-certified. The Music City Center is a great example of this, with its green roof that spans over four acres and mimics the rolling hills of Tennessee.

Part of the push for a healthier Nashville is to create "blue zones," or areas where people tend to live the longest. Healthways, a Nashville-based company that assists people in living healthier lifestyles in order to change our approach to healthcare and lower insurance premiums, has started the Blue Zones Project. With this project, they've identified different characteristics of blue longevity zones, like moving naturally (meaning walking instead of driving) and connecting with the people around you.

Several developers in Nashville are trying to build neighborhoods that will become blue longevity zones. These developments are largely focused on having high walkability scores and community resources. Zac Thomas of Luma Systems, LLC says, "With respect to Blue Zones, the challenge as a real estate developer is to placemake in a manner that strengthens communities, lengthens lives, and improves the quality of those lengthened lives. Nashville is a city where developers are thinking deeply about these issues and are creatively planning development that is increasingly aligned with Blue Zone principles."

Coda

Nashville has a legacy of strong leadership and smart political decisions. The consolidation of the city and county governments in particular has shaped the city, allowing Nashville to best leverage its resources for the good of its citizens.

Nashville's government leaders care less about politics and more about people. The current public sector initiatives reflect a focus on improving quality of life, through affordable housing, transportation, and green initiatives.

Another major factor in quality of life is the great food and drink available throughout Nashville.

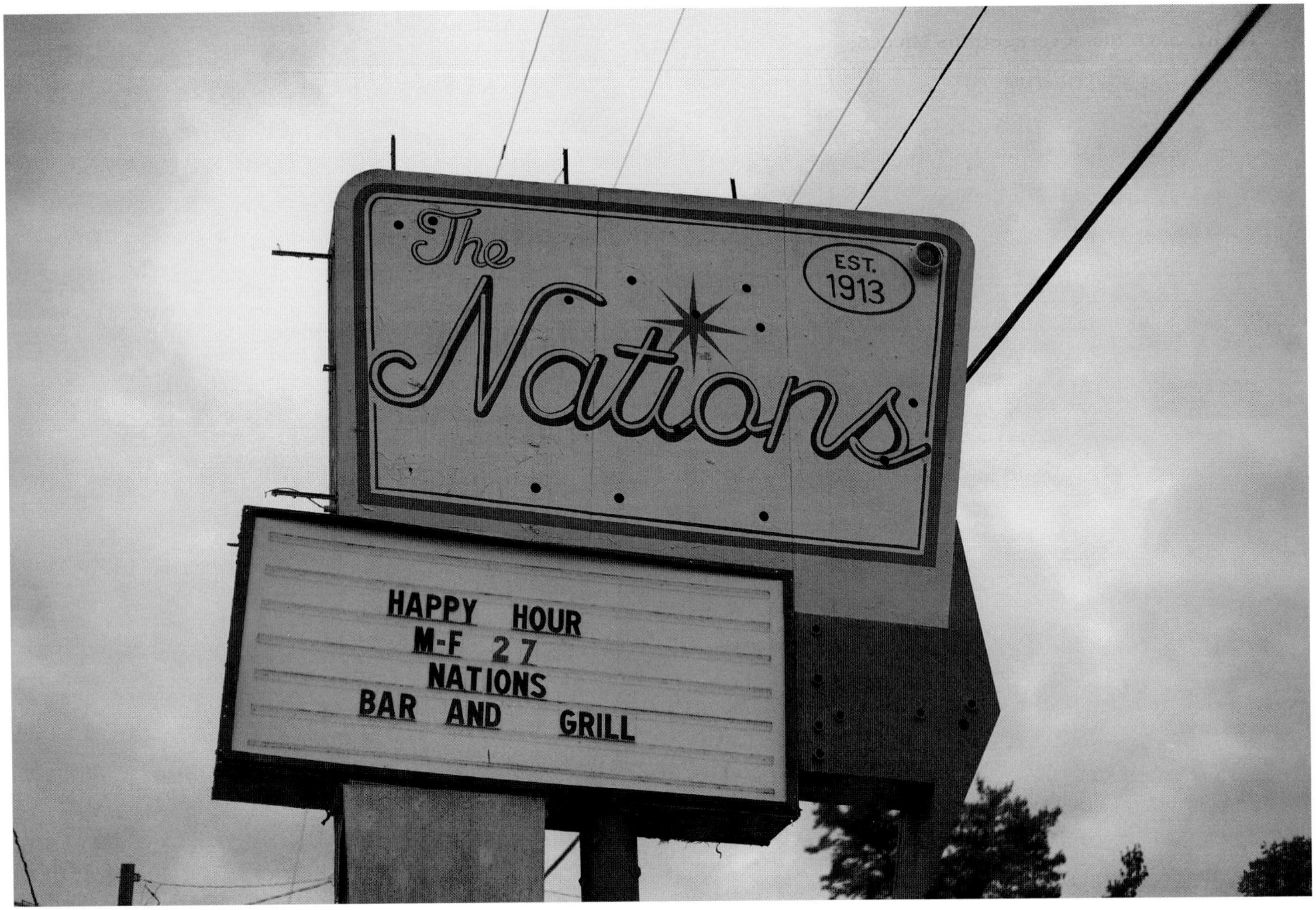
The
EST.
1913
Nations
HAPPY HOUR
M-F 2 7
NATIONS
BAR AND GRILL

CHAPTER 9

★

FOOD AND DRINK
Beyond Hot Chicken

Hot chicken is the country music of Nashville cuisine. It's a defining part of the Nashville culinary scene, but just as country music is far from the only genre represented in Nashville, hot chicken is one piece of a larger gourmet puzzle. Gastronomes have much to explore beyond hot chicken in Nashville. That said, the Nashville food story wouldn't be complete without mention of hot chicken.

The Origins of Hot Chicken: A Spicy Story

Hot chicken has spread beyond Nashville's borders, popping up across the nation and globe, but it has an especially firm foothold in Nashville. We even have a Nashville Hot Chicken Coalition and a Music City Hot Chicken Festival. Hot chicken has become such a phenomenon that people have memorialized it through song. (Yo La Tengo, a Brooklyn band that cut one of its albums in Nashville, has actually released *multiple* songs about hot chicken—our hot chicken is *that* good.)

The powerhouse of the Nashville hot chicken scene is Prince's Hot Chicken, which boasts the claim to fame of being the originator of this spicy dish. The story dates back over 80 years, to Thornton Prince. As André Prince Jeffries, Thornton's great-niece who now runs Prince's Hot Chicken, tells it, Thornton was "a very handsome man and quite the womanizer," who "married over five times."[301] While Thornton was not the one to create the famous hot chicken recipe, he was the first one to eat it and the one credited with starting the BBQ Chicken Shack (later renamed Prince's Hot Chicken) that first served it. The culinary mastermind behind hot chicken was one of Thornton's wives. Because Thornton was involved with quite a few women, her identity has unfortunately been lost to time.

As the story goes, Thornton returned home late after a long night of carousing to a very displeased woman. They say the way to a man's heart is through his stomach, and this woman decided that the stomach would be a good way to revenge as well. She whipped up the hottest possible fried chicken spice she could concoct. Hell hath no fury like a woman scorned, and she intended to bring the flames of hell to Thornton's stomach. She underestimated the strength of Thornton's stomach, and her plan backfired spectacularly: Thornton *loved* the chicken. Thus was born the BBQ Chicken Shack.

The chicken truly is so spicy it can be hard to eat. Plenty of people not only tolerate but crave that burn. You can now get hot chicken as far away as Thailand and Australia, but no one will ever do it quite like Nashville, the home of hot chicken.

The History of Nashville's Restaurant Scene

The food, drink, and hospitality industry of Nashville is a $5.7 billion enterprise that provides 87,500 jobs.[302] Tourism is a key driver of Nashville's economy, and if there's one thing tourists like to do, it's eat. For some people, vacation means hopping from one restaurant or bar to the next. In fact, much of Nashville's tourism is now driven by our restaurants, which can be hard to believe for longtime residents.

Today, Nashville's culinary scene is founded on independent restaurants and notable chefs, but in the late 1990s, chain restaurants were king. Nashville is the home base for several giant chains, including Shoney's, O'Charley's, J. Alexander's, and Captain D's. Of these, all except Shoney's are not only headquartered in Nashville but were founded here. Captain D's, under the name Mr. D's Seafood and Hamburgers, was the first to be founded, in 1969, in the Nashville suburb of Donelson.[303] Two years later, in 1971, O'Charley's was founded across the street from Vanderbilt.[304] That same year marked the relocation of Shoney's headquarters from Charleston, West Virginia, where it was founded, to Nashville.[305] J. Alexander's was the last to open, in 1991.[306] These chains formed a strong backbone for Nashville's restaurant scene at the height of the chain restaurant boom, and they are still an important part of Nashville's gastronomy economy, with hundreds of restaurants across the country.

By the 2000s, chain restaurants began to go out of style. Because of the preponderance of chains, Nashville had not developed a unique food identity. Even the family-run, non-chain restaurants tended to serve the same kind of food you could find at a chain restaurant anywhere in the country. In backlash to this ubiquity, Nashville, like many cities, jumped on the farm-to-table bandwagon that emphasized independent restaurants, fresh ingredients, and chef vision.

In Nashville, two farm-to-table pioneers were chefs Margot McCormack, with Margot Café, and Deb Paquette, with Etch. They created unique, interesting food that went beyond the typical meat-and-three cuisine then ubiquitous in Nashville. In the process, they raised the bar for fine dining in the city. When McCormack opened Margot Café, she served seasonal food. She didn't have a walk-in cooler, so she had to use whatever was fresh. The result was that her menu was constantly changing. Paquette followed similar concepts with Etch, focusing on organic, locally grown, fresh ingredients. It sounds like an oxymoron, but McCormack and Paquette's approach was to create healthy southern food.

The farm-to-table trend took off in Nashville, with many restaurants sourcing local ingredients and even growing their own. In a short amount of time, Nashville's food scene has catapulted from the commonplace to the extraordinary. By 2016, *USA Today* declared Nashville the third best local food scene in the country, placing it above even New Orleans and San Francisco, and Zagat ranked Nashville number 6 on its list of America's Next Hot Food Cities.[307] The velocity of the change has been remarkable, such that food now drives much of Nashville's tourism.

Biscuit Love vs. Biscuit House

In 2015, *Bon Appétit* named the East Nasty fried chicken biscuit sandwich at Biscuit Love the best sandwich in the country.[308] Many visitors to the city are eager to try a bite of culinary stardom, but they mistakenly end up at Biscuit *House* instead of Biscuit *Love*. The mistake can lead to confusion because while Biscuit Love is a trendy, industrial chic restaurant perfect for social media posts, Biscuit House is the least Instagramable restaurant in town. It's the kind of place filled with regulars, where you'll find eight policemen crowded around the same table. Fortunately, the food is excellent at both restaurants. Biscuit House recently won best breakfast in Nashville.[309] So whether you end up at Biscuit Love or Biscuit House, you can't go wrong.

The Restaurant Landscape Today: Quality and Collaboration

Nashville is now a culinary hot spot. The restaurant scene today is all about *more*—more quality, more quantity, more collaboration, more award recognition.

Twenty years ago, if you wanted to go out to eat in Nashville, you'd simply choose a restaurant and go. Today, because of the new eminence of our food scene, reservations are often required, and some restaurants are in such high demand that getting a reservation is no easy task. One time Steve tried to get a reservation at Moto two days ahead of time. "You mean *this* Friday?" she asked, a little amused. "No, I'm afraid we don't have any available tables." The Catbird Seat, with only 22 seats, is even more difficult to secure a reservation for and was named to *Vogue*'s list of 13 hardest-to-get restaurant reservations.[310]

Fortunately, in conjunction with rising quality and popularity, we've also seen an explosion of new restaurants. In 2014 and 2015, more than 120 new restaurants opened.[311] Twenty years ago, you might have only one option for a fine-dining restaurant in a certain neighborhood, and now you'll have six.

The chefs of Nashville have capitalized on the growing community to build bonds of collaboration instead of competition. Chef Margot McCormack has said that she doesn't care about "winning a James Beard award or being part of the Nashville food renaissance"; rather, she feels a "certain sense of responsibility."[312] This is a common theme among Nashville chefs. There is a strong sense of community within the culinary scene as well as ties that bind chefs with the larger Nashville community. As such, many of our chefs feel a responsibility to serve the community by supporting each other as well as local farmers.

As journalist Margaret Littman, who frequently writes about Nashville, says, "Nashville is known for being a collaborative town.

The basis of the economy—songwriters penning hits for country stars—revolves around multiple people working together on the lyrics for one song. That carries over into a supportive environment citywide."[313] The culinary world can be cutthroat, but in Nashville, competition takes a back seat. Chefs here truly want each other to succeed. They understand that it's not a zero-sum game, where one person's success directly reduces another's. Rather, the more Nashville restaurants that succeed, the more Nashville becomes known as a gastronomic city, which drives more foodie traffic and is better for the community as a whole.

These strong bonds of mentorship have helped to elevate the Nashville food scene. Paquette and McCormack, for instance, have trained many chefs who went on to open their own restaurants in the city. This is the true secret to what made them such revolutionary leaders in the farm-to-table movement. A single chef can have only so much impact—so many restaurants they can operate—but when they begin to train and work with others, their influence spreads. For this reason, when a chef leaves to pursue their own restaurant, it's not seen as a betrayal but as a source of pride.

The supportive community is attractive to both aspiring and established chefs, especially women. Maneet Chauhan, a judge on the popular TV show *Chopped* and the first female Indian contestant of *The Next Iron Chef*, chose Nashville for her restaurant because of the community. "Cooking is a form of art, and

Nashville…supports artists," Chauhan said. The strong female chefs here also played a role in her decision. "When I came here, it was easy to see who were the trailblazers. It was the women," Chauhan said. "If there were the same number [of female chefs] as there are in Nashville in a larger city, it would *still* seem like a large number," she said. "To have this many in the city, it is tremendous."[314]

Because of the welcoming nature of the community, culinary talent in Nashville has skyrocketed in recent years. In addition to great local chefs, like McCormack and Paquette, talented chefs from across the globe have begun to flock to Nashville, including celebrity chefs who can draw customers based on name recognition alone. Chef Jonathan Waxman, owner of Adele's in the Gulch, is one such example. The food scene and Waxman's restaurant in particular played a large role in Jimmy Kimmel's decision to visit Nashville recently. "I think for people who know a lot about food, Nashville is on their must-visit list," Kimmel said.[315] Dan Auerbach, of the Black Keys, has also pointed to the Nashville food scene as a major draw of the city, saying, "I gotta be honest…I moved here partly because of the food."[316]

With so much new talent, Nashville's chefs have begun to be recognized on a national scale, with nominations for James Beard Awards—the Oscars of the restaurant industry. In 2019, when semifinalists were announced, Nashville scored five slots: Margot McCormack (Margot Café & Bar) for Outstanding Chef, Josh Habiger (Bastion) and Julia Sullivan (Henrietta Red) for Best Chef: Southeast, Benjamin and Max Goldberg of Strategic Hospitality (associated with the Catbird Seat, Patterson House, Henrietta Red, Bastion, and more) for Outstanding Restaurateur, and Philip Krajeck's restaurant Folk for Best New Restaurant.[317]

Nashville routinely pulls in semifinalist nods and has had three wins. Jack and Rose Arnold (Arnold's Country Kitchen) and André Prince Jeffries (Prince's Hot Chicken Shack) have won Heritage Awards, and Tandy Wilson (City House) snagged the city's first Best Chef: Southeast win in 2016.[318] Also in 2016, Sean Brock (Husk) was a finalist for Outstanding Chef, the equivalent of Best Actor at the Oscars.[319] With this recognition, 2016 was a big year for Nashville's culinary scene, sparking national dialogue about our chefs and restaurants.

Nashville's food scene continues to advance, improving and refining while holding onto characteristics that make it uniquely Nashvillian.

Food Trends in Nashville

The major food trends that define Nashville's culinary industry are meat and three, barbecue, upscaling, food trucks, and pop-ups.

Meat and Three

The foundation of southern cuisine is the meat and three—one meat main dish and three side dishes. At the height of the fast-casual food trend, meat and three was the standard in

Nashville. With the rise of farm-to-table and more focus on fine dining in Nashville, restaurants moved away from meat and threes. Now, in reaction to the prevalence of fancy, sometimes ostentatious food, the meat-and-three concept is experiencing a revival. People, especially hipsters and tourists who want an authentic Nashville experience, have begun to once more embrace meat and threes.

Two of the best known and oldest meat-and-three restaurants in Nashville are Arnold's and Varallo's. Arnold's is a Nashville staple and frequently makes top-10 lists. Varallo's has received less media attention, but it's one of our favorite restaurants in Nashville. It was sold near the end of 2019, but until that point, it was Tennessee's oldest family-owned restaurant, dating back to 1907.[320] It's near the entrance to the Arcade, which is a block of covered shopping modeled after Italian arcades. It's close to where we used to work, so we'd grab lunch there nearly once a week.

Barbecue

Another cornerstone of southern cuisine is barbecue. In Tennessee, Memphis is the city that's always been known for barbecue, but Nashville has been catching up. One of the great things about barbecue is that each place in the South puts a slightly different spin on it, with a unique flavor palette. So even if you've had southern barbecue, it's worth giving Nashville barbecue a try.

Some of our favorite barbecue restaurants are Martin's Bar-B-Que, Peg Leg Porker, Edley's Bar-B-Que, and Jack's Bar-B-Que.

Upscaling

One of the biggest trends in Nashville is upscaling, where chefs take a popular food concept and elevate it to a new level. Much of the fine-dining scene is an extension of traditional food like meat and threes and barbecue. Chefs take the familiar and transform it into something new.

A great example of upscaling in action is the Capitol Grille, which is in our only five-star hotel, the Hermitage Hotel. On the menu alongside pan-seared scallops and filet mignon, you will also find hot chicken, which was previously found only in the strip-mall setting. Bartaco, Saint Añejo, and Superica are also upscaling experts, experimenting with unique flavors and twists on typical Mexican cuisine.

Food Trucks

Nashville tends to be quick to embrace revolutionary business models, like Uber and Lyft in the transportation industry. In the restaurant sphere, the innovative new business model is food trucks. True to character, Nashville was an early adopter of food trucks, and in the last decade, the city has seen the emergence of a vibrant food truck culture.

Tried-and-True Warhorse Restaurants

Some of Nashville's oldest restaurants are also the most popular. At these tried-and-true favorites, you will often find a line wrapping out the door, but they are well worth the wait.

- Pancake Pantry (Hillsboro Village)
- Jimmy Kelley's (West End)
- Prince's Hot Chicken Shack (Nolensville Pike)
- Sperry's (Belle Meade)
- Arnold's (8th Avenue)

Emerging fields, like Uber or food trucks, offer great opportunity but also great challenge. Whenever a new industry first appears on the scene, there's chaos. Everything is an experiment, with no blueprint to follow. There are no regulations and no support structures. Especially when that field involves something that people ingest, the lack of regulation can be a safety concern. To set food trucks up for success, the Nashville Food Truck Association formed. The association's mission is to "provide Leadership, Guidance, and Beneficial Support through Mentorship, Advocacy, and

114 ★ *Climbing the Charts: The Ascent of Nashville*

Charity via a network of like-minded business owners serving the Greater Metro Nashville/Middle Tennessee areas."[321] As with other industries in the city, from music to real estate to healthcare, the city has worked to provide structure and institutional support to the food truck community.

With low overhead and limited menus, food trucks have flexibility and opportunity that traditional restaurants do not. Food trucks tend to fit into a specific niche, like the Grilled Cheeserie, which only does grilled cheese sandwiches. Food trucks do one thing, and they do it well. With this specialization, food trucks have brought much more variety to the Nashville food scene, especially in terms of international offerings.

Since few people are required to operate a food truck, it's easier for food trucks to keep nontraditional hours. This is well appreciated by late-night crowds. Roaming Hunger, a website dedicated to all things food truck, says, "With a serious nightlife that tends to get out seriously late, food trucks in Nashville are more than a privilege, they're an essential utility."[322] After spending a night out on the strip drinking and listening to music, revelers can nearly always find a food truck to give them a pick-me-up.

Due to their mobile nature, food trucks are also a great choice for catering. With a food truck, you don't have to worry about transporting food and it getting cold because you can bring the entire kitchen to your location. We've been to birthday parties, open houses, and fundraisers that feature one or more food trucks.

Food trucks are a great tool for aspiring restaurateurs. It is much easier and cheaper to start a food truck than open a restaurant, so many chefs will first break into the restaurant scene with a food truck. After building a customer base, they then parlay the success of their food truck into a brick-and-mortar restaurant. Food trucks are essentially restaurant incubators.

Food trucks can be found all over the city. Some lay down roots in specific locations, and others travel. For special events, dozens of food trucks will gather together. Every Thursday, for instance, up to 20 food trucks will line Deaderick Street near downtown for the lunch hour. For an interactive map of food trucks in Nashville, you can visit www.roaminghunger.com/food-trucks/tn/nashville.

Pop-Ups and Supper Clubs

Like food trucks, pop-ups and supper clubs have become popular in Nashville as an innovative way to break into the food industry. A pop-up is a temporary restaurant, essentially like a traveling circus. The chef does not have a brick-and-mortar lease but instead operates temporarily in a provisional space, like a private home or event space. Sometimes the pop-up will be a collaboration, with a takeover of another chef's restaurant.

Restaurants are risky ventures, with a high failure rate. It can be difficult to secure loans, and in general, there are high barriers to entry. Similar to food trucks, pop-ups give chefs the opportunity to build name and brand recognition and develop a following with limited investment and financial risk before taking the plunge into a brick-and-mortar restaurant.

In addition to giving aspiring chefs a way to break into the industry, pop-ups add spice to existing restaurants. People always want to try the "new thing" of food, but it is not always clear which food trends are here to stay and which are fads—think of the rise and fall of the molecular gastronomy, foam, and deconstruction trends. A full-scale restaurant committed to a new trend could be shuttered within a few years. Pop-ups, on the other hand, encourage a creative spirit with much less risk. With a pop-up, chefs can experiment with new trends without long-term commitment. Sometimes it's not even a trend but simply a new style of food. An Italian restaurant, for instance, might feature a pop-up takeover from a Japanese chef specializing in ramen. The pop-up is a way to generate buzz and excitement for both the Italian restaurant and the Japanese chef, with each benefiting from the collaboration by expanding their typical target customer pool.

In Nashville, Vivek Surti is the apotheosis of what supper clubs and pop-ups can achieve. Surti is the culinary might behind Vivek's Epicurean Adventures, Nashville's longest-running pop-up restaurant. In 2010, after watching *The Four Coursemen*, about an Athens, Georgia supper club, Surti was inspired to do something similar in Nashville.[323] He hosted his first supper club at his parents' home. Six people attended.[324] Flash-forward a few years, and Surti had perfected his supper club to a science. He could only serve a max of 25 at his parents' home, so he began shifting from supper club to pop-up, hosting larger, rotational events at restaurants, where he could serve up to 250.[325]

Today, Surti has leveraged his success with supper clubs and pop-ups into Tailor, a brick-and-mortar restaurant in Germantown. With Tailor, Surti is bringing the supper club experience and concept into a restaurant environment. Dinner at Tailor is an intimate two- to three-hour curated experience, with 8 to 10 courses explained by the chefs.[326] For tourists and locals alike, it's a foodie experience not to be missed.

Locally Grown Restaurant Groups

Many of Nashville's restaurants are family- or chef-owned, but there are also two key restaurant groups making a big impact in Nashville: Strategic Hospitality and M Street. Typically, when the traditional restaurateur discovers a concept that works, they move toward franchising, opening a copy of the restaurant in a new location. Strategic Hospitality and M Street take a different approach. They're not interested in developing chains; rather, they seek to create one-of-a-kind restaurants that share a thread of entrepreneurial spirit and innovation without being carbon copies of each other.

Brothers Ben and Max Goldberg, the talent behind Strategic Hospitality, are responsible for an eclectic mix of bars and restaurants, including Nashville favorites like the Catbird Seat, Patterson House, Bastion, and Henrietta Red. Nashville natives, they have sought to fill a hole they personally saw in the city, assuming that if they wanted to see something new in the city, other people would too. With this approach, their properties mirror their own growth, with each serving as a "snapshot" of their life at that point in time.[327] Their evolution of ventures includes everything from nightclubs, to speakeasy lounges with bespoke cocktails (like the Patterson House), to multiuse social spaces geared toward creative professionals, like their Pinewood restaurant and bar with bowling alley and swimming pools.

Brad Smith, CEO and co-founder of Nashville's healthcare Aspire Health, said, "If you ask most of the folks in Nashville between their early 20s and mid 40s, everybody would probably know at least three or four of the Goldbergs' bars or restaurants," which shows how deeply woven Strategic Hospitality has become in the fabric of the city.[328] The Goldbergs have had a great influence on the city because the impact of restaurants extends beyond their own revenue generation. Restaurants can be a big draw for companies, who want to know they can recruit talent to the city. If you want to know what it's like to work and live in a city, looking at the restaurants and bars is a great place to start. As Ben Goldberg says, "It's a very visible, tangible way to see what's going on in a city."[329]

Restaurateur Chris Hyndman has had similar impact with M Street. Like Strategic Hospitality, M Street is not interested in starting chains, but their approach is different from the Goldberg brothers'. Where Strategic Hospitality has properties scattered across the city, M Street has clustered their restaurants along a single street, McGavock Street. They essentially built their own culinary destination in the city from the ground up. M Street became a top drop spot for Lyft and Uber, of enough scale to help entice Uber Eats to come to Nashville.

The M Street empire features six restaurants, with a wide range of cuisine represented, from Asian fusion, to Italian, to American steakhouse, and more. Though each restaurant operates based on a unique food concept, they are run on similar business models and have earned M Street a reputation for quality.

Craft Distilleries

Bourbon and whiskey have become so popular globally that Kentucky now rakes in billions of dollars in tourism on the merit of their bourbon trail alone. Before Prohibition, Tennessee had a similar level of distillery operations as Kentucky, but following the end of Prohibition, Kentucky re-embraced whiskey production in a way that Tennessee did not. In the intervening years, new craft distilleries sprang up across Kentucky, while in Tennessee, existing distilleries could operate, but it was essentially impossible to open new ones.

The Music City Chef Throwdown: Chefs Give Back

Like other Nashville business owners, a strong philanthropic streak runs through our area chefs. A great charity event top chefs participate in each year is the Music City Chef Throwdown. The fundraiser benefits the Martha O'Bryan Center, an antipoverty nonprofit, and it's quite popular. Wagon Wheel is a sponsor of the event, so we get 10 free tickets. We offer them to our employees first, and without fail, they are snatched up within a day.

The throwdown is set up as an *Iron Chef*-esque competition, with the added twist that all ingredients must be affordable to someone on limited income. The involved chefs, both the participants and the judges, donate their time and energy to raise money for a good cause. The event draws some of the best talent from the city. In 2019, contestants included Husk's Katie Cross and Taylor "Dip" Varnell from Dino's, which was featured on Anthony Bourdain's last season of *Parts Unknown*. Deb Paquette was also featured as a judge. The competition demonstrates the friendly rivalry between area chefs as well as the deeper ties that bind chefs to the larger community.

In 2009, Tennessee changed its laws such that new distilleries could once more form. The changes in the law also allowed new life to be breathed into old distilleries. As reported by *Whisky Advocate*, "Some distillers are breaking new ground, and others are reviving recipes passed down through generations."[330] It's another prime example of how Nashville takes an innovative, forward-thinking approach while also looking to the past for inspiration.

In the past decade, we've been playing catch-up. We now have enough distilleries to support our own Tennessee whiskey trail. (For details on the whiskey trail and a complete list of distilleries in Tennessee, including in the Middle Tennessee / Nashville area, check out https://www.tnwhiskeytrail.com/.) The trail features 30 distilleries, including small boutique operations, titans of the industry like Jack Daniel's, and everything in between.[331]

The Nashville area has over a dozen distilleries of its own, and of these, Nelson's Green Brier, Pennington Distilling, Leiper's Fork, H Clark Distillery, Heaven's Door, and Corsair are particularly noteworthy.

Nelson's Green Brier Distillery

With roots dating back to the 1860s, Nelson's Green Brier Distillery has a rich history. The distillery closed in 1909, when statewide Prohibition began in Tennessee, but nearly a hundred years later, in 2006, founder Charles Nelson's great-great-great-grandsons, Charlie and Andy Nelson, brought it back to life.[332]

The distillery's historical roots were important to Charlie and Andy, who are self-described history buffs. The brothers worked to preserve old photographs and even located and reused ad campaigns and branding from before Prohibition. The original distillery property is on the National Historic Register,[333] and they were able to keep the original distillery license, which was one of the state's first, predating even Jack Daniel's license.

One of the distillery's most popular labels is Belle Meade bourbon, which is a favorite among bourbon and whiskey connoisseurs. The bourbon has won many awards, including Double Gold at the 2019 San Francisco World Spirits Competition for the Honey Barrel-finished edition.[334] The bourbon, with special edition bottles edging into the triple digits, has become a collectors' item.

Constellation Brands, which makes Corona and Svedka vodka, recently bought a majority share in Green Brier. It's still early, but it appears that little will change in day-to-day operations. Charlie and Andy will simply have more resources and support in rebuilding the distillery to the heights it attained in its heyday, during which it was the country's largest producer and supplier of Tennessee whiskey.[335]

Pennington Distilling

Pennington Distilling opened in 2011, and as of 2017, they were aging three whiskeys.[336] Most whiskeys need to be aged for at least six years, so Pennington is just beginning to release its whiskeys. This is a common theme among new distilleries. Since the law only changed in 2009, we've only seen the beginning of what our distilleries can produce. The coming years are sure to be interesting as we see more 10-year-aged whiskeys released.

Pennington is most famous for their Pickers Vodka, which has begun to gain national popularity, and Whisper Creek Tennessee Sipping Cream, which is kind of like Irish cream. It is Tennessee whiskey, cream, and 30 other all-natural ingredients. People love to put it in coffee.

Williamson County Distilleries: Leiper's Fork and H Clark

Leiper's Fork Distillery is notable because it is the first distillery in Leiper's Fork, a nearby suburb of Nashville. The distillery features a 5,000-square-foot distillery with a tasting room in a 200-year-old cabin.[337] The distillery opened in 2016, so it is just beginning to release whiskeys.

H Clark Distillery, which opened in 2014, was the first distillery to be opened in Williamson County in more than 100 years, and the founder, Heath Clark, uses a direct-fire pot for distilling.[338] We used to work with Heath at our old law firm. He is a healthcare lawyer, so H Clark Distillery is an example of the unexpected impacts the healthcare industry has had on Nashville.

Clark's legal background came in handy, as he was instrumental in spearheading a law that made it easier to license distilleries in Tennessee (previously distilling was legal in only three Tennessee counties). Said Clark, "We didn't force alcohol on anyone that didn't want it; the dry counties stayed dry. But if you can drink whiskey from Kentucky, why can't you drink whiskey from Franklin?"[339]

Heaven's Door

Heaven's Door is Bob Dylan's joint venture with respected Kentucky-based Angel's Envy, which was started by Lincoln Henderson, the former master distiller at Jack Daniel's.

Dylan and Angel's Envy have bought an old church downtown, near the convention center—expensive, prime real estate. The location will include not just a distillery but also an arts center. It is set to feature a music venue as well as sculpture.

Corsair

Corsair was founded by Darek Bell and Andrew Weber in Kentucky in 2008. After the 2009 law change, which Bell played an influential role in, the distillery moved to Nashville, becoming the first new craft distillery in the city since Prohibition.[340]

With a background in graphic design, Bell brought a unique eye for marketing to the distillery. The brand has a *Mad Men* vibe, with the slogan "Booze for Badasses." In addition to whiskey, they also brew gin, absinthe, rum, craft beer, and, during the COVID-19 pandemic, hand sanitizer. They've called themselves a brewstillery as well as distillery.

Whisky Advocate has praised their "highly imaginative whiskeys crafted with unconventional ingredients and distilling techniques."[341] They may be the first and only distillery to make a quinoa whiskey, which is apparently quite popular in Japan. With their innovator spirit, Corsair has won more than 150 awards at international spirits competitions and is well on the way to building national brand awareness.[342]

Craft Beer and Cocktails

Thrillist has named Nashville the best drinking city in America.[343] Indeed, quite a lot of booze flows through the city. In addition to craft distilleries, we have a plethora of craft breweries and cocktail innovators.

Our favorite cidery is Diskin Cider, and some of our favorite breweries are Black Abbey, Jackalope, Yazoo, and East Nashville Beer Works. Yazoo was one of the city's first craft breweries and has grown into a widely distributed brand. East Nashville Beer Works is one of the top-awarded breweries in Nashville. Their Cumberland Punch wheat beer recently won silver in the American-Style Wheat Beer category at the Great American Beer Festival. With 2,295 breweries and 9,497 competing beers, this was a high honor. In fact, East Nashville Beer Works was one of just three Tennessee breweries to take home an award.[344]

The bespoke cocktail scene is centered around East Nashville, which is frequently compared to Brooklyn. The neighborhood has at least one direct tie to the New York borough in the form of Attaboy. The Attaboy cocktail bar in Brooklyn has been named the seventh-best bar in the world,[345] and they have since opened up a second location—right here in East Nashville.

Patterson House, though not in East Nashville, was one of the pioneers of the cocktail scene, with their claim to fame being a Japanese ice-cutting machine that could cut giant oval ice cubes. When Patterson House first opened, only a handful of those machines had made it outside of Japan, making it quite the novelty.

The Soler sisters are perhaps the most well-known leaders of Nashville's craft cocktail movement. They own a total of three bars—No. 308, Old Glory, and Flamingo Cocktail Club / Falcon Coffee Bar—all specializing in serving up unique concoctions, like the Beet Happening, made up of mezcal, Greek yogurt, fresh beets, citrus, a touch of agave, and a sprig of dill.[346]

Coda

Nashville's restaurant scene has undergone a rapid transformation in the past 20 years, beginning with the farm-to-table movement. In addition to traditional favorites like hot chicken and barbecue, new trends have taken hold in the city, including an extensive food truck network and pop-ups. Nashville's restaurant scene is now befitting of the cosmopolis the city is, and culinary tastemakers are taking notice. Craft distilleries, breweries, and cocktail bars have experienced a similar renaissance in the past decades.

The new quality of food and drink has boosted tourism as well as made life in the city more enjoyable. In the next chapter, we'll review another aspect of Nashville that has brought money to the city while also improving the lives of its citizens: sports.

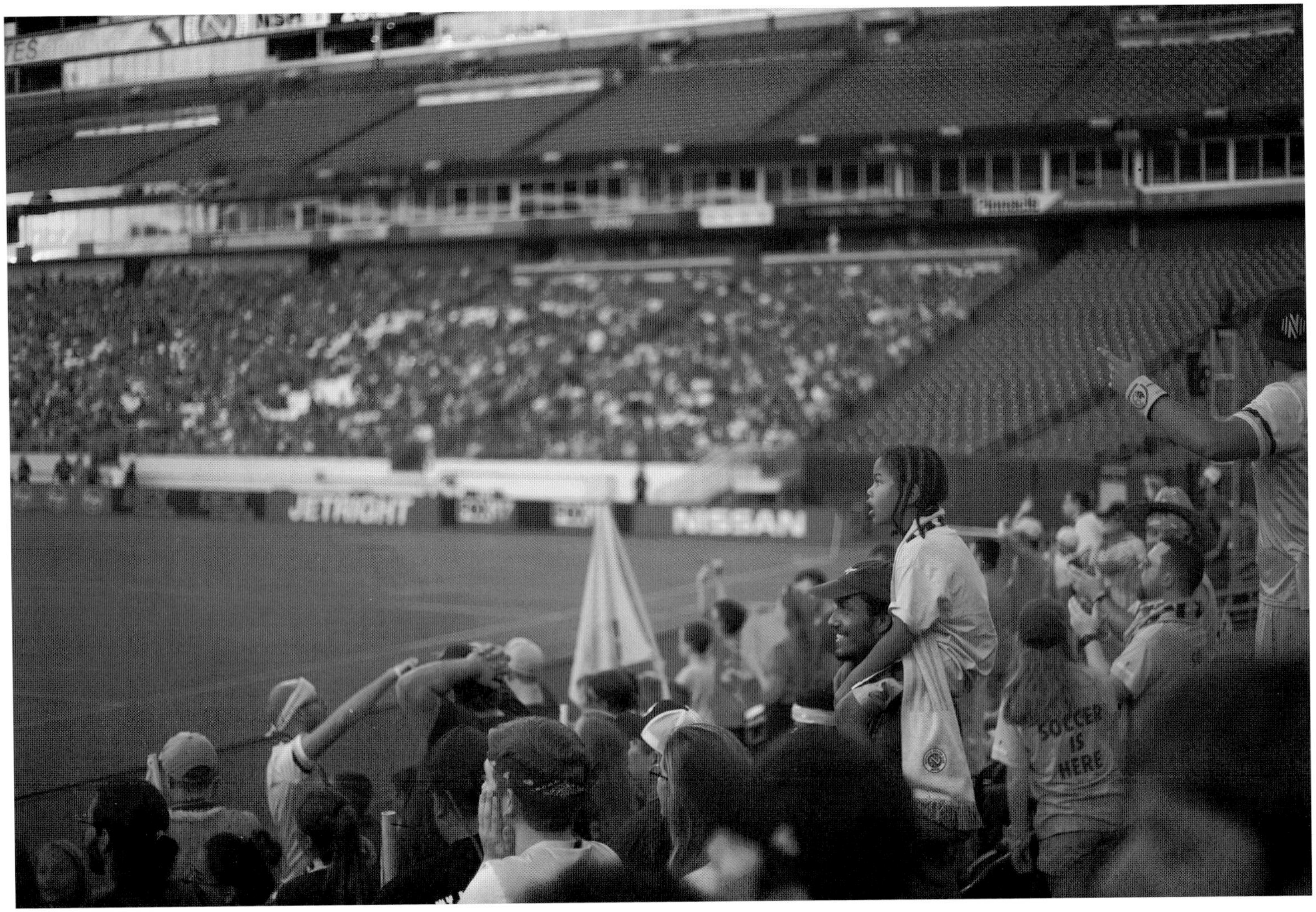
NISSAN
SOCCER IS HERE

CHAPTER 10

---★---

SPORTS
Predators, Titans, and Soccer

Thirty years ago, the sports landscape in Nashville consisted of college athletics, especially basketball, and a Minor League Baseball team, the Nashville Sounds. The Nashville Sounds still play today, and college athletics are as important as ever. At home basketball games, Vanderbilt's Memorial Gym is filled with enthusiastic fans in black and gold—what we call Memorial Magic. Vanderbilt plays in the highly esteemed Southeastern Conference, and thanks to Nashville's central location, we are one of the most frequent hosts of the SEC Tournament. Vanderbilt's baseball team has also risen to prominence, winning the College World Series twice in recent years, in 2014 and 2019.

Though college athletics are celebrated here, they are now just a small portion of Nashville's sports landscape. With an NFL, NHL, and MLS team, Nashville is a new professional sports mecca. In fact, in 2019, Street & Smith's Sports Business Journal named Nashville the best sports city in the United States.[347] You can tell when it's game day based on how many jerseys you see around town. With how diehard the fans are, it's surprising that our three major professional teams have a relatively short history in the city. The Titans relocated from Houston to Nashville in 1997, the Predators came in 1998, and the Nashville SC expansion team was awarded to Nashville in 2017. Nashvillians love their sports so much that they are already itching to secure an MLB team as well, with a group led by World Series hero and former Arizona Diamondbacks General Manager Dave Stewart, rumored to be pursuing an expansion team for Nashville.

Though Nashville boasts some of the most energetic, passionate fans in the nation, that was not always the case, especially for the Predators.

Nashville Predators

As you might imagine, prior to 1998, Nashville was not a hockey city. The city typically sees only a few inches of snow a year, so winter sports were not that popular. Even after the Predators team was announced, interest in hockey remained low in Nashville. When you went to a home game at Bridgestone Arena, it would often look like it was the other team's home ice.

The Predators actually weren't Nashville's first hockey team, though. We had a string of minor league teams: the Dixie Flyers, the South Stars, the Knights, the Nighthawks, and the Ice Flyers.[348] So there was something of an underground hockey scene, primarily composed of transplant fans. The majority of the population, however, did not care about hockey or understand it. Local sportscaster Rudy Kalis worked to change that.

Being from Wisconsin, Kalis knew more about hockey than the average Nashvillian, but he took on the role of "dummy."[349] He asked the dumb questions others were too afraid to ask: What's icing? What does offsides mean? In this way, he began to educate the local population.

The other challenge was building emotional investment. Kalis, for his part, did stories on the players, who he described as "down-to-earth guys" with "virtually no ego."[350] Fans began to develop favorite players, and the more people attended games, the more they fell in love with the sport. If you've ever had a chance to see a hockey game live, you understand the intensity of speed and skill on display that simply doesn't translate to a television screen. The Predators also did a great job of building youth hockey leagues, drawing children and their parents into the game. The Predators have been here for more than 20 years now, so those five-year-old kids who started playing hockey in the '90s are now in their 20s and 30s. It's a whole generation of fans who grew up watching and playing hockey. Now those fans are starting to have children of their own and are passing on their emotional connection to the game.

Today there is a large fan base, but early on, the Predators were a shoestring operation. They were always right on the edge, struggling to break even. There were nearly constant news stories about how they needed to sell more tickets.

In the 2006–2007 season, the Predators made the playoffs. There was terrible attendance during the playoff games, and they lost in the first round. Fans were disappointed by the poor performance, and the Predators' owner at the time, Craig Leipold, essentially said, "Look, if you want to have a hockey team, you have to come to the games." He had a point, but it rubbed people the wrong way. They were already frustrated about losing, and now they were being scolded by the owner.

Next thing you know, Canadian billionaire Jim Balsillie, co-CEO of Research In Motion (which was responsible for Blackberry), puts in an offer to buy the team. There was a lot of local news coverage, with questions of what would happen to the team if Balsillie bought it. Fans hoped he would keep the team in Nashville, but it slowly dawned on them that of course he wouldn't do that; he'd move it to

Hamilton, Ontario, where he lived and where the general population loved and supported hockey.

With the city on the verge of losing the team, fans sprang into action. George Plaster, a prominent local sportscaster and later athletic director at Belmont University, led the charge. He helped to organize a rally where they would try to sell a certain number of season tickets to demonstrate support for the team and prevent it being sold. They went into the rally with low expectations. They wanted to sell just a hundred season tickets.

Fortunately, Nashville proved everyone wrong. About 8,000 people attended the rally, and 700 season tickets, close to $2 million worth, were sold.[351] Plaster was stunned and told the crowd something along the lines of "I don't know what's going to happen, but this team's not going anywhere."[352]

A group of local business leaders came together to buy the team and formed Predators Holdings LLC. The largest investor was attorney and businessman David Freeman, whose contribution was instrumental in keeping the Predators in Nashville. Many of the other members of the LLC were prominent players in the healthcare sector, including Tom Cigarran, CEO of Healthways, and Herb Fritch, chairman of Healthspring, which is now part of Cigna. Other investors included venture capitalists and real estate developers. The group bought the team from Leipold in late 2007 for $193 million.[353]

At the time, there was some doubt about the decision. "Do these guys know anything about running a hockey team?" people asked. "Do they even have enough money to run a professional sports franchise? Is this really going to work?" The answer to all three questions has been a resounding yes. Following the purchase, Herb and Tom became fixtures at the games, cheering as loud as anyone else. They were already beloved local leaders, and now they were putting a face on the ownership of the team. It galvanized Nashville around the team. Predators Holdings LLC is a success story of local people saving a local institution. As of 2018 the Predators were worth an estimated $420 million, up from $270 million in 2016, so it was a good investment.[354]

After conquering the challenge of building a fan base, the Predators still faced an uphill climb to gain respect in the league. They were an underdog for years, routinely underestimated. Then in 2017, they made their Stanley Cup run, and traditional hockey markets—like Toronto, Detroit, Chicago, New York, and Boston—sat up and started paying attention. They realized that both the Predators and Predators fans were a force to be reckoned with.

Throughout the Stanley Cup, the entirety of Broadway downtown was filled with yellow-clad fans watching the games on giant screens. For Game 3, a total of 17,283 fans filled Bridgestone Arena, and an additional 50,000 took to the streets outside the arena.[355] Though the Predators ultimately lost the Stanley Cup, it has only invigorated fans, who are already looking forward, itching for a Stanley Cup win.

Q&A with David Poile, General Manager of the Nashville Predators

Q: What do you think makes Nashville unique as a market for professional sports teams, particularly the Predators?

A: The community's total support and commitment to their teams, specifically the Predators, makes the city special. There's very little negativity, and the fans have real belief in our individual players and our team and how we play the game. Nashville simply loves hockey right now.

Q: You've been with the Predators since the beginning and have had the opportunity to see Nashville evolve as a city. Especially in the last five years, how do you think Nashville has changed?

A: To me, the city and the Predators have evolved together. Nashville was a nice, unassuming, quiet city that has exploded in terms of everyone's awareness of what the city is all about and what it has to offer. It aligns with how the Predators have transformed from a team that was competitive but not threatening to one of the best teams in the league. In the last few years, we've been growing as a team, both in terms of our fan support and our competitiveness.

Q: When you're recruiting players and negotiating deals, what role does the team's location in Nashville play?

A: When we first started, our location in Nashville wasn't really a plus because no one knew anything about Nashville. But in the last few years, with Nashville becoming the "it" city and the Predators getting better and better and having success in the playoffs, we've become a top choice for where players want to play. After 20 years of the franchise, coaches, players, and the media now know how special Nashville is.

Q: How do you "sell" Nashville to players? What do you think makes Nashville, "Nashville"?

A: To me, we just need to get the player to come to Nashville and take them to different places. The city sells itself. It's not just one thing that makes Nashville, "Nashville"; it's a whole bunch of things. From the Predators to the Titans to the music entertainment to the restaurants—there's a lot still under the radar here.

When a player is deciding where to go, they write down all the factors important to them: size of the city, location, temperature, competitiveness of the team, how easy it is to move around, what would it be like for their family living there. Because Nashville is a smaller city with a big-city feel and all the big-city amenities, it's easy to check off all the boxes on a player's list.

Q: In your 20 years with the Predators, what are the highlights for you?

A: The highlight, so far, is being in the Stanley Cup Finals, but there have been so many special moments—from earning the Presidents' Trophy to Pekka Rinne winning the Vezina Trophy for the first time. One of the highlights is simply where we are today—the accumulation of everything over the past 20 years, both the successes and the missteps, that has led us to this point. It's an exciting and fun time for our franchise. We are in the entertainment business, and we are one of the most entertaining teams in the league to watch. To see where we are today is very, very satisfying.

Part of the Predators' success is due to the stability of the team's management. President of Hockey Operations and General Manager David Poile, who has been declared Executive of the Year in the NHL multiple times, has been the Predators' general manager for their entire existence, and the team has had only three head coaches: Barry Trotz, Peter Laviolette, and John Hynes.

Other teams are interested in the Predators' secret sauce that has propelled them to such success. In keeping with Nashville's spirit of collaboration, CEO and President Sean Henry shares what he can with other general managers. In his thinking, the healthier all the teams are, the better the league does, and the better we do.[356]

Today, the Nashville Predators have come a long way from their humble, uncertain roots. ESPN has ranked them as the number one franchise across all sports.[357] If you go to a Predators game now, you will find a sea of yellow and some of the loudest fans in the nation. We've broken records for our volume, hitting *129.4 decibels*.[358]

Nashville Soccer Club

Soccer is the most popular sport in the world, and in the United States, it is quickly closing in on baseball as the third most popular sport (after football and basketball). More Americans bought tickets to the 2018 World Cup than any country other than Russia, and among the 18–34 age range, soccer has already surpassed baseball and is tied with basketball as the second most popular sport to watch.[359]

In 2016, Major League Soccer (MLS) sought to add several expansion teams. Will Alexander, formerly the chief of staff for the Tennessee Department of Economic and Community Development and now the chief revenue officer for Nashville Soccer Club (Nashville SC), felt that securing one of these expansion slots for Nashville would help establish Music City as not just a top US city but a first-tier *international* city. Bill Hagerty—native Nashvillian, former US ambassador to Japan, and current US Senator from Tennessee—agreed with him. The two of them would become key leaders in the coalition to bring an MLS team to Nashville.

MLS had announced that the 2016 expansion round would likely be its last, so this was presumed to be Nashville's only chance at a team. With that in mind, Alexander and Hagerty began by formulating a list of potential owners. Ownership is one of the most important factors driving a professional sports team's success, and as such, it was a key element MLS considered in evaluating cities. Ideal owners needed to have business acumen, deep community ties, a long-term time horizon, and passion about the opportunity. Alexander and Hagerty's number one choice met all of these criteria: John Ingram, billionaire son of the beloved philanthropist Martha Ingram (mentioned in Chapter 4) and former chairman of Ingram Industries.

Ingram loved the idea of a Nashville soccer team and said yes. From that point, he and the Ingram Industries team began leading the bid. As the expansion bid gathered steam, the ownership group expanded. The Turner family, known for Dollar General and their critical role in the redevelopment of the Gulch, and the Wilf family added their financial support to Ingram's. The Wilfs, especially Mark Wilf, were an important addition because of their experience as owners of the Minnesota Vikings. The Wilfs' history of successful, well-managed ownership of a major sports franchise, as well as their experience building US Bank Stadium (where they hosted a Super Bowl), lent credibility to Nashville's bid.

Compared to other cities, Nashville was throwing its hat into the ring late in the game. Other cities had been pursuing a team for over a decade. Partly for this reason, Nashville was initially viewed as the longest-odds, dark-horse candidate among the 12 cities vying for a spot. Many sports observers questioned how Nashville could compete at all. As the *Tennessean* reported, "Detroit is a significantly larger market. Cincinnati has a successful United Soccer League team that packs the stands. And Sacramento has been on Major League Soccer's radar for years."[360]

But Nashville had a secret weapon. As John Ingram put it, Nashville is "a city that works together and a city that thinks big."[361] A diverse committee made up of community leaders was formed to push for the team. The committee included business and political leaders and even celebrities, like Titans running back Eddie George and Victoria's Secret model Lily Aldridge.[362] The committee also included the leaders of the Predators and Titans. Despite the fact that another pro team could create competition for fan support and ticket sales, both the Titans and the Predators were—and continue to be—supportive of the MLS expansion team, refusing to see Nashville SC as only a rival.[363]

The Catfish Toss

If you go to a Predators game, you may notice someone slinking around in sweatpants, creeping down toward the ice. He'll stand there awkwardly for a few moments, and then when there's a break in the action, he'll pull a catfish out of his pants and toss it over the glass barrier onto the ice. Gameplay will pause as the referees skate out to shovel the catfish off the ice. It's never the same fan, and it's usually only during big games, but it happens with enough regularity to have become a tradition. Ahead of the Stanley Cup playoffs in 2018, Bridgestone Arena even installed a catfish tank, to the delight of fans.

This catfish toss may seem like an incomprehensible act, but hockey fans are sure to recognize the tradition's roots in the Red Wings franchise. Long before the Predators' catfish toss, Red Wings fans had a tradition where they would throw an octopus on the ice during playoff games. Perhaps because of the density of Red Wings fans in Nashville, the Predators' fan base has adapted the tradition, putting a southern spin on it.

The tradition has ruffled a few feathers. Many oppose the use of live catfish for the tradition and encourage fans to throw plush catfish instead. The greatest controversy related to the tradition took place during Game 1 of the Stanley Cup, which was held in Pittsburgh. Ahead of the game, local fish markets tried to avoid selling catfish to Tennesseans in an effort to prevent one ending up on the ice.[364] Predators fan and Nashville native Jacob Waddell had thought ahead, though, and brought a catfish with him from Nashville.[365] He managed to get it out on the ice and was arrested for it. The charges were later dropped, but by that time, Waddell had earned himself local celebrity status and the nickname "Catfish Jake."

The Predators actually contributed to the MLS's decision to bring an expansion team to Nashville. Just months before the MLS decision was made, the Predators made it to the Stanley Cup, and the high-energy zeal of Nashvillian fans played out on a national stage. Ticket prices for the Stanley Cup final were the highest ever sold for the final of a professional supporting event, with the average price coming to $2,116.[366] Nashvillians thus showed MLS that they were willing to support their teams, both with fan loyalty as well as their wallets. If there was any remaining doubt, Nashville shattered it the next month, when the CONCACAF Gold Cup match at Nissan Stadium earned the record for the largest soccer game attendance in Tennessee.[367] Just weeks later, Nashville broke the record again for an English Premier League preseason match.[368] The fact that Nashville could draw such large crowds for rather unexceptional games like these pointed to a promising future for Nashville SC.

Public-private cooperation was also critical in launching Nashville from underdog to front-runner. The committee pushing for the team worked closely with Mayor Megan Barry and the city to form a unified front. The MLS wanted the expansion teams to have state-of-the-art outdoor stadiums designed specifically for soccer. Several leading cities struggled to get the needed stadium financing approved. St. Louis, for instance, voted not to finance a stadium, Charlotte failed to reach a public-private financing agreement, and San Diego also faced a referendum setback. In contrast, as other cities fumbled the ball, Nashville's Metro Council approved a $275 million soccer stadium proposal (mostly publicly funded, but to be paid back through a long-term lease with the team) by a vote of 31 to 6.[369] The proposal will allow for a 30,000-seat stadium to be built at the fairgrounds in the Wedgewood-Houston neighborhood.[370] The new soccer stadium is scheduled to be ready in 2022, and until then, the Titans will share Nissan Stadium with Nashville SC.[371]

With the stadium financing approved, Nashville went from an afterthought to a solid front-runner, but there was one last factor that helped Nashville cinch an expansion team: the city's brand made it a good fit for a soccer team. We're a dynamic, growing city of young and increasingly diverse people. Especially with the recent influx of international Nashvillians, we have the building blocks for an avid soccer fan base that can support a major league team. MLS commissioner Don Garber said of Nashville, "This is a city we've fallen in love with ... Everything about it fits our brand; we're young; we're on the rise; we're very diverse; we're very interested in trying to do things a bit differently than the other pro leagues have done."[372]

With a kismet chain of events, everything came together to send Nashville from dead last to becoming the first city awarded an MLS expansion team.

Tennessee Titans

Nashville's first pro sports team was the Tennessee Titans. The story of how the city lured the team from Houston is a master class in business and political maneuvering.

Goodbye, Houston—Hello, Nashville

In the summer of '95, Phil Bredesen was preparing for his second mayoral campaign, and Bud Adams was looking to find a new home for his Houston Oilers.[373] When Adams called up Bredesen to suggest moving the Oilers to Nashville, Bredesen wasn't surprised, but he was skeptical.

Nashville SC Colors and Crest

In picking the team colors and logo, Nashville SC wanted something that represented the city and culture. Because of the strong influence of music on Nashville, the colors will be "acoustic blue" and "electric gold," and the crest is meant to "evoke sound waves."[374] The colors serve the dual purpose of visual consistency with another of the city's pro teams, the Predators, whose colors are blue and yellow. John Ingram said of the colors and crest, "The Nashville SC name and primary gold color, along with the themes of sound and energy in the logo, embody our city and our fans who have been with us from the start."[375]

---

130 ★ *Climbing the Charts: The Ascent of Nashville*

Nashville was in the midst of the final stages of construction of the downtown Bridgestone Arena, a venue designed for hosting concerts and hopefully a basketball or hockey team. With the arena's impending completion, Adams was far from the first to express interest in moving a sports team to Nashville. However, many teams had expressed interest only so they could leverage an offer from Nashville to pressure their home cities into committing more funding. Bredesen had bet a lot on this new arena, and he was worried it would become the next Memphis Pyramid: a defunct, teamless facility on the city's skyline.

The Bridgestone Arena wasn't suitable for a football team, so Adams was asking Bredesen and Nashville to build a brand-new stadium for his team. Especially with an election on the horizon, Bredesen couldn't afford to have media coverage about yet another team courting Nashville only to leave the city jilted at the altar. So a Nashville delegation and a group representing the Oilers began to clandestinely work on a deal out of the spotlight.

Nashville was facing stiff competition from another city seeking to secure the Oilers: Baltimore. Since losing the Colts in the 1980s, Baltimore had been trying to lure another NFL franchise to the city. Their bait was $450 million earmarked for a new stadium and a signing bonus of $50 million to whatever team would relocate there.[376] It was a tempting offer. Steve Underwood, Adams's right-hand man, thought Baltimore was the best choice. Adams disagreed. He liked Nashville. He joked that it was because he didn't want to have to fly the extra 45 minutes it took to get to Baltimore from Houston, but in truth, Nashville had won him over.[377]

Now that Bredesen and other city leaders had won over Adams, they needed to win over the people of Nashville. A new stadium would require a lot of money, at a time when the city had already poured millions of dollars into the Bridgestone Arena with no return on investment guaranteed. One of our developer clients, Rob Shuler, was a business owner at this time, and he, like other business leaders, was initially opposed to the idea. Rob loved football and had even played in college—he was an offensive tackle at SEC powerhouse Auburn—but he didn't think that building a football stadium to lure an NFL team to the city made sense. Then he attended a speech in which Bredesen essentially said, "Look, I've never been to a professional football game, and I know little to nothing about the NFL. But I've studied this carefully—studied the impact of stadium building and professional sports franchises in a city of our current size and scale. And my strong conclusion is that this will be very good for the city, especially economically." That was all it took for Rob. He knew that Bredesen didn't make decisions based on emotions, and he had a proven track record in business. So if Bredesen said it made smart economic sense, then Rob believed it. Not everyone was convinced, though. In particular, there was significant opposition from the religious community, which was "concerned with what would happen to their congregations if Sunday mornings were spent tailgating, rather than at worship."[378]

Initially, support for the referendum to approve the stadium appeared low, but it ultimately passed, with 59 percent in favor.[379] Thus, in 1997, the Oilers said goodbye to Houston and became the Tennessee Oilers.

The Music City Miracle

When the Oilers first moved to Nashville, their performance left much to be desired. Considering the circumstances, this wasn't surprising. They did not yet have a stadium or practice facilities, so they practiced on a stretch of grass behind a Wendy's restaurant. For the people watching practices as they sat in the fast-food restaurant's drive-through, the thought that this team would be at the Super Bowl in just two years was laughable.

To put it lightly, the Nashville relocation was difficult. In addition to subpar practice facilities, the Tennessee Oilers had to play all their games on the road. Their "home" games were played in Memphis, more than three hours away. Many Nashville fans were unwilling to make the drive. Memphis football fans were not quick to support the team either. Ultimately, they knew the Oilers would only be playing in Memphis for a couple of years, and it did not seem worth any emotional or financial investment.

Attendance in Memphis was so terrible that the team decided to instead begin playing at Vanderbilt. Vanderbilt Stadium had far fewer seats, but at least the Oilers would not have to be on the road so much. In 1999, Adelphia Coliseum (now called Nissan Stadium) was completed, and the team finally had a permanent home and not a moment too soon. In four years, the team had played home games in three different cities and four different stadiums. The stability after years of volatility did a world of good for their performance. In the 1999 season, they were undefeated at home and lost only three regular season games.[380]

Along with the new stadium, they also got a new name and new uniforms in 1999, becoming the Tennessee Titans. Adams wanted a name that reflected "power, strength, leadership and other heroic qualities." "Titans" accomplished just that, with the added perk of being a nod to Nashville's "Athens of the South" nickname, with titans being deities in Greek mythology.[381] After the new stadium, new name, and new uniforms, the Titans had yet one more new experience waiting for them in 2000: their first Super Bowl appearance. To get there, they first needed to win the Wild Card playoff game against the Buffalo Bills.

The game took place at Adelphia Coliseum. The Titans led 12–0 at the end of the first half, but the Bills came out roaring in the second half. After two touchdowns and a failed two-point conversion, the Bills had a lead of 13–12. The Titans retook the lead in the final quarter with a field goal: 15–13, with 1:48 to go. It was short-lived, with the Bills soon reclaiming the lead with a field goal of their own: 16–15. Only 16 seconds remained on the clock.[382]

Bills fans had already begun to celebrate when the Titans launched their "Home Run Throwback" play. On the kickoff return, Titans tight end Frank Wycheck threw a lateral pass to Kevin Dyson. The Bills defenders were all clustered around the action near Wycheck, leaving Dyson with a wide-open path to the end zone. Dyson ran 75 yards for a touchdown, clinching a 22–16 victory.

In the Super Bowl, the miracles were on the Rams' side as the Titans made a play in the fourth quarter for a potentially game-tying or game-winning touchdown (depending on whether they kicked a field goal or went for the two-point conversion). Within yards of the goal line, Dyson was tackled. Dyson rolled and outstretched his arm, but the ball fell a few inches short. It was one of the most famous game-ending plays of all time, known simply as "the Tackle." Though the Titans team did not come away with Super Bowl rings, they went down in history for being involved in two of the most exciting games of all time.

The Titans Today

Following their 2000 Super Bowl run, the Titans reached the playoffs three of the next four seasons, but they have not (yet) made it back to the Super Bowl.

Bud Adams died in 2013, and his daughter Amy Adams Strunk now runs the team. She has been making a big impression in the community and helped bring the NFL draft here. In 2019, the Tennessee Sports Hall of Fame named her Tennessean of the Year.[383]

The Titans ended the 2019 season on a positive note, making it to the AFC Championship Game behind the unstoppable running of Derrick Henry before losing to the eventual Super Bowl LIV champion, the Kansas City Chiefs. Titans fans are optimistic that great days are ahead for the two-tone blue.

Coda

Nashville's three sports teams—the NHL's Nashville Predators, the NFL's Tennessee Titans, and the MLS's Nashville SC—have helped to raise the city's reputation, putting it into a new league. Now, in addition to being known for music, we're also known for our professional sports teams.

In the next chapter, we'll review another of Nashville's claims to fame, our status as the Athens of the South.

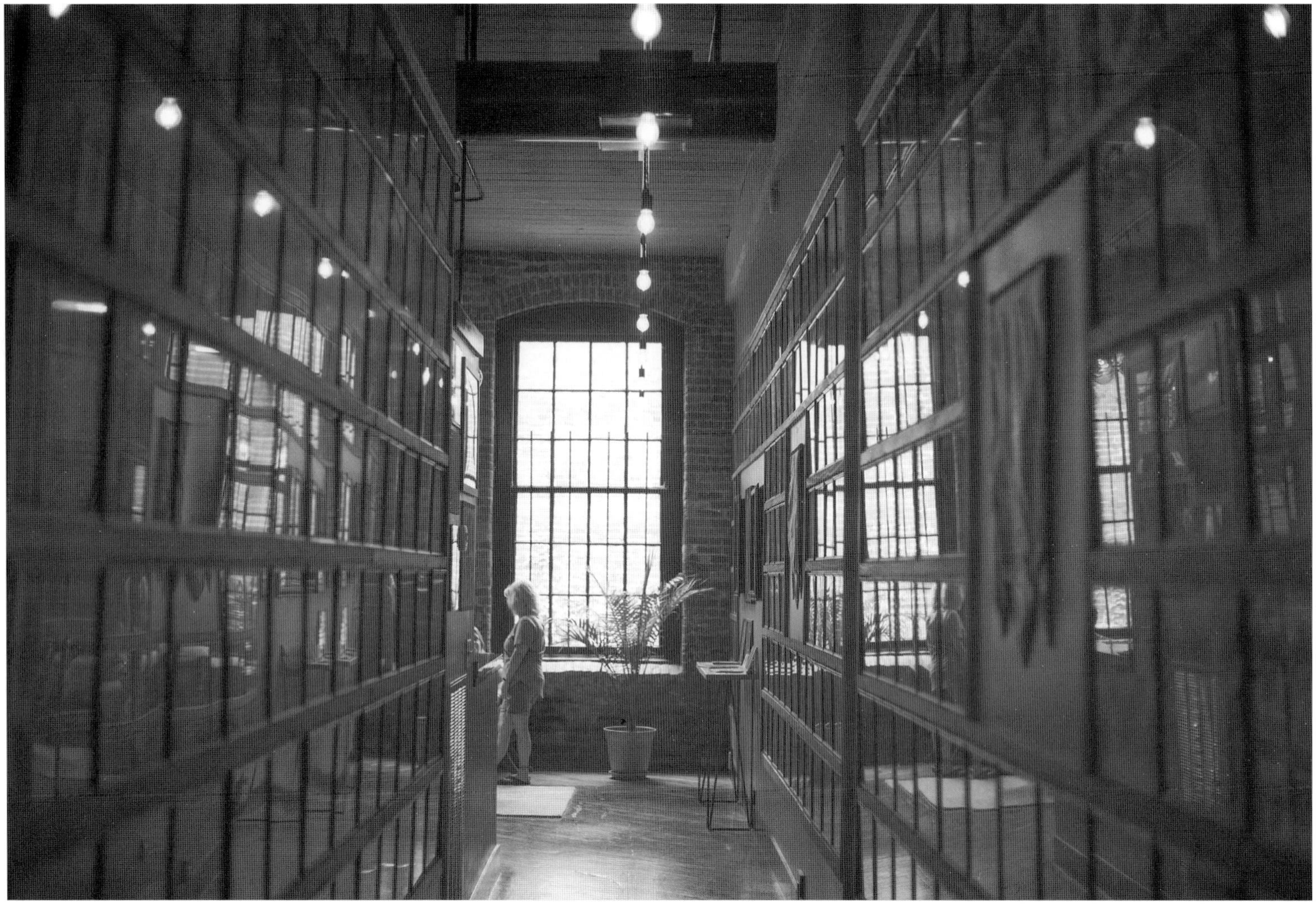

CHAPTER 11

EDUCATION
The Athens of the South

Before Nashville became the "it" city, its moniker was the "Athens of the South." Ancient Athens was the educational center of Greece, and Nashville is the educational center of the South. The nickname first arose in the 1850s because Nashville had the most higher-education institutions in the country and was also the first southern city to create a public school system.[384]

Further reinforcing the nickname, in 1897, as part of Tennessee's hundredth anniversary celebration of statehood, a full-scale replica of the Parthenon was constructed in Centennial

Park in Nashville.[385] Built of plaster and wood, it was initially meant to be temporary, but people loved it so much that the city decided to keep it, rebuilding a more permanent version in concrete in 1931.[386] The original Parthenon, being thousands of years old, is in ruins, so Nashville's Parthenon is actually the best way to see the Parthenon as the ancient Greeks would have, especially since the 1990 addition of the 42-foot-tall golden replica of the statue of Athena—the tallest indoor sculpture in the Western world.[387]

Nashville is home to 24 accredited four-year, two-year, tech schools, and post-graduate schools, with Vanderbilt being the best known.[388] We retain 60 percent of students who graduate from these schools, and more than 34 percent of residents over 25 have a bachelor's degree or higher, with more than 150,000 Nashvillians having graduate or professional degrees.[389]

Rising Prominence of Local Higher Education Institutions

Vanderbilt is Nashville's most well-known university. It has an extensive history of academic excellence, and as of 2019, *U.S. News & World Report* ranked it number 14 among National Universities and number 7 for Best Value Schools.[390] The university consistently ranks on top-10 lists, and its graduates include six Nobel laureates, including Al Gore.[391]

Amazon Future Engineer Program: A Boost to Computer Science Education in Nashville

An unexpected and oft-overlooked benefit of Nashville's pro-business agenda is business investment in local education. Businesses located in Nashville have a stake in the city's education system because it directly impacts their future talent pool. Many businesses thus choose to give back to the community through education programs.

In 2019, Amazon became the latest in a long line of businesses that have invested in Nashville's education system. As reported by the *Nashville Business Journal*, Amazon's partnership with Metro Nashville Public Schools "will bring computer science courses and robotics teams to underserved communities. The Amazon Future Engineer program will fund robotics programming at 21 elementary, middle and high schools, and will give an additional $10,000 each to expand computer science education at 24 schools."[392]

Vanderbilt has a huge impact on the Nashville community, with Vanderbilt University Medical Center being the number one employer in the area.[393] For 2015–2016, the university had a $9.5 billion impact on Tennessee's economy and brought 600,000 visitors to the area for Vanderbilt-related activities.[394]

Vanderbilt has long since made a name for itself, but it's far from the only impressive university in Nashville. Fisk University has a rich history (in fact, its campus is listed on the National Register of Historic Places) and is ranked number 6 of *U.S. News & World Report*'s Historically Black Colleges and Universities.[395] Another historically Black institution, Tennessee State University (Oprah's alma mater) has been thriving under the leadership of its excellent president since 2013, Dr. Glenda Baskin Glover. Two other Nashville universities, Belmont University and Lipscomb University, have been increasing in prominence in recent years.

Belmont University is one of the fastest-growing universities in the country. Belmont, a Southern Baptist college, had record enrollment in fall 2018 for the eighteenth consecutive year.[396] Total, over the last decade, it has seen a 65 percent increase in enrollment.[397] Throughout this explosive growth, the university has not lowered but *increased* its standards. In 2018, its incoming class had an average ACT score of 27.[398] It is now ranked number 6 on *U.S. News & World Report*'s 2019 Regional Universities South list.[399]

As Belmont has grown, it has popped up with more frequency in the media. In 2008, Belmont received national attention for hosting a presidential debate, which Belmont University President Bob Fisher described as "the Super Bowl of higher education."[400] The event helped put Belmont on the nation's radar, and the university repeated the honor once again for the 2020 election. The university has also received increasing media coverage—and a spike in enrollment—for the quality of its music business program, with Billboard naming it one of the top programs of its kind in the nation.[401]

Another way Belmont has raised its profile and attracted more students nationally is through its sports program. In the past, Belmont competed in the National Association of Intercollegiate Athletics (NAIA), where it played small schools without national name recognition, but in 2004, it switched to the NCAA. Most thought the move would be a double-edged sword. In the NAIA, Belmont had been the big fish in a little pond; in the NCAA, it would be a small fish in a much larger pond. Many assumed that it would be annihilated by the greater competition, but the Belmont Bruins basketball team rose to the challenge. They started in the Atlantic Sun Conference and immediately began dominating. They then moved to the Ohio Valley Conference and continued to dominate. Since becoming Division 1, they've won their conference 12 times, and qualified for the NCAA March Madness tournament 8 times out of 17 total chances.[402]

Lipscomb University is one of the fastest-growing private doctoral universities in the country, with an enrollment growth of 80.6 percent from 2006 to 2016.[403] In that time period, it doubled its number of colleges, from 5 to 10.[404] One of the biggest draws of the university is its job-placement success rate. For the 2016–2017 bachelor's degree graduates, 96 percent were employed or pursuing graduate school within six months.[405] Lipscomb's accounting program in particular is excellent. It is the number one accounting program in Tennessee and has an astounding 100 percent placement rate.[406]

K–12 Education

K–12 education is one of the hottest issues in Nashville right now. We've long been a bastion of higher education, and we now want to bring our K–12 education up to the same level.

Nashville's current K–12 education system is notable for the great variety of options. Our public schools have made great strides in the past decades with the introduction of magnet schools, but historically, their performance was lackluster, leading to the rise of an impressive private school system. A charter school movement has also been gaining momentum in the city. Not every charter school has been a success, but several have been doing some innovative work.

Today, thanks to healthy competition between schools, parents and students have many excellent options, whether they choose a public, charter, or private school.

Free and Low-Cost Education

As the educational center of the South, Nashville believes that education is a right, not a privilege. In addition to our K–12 public school system, Nashville Community Education provides extremely low-cost classes for adults, with over 160 classes offered, in topics ranging from dance to estate planning to salary negotiation to Mandarin.[407] As the fall 2019 brochure states, "costs should never get in the way of enrichment," so scholarships are available to help with the class fees.[408]

The state of Tennessee is also pioneering a free community college program, Tennessee Promise. The program allows any student to attend a two-year community college tuition-free, and under another program, UT Promise, high-achieving students from families that make $50,000 or less can attend the University of Tennessee for free.[409]

The Academy Model

An interesting new trend in Nashville K–12 education is the academy model, where the traditional high school curriculum is split up into "majors." For example, students could choose to pursue a healthcare track that will provide them with tangible skills and a certification that they can leverage to enter their desired field. The thought process behind this approach is that while a general high school diploma is beneficial, it is even better to develop marketable, practical vocational skills.

There are currently 12 schools participating in the academy model pilot program in Nashville. Two of these are Stratford STEM Magnet School and McGavock High School. Stratford has two academies, the Academy of National Safety and Security Technologies, which focuses on computer programming and criminal science, and the Academy of Science and Engineering, which includes biotechnology, engineering, and interdisciplinary science and research.[410]

McGavock, which Angie and Steve had the opportunity to tour, offers four academies: Gaylord Opryland Academy of Hospitality and US Community Credit Union Academy of Business and Finance; Academy of Aviation and Transportation; Aegis Sciences Corporation Academy of Life Science and Law; and CMT Academy of Digital Design and Communication.[411] While Angie and Steve were there, they observed students practicing blood draws on a fake arm and visited the fully operational student-run US Community Credit Union branch within the school. They were impressed by how hands-on and intensive the education was.

Magnet Public Schools

There are 88,000 students enrolled in Metro Nashville Public Schools, with more than 120 different languages spoken by the student body.[412] Like most cities, Nashville's public schools, with a mandate to educate all comers, have struggled to compete with the area's private schools academically. However, magnet schools have been steadily raising the bar. In 2017, Tennessee had zero National Blue Ribbon Schools (as determined by the US Department of Education), but in 2018, we had six, with four lying in the Nashville MSA and one—Hume-Fogg High School—in Nashville proper.

Nashville's two best magnet public schools are Hume-Fogg High School and Martin Luther King Jr. Magnet School. They were the city's first flagship magnet academic schools, developed under Bredesen's mayoral term. Hume-Fogg is known as the liberal arts magnet school, and MLK is known for science and engineering.

The original incarnation of Hume-Fogg—the Hume School—was the first public school in Nashville, and today's Hume-Fogg occupies the same historic downtown campus. Niche ranked Hume-Fogg as the number 1 public school in the state of Tennessee,[413] and *U.S. News & World Report* ranked it number 60 in the country.[414] If given the choice between Hume-Fogg and any of Nashville's private, most parents will choose to send their child to Hume-Fogg because it is of the same caliber as the private schools but free.

MLK also has a great reputation. Niche ranked it number 5 in the state,[415] and *U.S. News & World Report* ranked it 166 nationally.[416] (This rank may not seem impressive at first, but *U.S. News & World Report* ranks more than 17,000 schools in their list. For further context, MLK received an overall score of 99.04/100, and Hume-Fogg had an overall score of 99.65/100.[417])

Charter Schools

With the current political environment, it's likely that we will see increasing numbers of charter schools. Not all charter schools are created alike, but Nashville has two in particular that are taking innovative approaches to education: Nashville Classical Charter School and Valor Collegiate Academy.

Nashville Classical was started by Yale alumnus Charlie Friedman, who has a master's in urban education. Friedman did not have previous ties to Nashville and chose the city based on what he'd read of our charter school movement. Under Friedman's guidance, the school, which has a large minority population, has been thriving. Test scores have skyrocketed, and the school has grown so much that it's now moving into its third facility to accommodate the larger student population. We're a little sorry to see them go. Their previous location was close to our office, and we (as Wagon Wheel) sponsored their playground. Though we will miss their presence in the neighborhood, we're thrilled that they've grown so much that the move is necessary.

When we talked to educators, the school they brought up again and again was Valor Collegiate Academy. Vince Durnan, the head of the University School of Nashville (which will be discussed under private schools), and Elissa Kim, who is a Tennessee State Board of Education member and Senior Vice President of Global Strategy and Talent at the College Board and who previously served as a Metro Nashville School Board Member and Executive Vice President of Recruitment and Admissions at Teach for America, both told us essentially the same thing: if you want a model of who's getting education in the charter school space right, Valor Collegiate Academy is a good choice. We know a parent whose kids attend the school, and he thinks the Valor Collegiate approach to education is the greatest thing ever invented.

The founder and CEO of Valor Collegiate is Todd Dickson, who is highly regarded in the education space as a pioneer of social and emotional learning (SEL). The cutting-edge SEL curriculum at Valor Collegiate is designed to teach students both academic and

140 ★ *Climbing the Charts: The Ascent of Nashville*

Q&A with Vince Durnan, Head of the University School of Nashville

Q: If someone is brand-new to town and trying to evaluate what school is best for their child, what factors should they consider?

A: Start with what environment suits the child best, with what brings out the child's best in terms of people, program, culture, and academic press. Walk the halls, ask the same questions to different people, and listen closely. See the school through the child's eyes.

Q: Nashville is well known as a leader in higher education, but what factors make the city a leader in secondary education?

A: Perhaps the most important factor is the tremendous variety in school types, with exemplars in single-sex, charter, and faith-based school types. As public school enrollments still strain to return to pre-1971 busing levels, many alternatives to neighborhood schools have been created—sometimes at great cost to the original system, but they do present options for those who can avail themselves.

Q: Nashville attracts talent from areas with some of the most elite schools in the country. What will they find upon moving to Nashville, in terms of private school options?

A: They will probably find fewer options of the nonsectarian, coeducational variety, but price points are typically significantly lower than those that prevail on the coasts. But change is happening by the day.

non-academic skills, like curiosity, kindness, and determination. In its first year, the school proved the validity of its model by "outperforming all Metro Nashville Public Schools and 99 percent of schools in Tennessee on state testing in its first year."[418] If the school continues on its trajectory, it very well may overtake Hume-Fogg as the top school of the state.

Private Schools

Nashville has several high-performing private schools. The main drawback to private school is, of course, the expense. However, while a private school in Nashville could run you $15,000 to $25,000 a year, a comparable school in New York or Washington, DC, could easily cost $60,000 to $70,000. Several of the best private schools in Nashville also have endowments that allow them to award need-based scholarships. Additionally, Nashville has several good parochial schools that are subsidized by their churches and thus have cheaper tuition, which puts downward price pressure on other private schools.

Of the private schools, University School of Nashville and Episcopal School of Nashville are particularly noteworthy.

University School of Nashville is one of the oldest private schools in Nashville and was the second school in Nashville to be desegregated. It was originally a demonstration school for Peabody College, part of Vanderbilt, but today it is an independent institution, though it is still on Vanderbilt's campus. As ranked by Niche, it is the top private school in the state,[419] and Best Schools ranked it in the top 50 of private day schools in the United States.[420]

Episcopal School of Nashville was co-founded by Ketch Secor, lead singer of Old Crow Medicine Show. On the surface, that may seem unusual, but Secor's father was a leading educator in Virginia, including serving as a headmaster at several Episcopal Schools. Though Episcopal School of Nashville is religiously affiliated, it tends toward the liberal end of the Episcopal spectrum. The school is a reflection of the Nashville community in that it is very diverse, both socioeconomically and racially, and features multiple languages on its school sign, including Arabic, Spanish, and Hebrew. The school also places a great emphasis on scholarships for underprivileged students.

Another private school we're partial to is St. Bernard Academy, which Angie's kids attend. The school has a ratio of 1 teacher to every 10 students, and it is more affordable in comparison to schools like the University School of Nashville while still maintaining high academic standards.

Focuses for Improvement

In the 2019 mayoral race, education, along with transit, was at the top of the list of the issues people care about. Education is on the radar for every major government leader in Nashville, and in 2018, Metro Nashville Public Schools released a new school improvement plan with a "four-prong strategy": "refining supports to school leaders, strengthening instructional coaching, developing student and family supports through a community school partnership model and growing teacher talent."[421]

While Nashville may not earn an A for every dimension of its current K–12 education system, it certainly gets an A-plus for innovation. We are committed to providing the best education we can. To that end, we are thinking outside the box in order to utilize our resources to the fullest. The city is a great microcosm of different methods and approaches being tried and tested. It's like we're in an educational laboratory. Granted, most parents don't want their children to be the test subjects in the Petri dish, but Nashville is taking a thoughtful, empirical approach to this experimentation. We aren't trying to reinvent the wheel, and we're not throwing out minimum standards. We're simply introducing new approaches in a slow, controlled way and then measuring the outcomes to determine what works and what doesn't.

It's not just educational methods that leading educators want to tinker with; they also want to infuse schools with money, sometimes in nontraditional ways. Elissa Kim, for instance, thinks we need to revamp the salary structure for principals and teachers. "A school's success hinges heavily on the leadership throughout the building," she says. "The culture of a school and the quality of instruction in each classroom drives student outcomes, so we need to recruit world-class leaders who can do this difficult work."[422] Yet when teacher pay caps out at $50,000, it's difficult to attract the best talent. As such, Kim is a proponent of rewarding results: if student outcomes rise, so does pay. She thinks amazing teachers should have the potential to make six figures given the outsize role they play in shaping futures. "There are ways to reallocate spending and build public-private partnerships to drive innovation in this space so more of our investments are going straight to the classroom."

The biggest battle in the education sphere of Nashville is funding. "If you want to learn about a school, the first place to start is how much money they have per student," Vince Durnan told us. For 2017–2018, Metro Nashville spent around $13,376 per pupil.[423] "Until that number is more in line with what the private schools can do for their students," Durnan says, "there's not a whole lot that can be done to bridge the gap."[424]

Q&A with Chuck Sabo, Head of St. Bernard Academy, a 2017 National Blue Ribbon School

Q: If someone is brand-new to town and trying to evaluate what school is best for their child, what factors should they consider?

A: I think they must first ask themselves what they are looking for. Is there a religious connection they want to make? Is location going to be a challenge? Is class size a consideration? What do they expect the school to provide (additional academic support services, for example)? Then they should look at academic reputation and recommendations from others.

I think touring each school they're considering is a key to finding the fit for their child. Not every school is a fit for every child.

Q: Nashville is well known as a leader in higher education, but what factors make the city a leader in secondary education?

A: It's the variety of options available for families. They can pick from single-sex, religious, charter, and so on.

Q: Nashville attracts talent from areas with some of the most elite schools in the country. What will they find upon moving to Nashville, in terms of private school options?

A: First, they can pay from $13,000 all the way up to $30,000 or $40,000. The Nashville area is rich in traditions, in academic or athletic options. Nearly anything they could want, I feel they could find here. Soon there will be a boarding school option as well at Currey Ingram.

Q: What makes St. Bernard Academy stand out as a leading option?

A: People say that there is a feeling they get about St. Bernard Academy when they walk through the door. I think with our small class sizes, the teachers really get the opportunity to get to know the kids at a whole different level. Also, we can provide academic support that others do not. We are proud of our academic reputation and the connections we have with the families.

Increasing government education spending is one way to address this financial gap; community fundraisers are another. KIPP (Knowledge Is Power Program) Nashville is an example of how successful fundraisers can be here. KIPP is a nationwide network of free, college-preparatory public charter schools that primarily serve low-income communities. KIPP schools work to take the bottom 10 percent of students and transform them into the top 10 percent of students. With the help of a local digital agency who created a short video about the school, KIPP Nashville recently raised $200,000 at their annual breakfast fundraiser, as well as an additional $50,000 through an email campaign.[425]

Coda

There is certainly room for improvement in Nashville's education system, but area schools have been steadily moving the needle forward. There's a great variety of choice—from public to private to charter schools—and there is a lot of dynamism and exciting work happening right now, including several innovative schools that are operating at the forefront of educational theory.

In the final chapter, we will look at all the sundry, not-yet-mentioned activities available in Nashville that make life in this city such a full, rewarding experience.

HANGING AROUND
in Nashville
SMASH VILLE
TITANS
709-KDO
LYNWOOD
8TH Av S.
@hangingaroundinc
@shopwheretheartis

CHAPTER 12

--- ★ ---

KEEPING BUSY
Life in Nashville

In addition to the amazing live music, the popping restaurant scene, and the year-round sporting events, Nashville offers all the amenities you'd expect from a world-class city. From parks to shopping to art and theater, we have it all. The only challenge is finding enough free time to do it all.

Outdoor Nashville

Geographically, Nashville is in a neat location. The Cumberland River flows right through downtown, and around 200 miles to the east are the Great Smoky Mountains. The city and surrounding area have an interesting topography. We're not quite in the foothills, but we are close enough to the Smokies to have beautiful rolling hills that are a blaze of color in autumn. And thanks to the Tennessee Valley Authority—a Great Depression–era public works program to bring electricity to rural areas in the southeast—several nearby rivers have been dammed to create well-loved lakes.

The Cumberland River

No geographic feature has had more impact on Nashville than the Cumberland River. The city likely would not even exist today without the river. While Nashville's economy no longer relies on river shipping, the Cumberland River has remained a key part of the city.

There are two downtown parks along the Cumberland River: Riverfront Park on the west bank and Cumberland Park along the east bank, next to Nissan Stadium. Riverfront Park hosts frequent concerts and events, and Cumberland Park features a splash pad popular with kids. Both offer great views of the city.

Twenty years ago, no one would have dared swim in the Cumberland River. People thought it was too dangerous. It turns out that's not true, and attitudes here changed. Now, multiple outfitter companies have made it possible for people to canoe or kayak down the river to Cumberland Park. That puts you on the opposite bank from downtown, but don't worry: no swimming is required. Downtown is just a walk away across the nearby pedestrian bridge.

> # Weekend Trip: The Great Smoky Mountains National Park
>
> The Great Smoky Mountains National Park is the most visited national park in the United States, with even more visitors than the Grand Canyon. Just a three-hour drive from Nashville, it's a perfect weekend destination. The verdant mountain peaks, characteristic blue haze, and plentiful wildlife make it a great place to unplug and unwind.

Lakes

On a sunny (or even rainy) weekend, you'll find many locals at one of three major reservoirs around Nashville: Old Hickory Lake, Percy Priest Lake, and Center Hill Lake.

Old Hickory Lake was made by damming the Cumberland River. Just a 10-minute drive from Nashville, it's a popular destination and receives tons of boat traffic. You can build right on the water there, so a lot of beautiful lake homes with private docks have popped up in recent years.

Percy Priest Lake is managed by the Army Corps of Engineers, and home construction is not allowed. It can be fun to look at all the houses on Old Hickory Lake, but Percy Priest Lake offers a different kind of beauty: unmarred forest and shoreline.

Another popular lake is Center Hill Lake, which is a little bit east of the city. It is known for being a really deep, clean, clear-water lake. Like Percy Priest Lake, it doesn't have any houses, with one notable exception: Alan Jackson's lake house. You can't get a permit to build a house on the lake, but Jackson decided it was better to ask for forgiveness instead of permission. He went ahead and built the house and then said sorry later. Jackson has since sold the house, so you won't catch sight of him there. However, in Nashville, you never know when you'll run into him or another famous musician out and about on the town.

Parks

Nashville has a lot of parks, of two varieties: urban parks and wilderness parks. The urban parks are the green spaces right in the city, and the wilderness parks are outside of town, in more expansive natural areas.

The most famous and popular of our urban parks is Centennial Park, which is where our Parthenon replica is. Within the Parthenon is the colossal Athena statue as well as an art gallery, with permanent and rotating exhibits. Centennial Park features an idyllic reservoir complete with ducks, and the park is the location for many popular events and festivals, like the free music series Musicians Corner and the Shakespeare in the Park performances.

Bicentennial Mall is another popular urban park. It's right downtown and has a great view of the Capitol. It includes a splash pad and intricate water fountains, but what makes it really stand out is its large stone columns inscribed with important historical dates and facts for Tennessee. As you stroll through the park, you can get a free history lesson by reading the stone columns.

Two of the major wilderness parks are Percy Warner Park and Beaman Park. These are the places people go to hike and disappear into nature. In these parks, you can feel as if you are a million miles away from the city.

Aside from urban parks and wilderness parks, the city also has its share of dog parks, golf courses, and gardens. Our favorite garden is Cheekwood, which is an old mansion that has been converted into a museum. Cheekwood has a beautiful botanical garden and rotating art exhibits. We also love the arboretum on the Vanderbilt campus.

Outdoor Activities

We have a little bit of everything when it comes to outdoor activities. With our abundance of lakes and rivers, fishing, boating, and kayaking/canoeing are popular. Besides the Cumberland River, the Harpeth River and Caney Fork River are the favorite spots for kayaking and canoeing. There's also good rock climbing in the area, and hiking is popular, especially at Radnor Lake Natural Area and the Cumberland Plateau. Radnor Lake is great because it has a wide variety of trails. You can hike up into the hills, or you can stick to one of the paved trails that are accessible to wheelchair users and ideal for baby strollers.

"Let Freedom Sing!": Fourth of July in Nashville

Nashville's "Let Freedom Sing!" event is one of the largest Fourth of July fireworks shows in the nation. In 2019, 343,000 people reportedly attended,[435] and in 2018, *Condé Nast Traveler* ranked Nashville's as 1 of the 11 best shows in the country.[436] The Nashville Symphony plays on the river for the celebration, synchronized with the fireworks, and it really is an incredible experience.

Shopping

When we first moved to Nashville, the shopping options were somewhat limited. Nordstrom wasn't even a thought. Today, you could spend weeks shopping and still not have time to visit all the stores.

The Mall at Green Hills is our luxury, high-end shopping mall, with stores like Louis Vuitton, Tiffany's, Restoration Hardware, and Nordstrom. It has more than a hundred stores and eateries. It's a beautiful mall with lots of windows and natural light, and it recently underwent a $200 million renovation that added a new wing, more stores (including more every-man stores, like Abercrombie and Forever 21), and more parking.[426] The expansion also included a new four-story, 70,000-square-foot Restoration Hardware experience store—one of the few stores of its kind in the country.[427] With its chandelier and wine bar, the store feels more like an elegant furniture gallery and café than a store.

Two other malls of note are Opry Mills and the Hill Center Green Hills. Opry Mills, an outlet mall, is located near the Grand Ole Opry, so you can shop all day and then hop over to the Grand Ole Opry when you're done. The mall is known for its IMAX, Rainforest Café, Madame Tussauds wax museum (complete with a wax Taylor Swift!), and giant stuffed grizzly bear that is perfect for photo ops. The IMAX is now 1 of just 19 in the country to offer immersive 4DX (which includes moving chairs and special effects like wind and rain) and ScreenX (multi-projection theater that offers a 270-degree view) experiences.[428] The Hill Center Green Hills is our open-air mall and features stores like Anthropologie, Lululemon, and Whole Foods.

Aside from traditional malls, many neighborhoods have thriving shopping districts, with an emphasis on boutique shops. The Gulch and 12 South are especially popular. One interesting dimension of Nashville shopping is the proliferation of celebrity-owned stores. Reese Witherspoon has a boutique, Draper James, in 12 South; Holly Williams, singer-songwriter and granddaughter of Hank Williams Sr., owns White's Mercantile, which has a store in 12 South as well as Franklin; and the *American Pickers* store Antique Archaeology is in Marathon Village, a former turn-of-the-century automobile factory.

Nashville also has numerous farmers' markets, including a year-round market in downtown, and a monthly flea market at the fairgrounds.

Nashville has every kind of shopping you could want. You can gorge yourself on cheap outlet shopping, unearth unique finds in boutiques and at the flea market, or splurge on high-end luxuries.

Family Activities

Butch Spyridon, CEO of the Nashville Convention and Visitors Corporation, has said that he wants Nashville to be Disney World during the day and Las Vegas during the night. While many of the city's activities are designed for those 21 and over, there's fun to be had for the whole family.

While Broadway is not kid-friendly at night, it's a great place for families during the day. Several of the honky-tonks allow children before a certain time, usually about six o'clock, so you can go and hear live music.

The Nashville Zoo is popular. They recently put in a new bear exhibit, and the zoo is a good size—not so massive that you wind up with tired, cranky kids but big enough to spend an afternoon or day there.

For hot days, there are several water options, including splash pads and water parks, like Nashville Shores on Percy Priest Lake, SoundWaves at Gaylord Opryland Resort, and Wave Country Water Park.

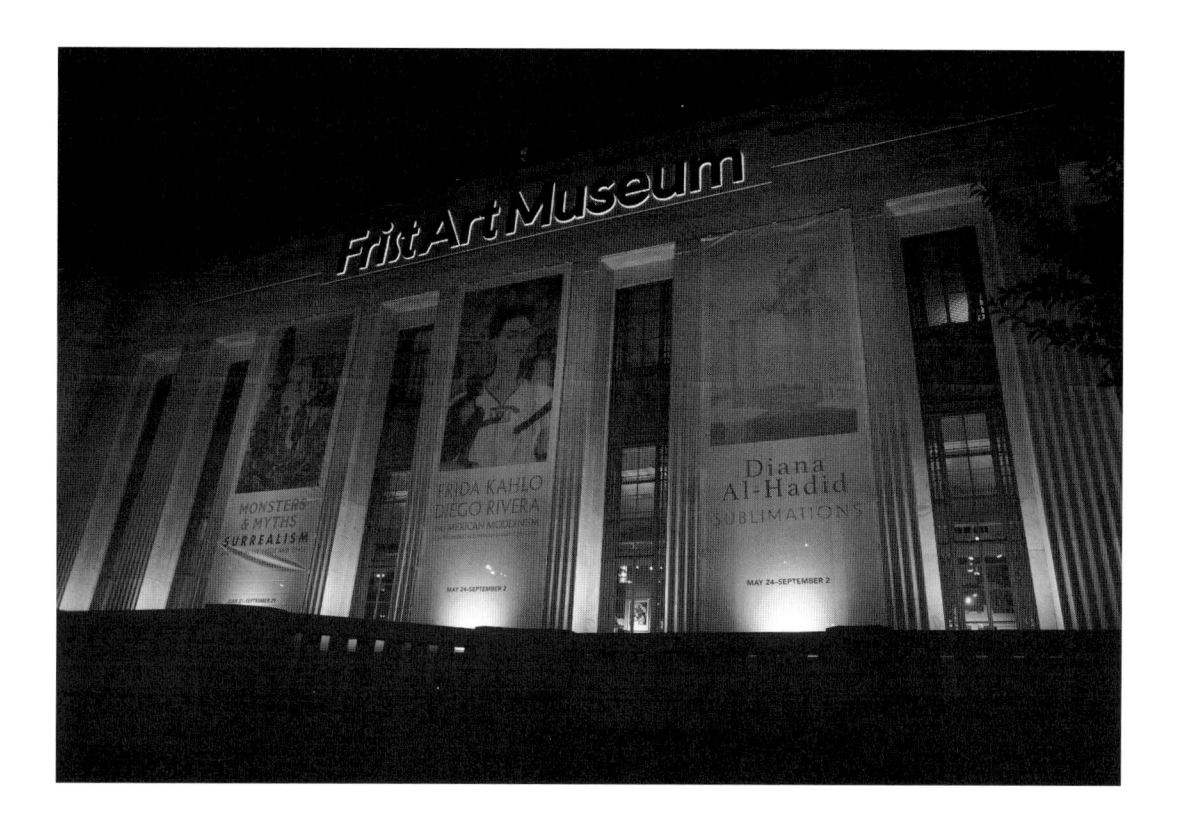

Another great place is Phillips Toy Mart. It's a mom-and-pop toy store with a good mix of classic and new toys. It's a yearly tradition for Angie to take her kids there around Christmas, and it's always a special treat.

There are plenty more fun things we like to do with our kids:

- Titans open practices
- Farmer's markets
- Hop-on, hop-off trolleys
- Lucky Ladd Farm, which has a pumpkin patch and hayrides in the fall
- Nashville Children's Theater
- Adventure Science Center
- Sudekum Planetarium

Art and More

Nashville has a vibrant art scene, from the classic to the modern. For the classic arts, we have the Frist Art Museum, Noah Liff Opera Center, Nashville Ballet, Schermerhorn Symphony Center, and Tennessee Performing Arts Center, which is where touring Broadway shows perform. In the contemporary art space, OZ Arts Nashville is a flexible performance and installation space. It's housed in a former cigar warehouse, and you never know what you're going to see there. It's an endless stream of new, eclectic art. We also have a slew of neighborhood art crawls staggered through each month:

- First Saturday Art Crawl Downtown (first Saturday)

- Art & Music at Wedgewood Houston (first Saturday)

- East Side Art Stumble (second Saturday)

- Germantown Art Crawl (third Saturday)

- Jefferson Street Art Crawl (fourth Saturday)

- Nashville Night (first Friday)

The Belcourt Theatre is Nashville's nonprofit cinema. It opened in 1925 and is dedicated to presenting the best of independent, documentary, world, repertory and classic films, 365 days a year.[429]

Coda

There is always something going on in Nashville. Though the city is known for music, we also have a strong visual and performance arts community. There are plenty of outdoor and family activities, and festivals are held year round. To get the full Nashville experience, we encourage you to check out an events calendar to find out what's happening in the city. Nashville Guru has one we like: www.nashvilleguru.com/nashville-events.

Favorite Nashville Festivals

Music Festivals

**CMA MUSIC FESTIVAL:
WWW.CMAFEST.COM**

This four-day festival has exploded over the last 10 years, becoming an international event. In 2019, it generated $65 million in direct visitor spending for the city of Nashville, with more than 50,000 people in attendance each night.[430]

TIN PAN SOUTH: WWW.TINPANSOUTH.COM
This festival has been going on since 1993 and is the world's largest songwriters' festival. Music fans from all over the world come to see these performances. The festival runs over the course of five days and is held at nine different venues around town. Typically held at the end of March.

**JEFFERSON STREET JAZZ & BLUES FESTIVAL:
WWW.NASHVILLEJAZZANDBLUESFEST.COM**

Founded in 1994, the Jefferson Street Jazz & Blues Festival is at the heart and soul of the African American community in Nashville. Happens annually in June.

**LIVE ON THE GREEN MUSIC FESTIVAL:
WWW.LIVEONTHEGREEN.COM**

Held at Public Square Park, this annual festival is produced and presented by Lightning 100. It has become a widely known public event that showcases well-known national artists as well as Nashville's emerging talent. Takes place over the course of two weekends at the end of August into the beginning of September. Go kiss summer goodbye at this free festival!

**AMERICANA FEST:
WWW.AMERICANAMUSIC.ORG/EVENTS/AMERICANAFEST**

Over the course of the past 20 years, this annual event brings together fans and music industry professionals. This festival usually takes place over the course of six days and offers networking opportunities and seminars as well as live showcases and performances. Takes place in September of each year.

Food and Drink Festivals

**NASHVILLE COCKTAIL FESTIVAL:
WWW.NASHVILLECOCKTAILFESTIVAL.COM**

This is a citywide celebration of craft cocktails and bartenders. This festival has three main events in addition to countless intimate opportunities throughout the week. Takes place every April.

**MUSIC CITY BREWER'S FESTIVAL:
WWW.MUSICCITYBREWERSFEST.COM**

Having been around for about 20 years, this festival has become one of the biggest and best of its kind in the country. Goers have the opportunity to sample some of the most respected brews from over 40 local, regional, national, and international breweries. Takes place every year toward the end of July.

**WINE ON THE RIVER:
WWW.WINEONTHERIVERNASHVILLE.COM**

Also around for about 20 years, this festival still has a focus on great-tasting food and wine from around the globe. They shut down one of the bridges over the Cumberland for this event, so it is more accurately *over* the river as opposed to *on* the river. Takes place in September.

Other Festivals

Nearby Festivals

TOMATO ARTS FESTIVAL:
WWW.TOMATOARTFEST.COM

The motto of this festival is "The Tomato—a unifier not a divider! Bringing together fruits and vegetables." This one started out as something of a joke, but in 2018, more than 60,000 people attended.[431] During this festival, you can walk the streets of the East Nashville neighborhoods to look at tomato-inspired art, eat food, and watch live music performances. Takes place every August.

TASTE OF MUSIC CITY

This is an all-inclusive food-tasting event with a one-price admission. Attendees have the opportunity to take a culinary tour of Nashville and enjoy samples from popular local restaurants. Takes place in June.

MUSIC CITY FOOD AND WINE FESTIVAL

This festival was cultivated by Grammy Award-winning artists and Nashville residents Kings of Leon and world-renowned chef Jonathan Waxman. This festival takes place in historic venues and outdoor spaces in downtown Nashville. Typically takes place in September.

OKTOBERFEST:
WWW.THENASHVILLEOKTOBERFEST.COM

This festival, which spans 10 blocks in the heart of Nashville, celebrates the traditions of Oktoberfest. This event has been going on for 40 years, and admission is free. It's not just a beer festival; there are arts and crafts, live German music, and much more. Always runs in the month of October.

IROQUOIS STEEPLECHASE:
WWW.IROQUOISSTEEPLECHASE.ORG

Since 1941, this event has been known as Nashville's rite of spring. Annually, it attracts over 25,000 attendees, combining horse racing with the spirit of community. Usually held at the beginning of May.

BONNAROO:
WWW.BONNAROO.COM

A quick 45-minute drive outside of Nashville is the legendary Bonnaroo Music and Arts Festival. It features a lineup of over 150 musicians and more each year. Typically held in June.

PILGRIMAGE FESTIVAL:
WWW.PILGRIMAGEFESTIVAL.COM

Taking place in Franklin (less than an hour from Nashville), Pilgrimage Festival features a diverse, renowned lineup of rock and roll, Americana, alt country, bluegrass, jazz, indie, gospel, pop, and blues. The festival is usually held in September.

BOBFEST

An hour north of Nashville, nestled on a lush 15 acres along the Red River in Adams, Tennessee, BobFest is a four-day music and arts camping festival. Usually takes places in September and is hosted by Cold Lunch Recordings and Nashville Psych Alliance.

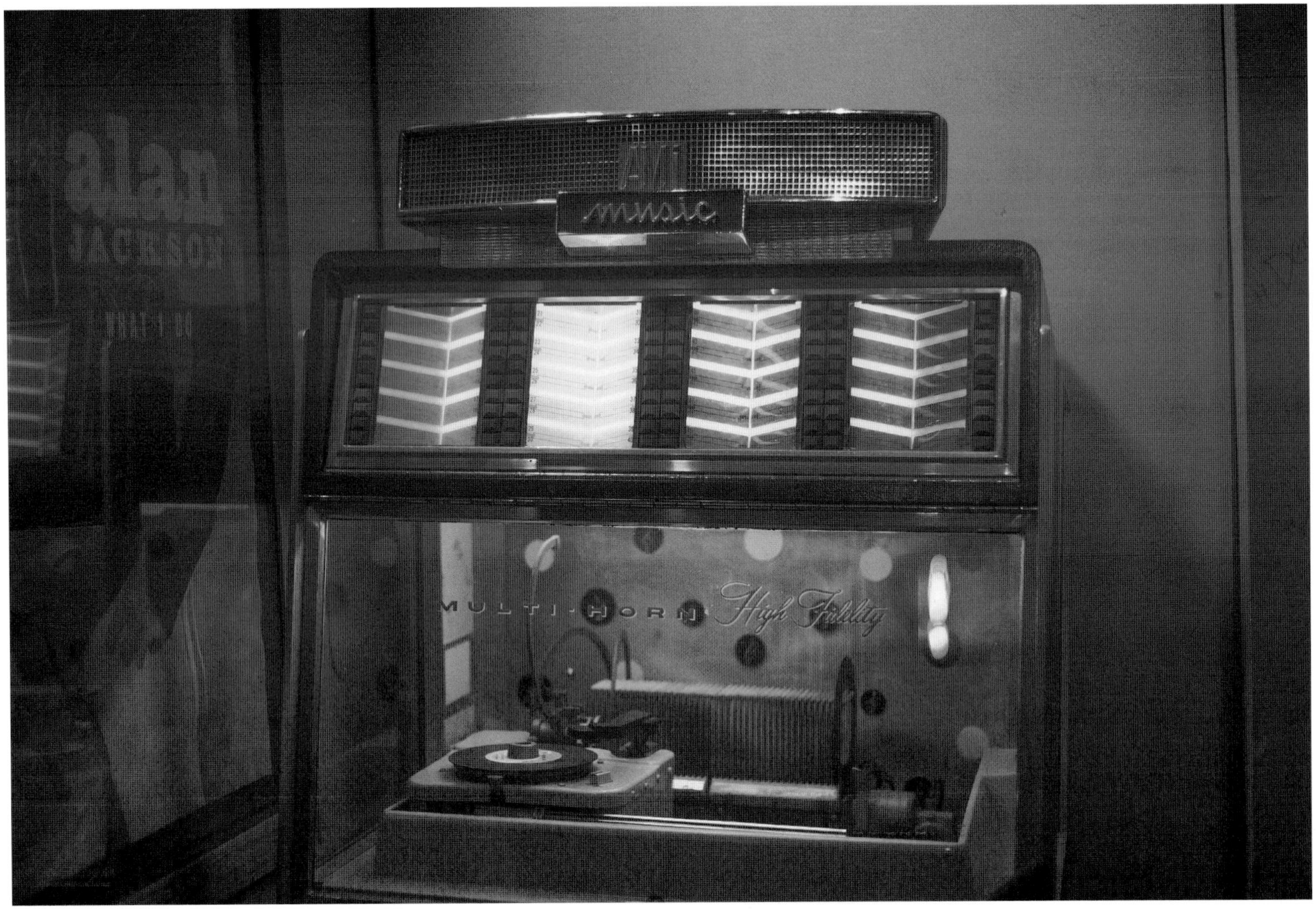
alan
JACKSON
AMI
music
MULTI-HORN High Fidelity

CONCLUSION

WHAT'S NEXT FOR NASHVILLE?

The future for Nashville is brighter than ever. Development and investment are taking place throughout all corridors of the city on a larger scale than ever before, and the city shows no sign of yielding the "it" city title. As Anthony Bourdain described it in the final season of *Parts Unknown*, "People who grew up [in Nashville] will tell you the city is in a state of perpetual, never-ending change, and the rate at which things are changing is accelerating."[432]

Even in the time we've spent revising this book, the city has gone through many changes. In early March 2020, a tornado ripped a path through Nashville, and on its heels came closures and disruptions due to the COVID-19 pandemic. In the face of devastation and uncertainty, Nashvillians rose to the challenge as they have many times before. People came out en masse to volunteer for tornado relief, and while the lasting effects of the pandemic are still to be seen, real estate developments have continued, and businesses are rebuilding.

We cannot say for certain what the future holds for Nashville, except that it will be different from today. Even from the time you picked up this book to when you put it down, something new has probably happened in Nashville. That's one of the things we love most about this city: as soon as Nashville reaches the peak of one mountain, we're already looking forward to the next mountain to climb, and that's how you stay on top.

The City's X Factor

Obviously, there is something special about Nashville, and everyone wants to know the secret. "From Australia to Austin," says Butch Spyridon, CEO of the Nashville Convention and Visitors Corporation, "people are wanting to learn from us."[433] The city's secret sauce is difficult to define. The best-known ingredients of the secret sauce are the music scene and the area's economic growth and stability, but there is more than immediately meets the eye. We also have a strong infrastructure and a confluence of increasing cosmopolitanism while retaining small-town sensibility.

If we had to choose just one catalyst for the city's ascent to the top of the charts, we'd point to our culture of collaboration and innovation. But ultimately, there is no one factor responsible for the city's climb. Ken Levitan, founder and CEO of Vector Management (whose clients include Kings of Leon, Hank Williams Jr., Emmylou Harris, Lynyrd Skynyrd, and Trace Adkins), described Nashville's recent rise thusly: "Nashville is on fire right now. All of sudden everything converged. The music, the food, the arts and culture, the political willpower, the gentrification of all of these downtown neighborhoods. Now everyone's falling in love with Nashville. It's about time."[434]

Nashville's persona is a carefully cultivated blend of spices. Any one ingredient on its own would be unremarkable, but together, they sing. Music, development, entrepreneurship, sports, arts, culinary achievement, healthcare, education—it all combines to create an unforgettable city.

What Newcomers Should Know

The most important thing Nashville newcomers should know is that we welcome outsiders. The way we see it, every outsider is simply a chance for us to gain a new Nashvillian. Many visitors are inspired to return to the city, already planning their next trip before the first one is over. Some of them even make a more permanent relocation.

Our city embraces businesspeople and real estate developers. Businesspeople can spot a great opportunity when they see one, and many have recognized Nashville as a great opportunity. But it's not just about the opportunities the city provides. It's also about what the city receives. We love outsiders because they infuse new life into the city, through developments, businesses, and innovative ideas.

Come Visit!

If you've been thinking about visiting Nashville, stop thinking and start planning your trip. The city's secret sauce really must be experienced, not just read about. So come see the city for yourself. Attend a live music performance, eat at one of our award-winning restaurants, taste our world-famous whiskeys, catch a sports game, walk around our parks, and stop by Wagon Wheel to say hi to some real Nashvillians and get some more insider tips. With just a few days in the city, you'll better understand what makes Nashville tick. Be careful, though: once you arrive, you may never want to leave!

ENDNOTES

1. Dave Paulson, "Dave Grohl, Foo Fighters Discover Nashville," Tennessean, October 30, 2014, https://www.tennessean.com/story/entertainment/music/2014/10/30/dave-grohl-makes-nashville-stop-hbos-sonic-highways/18209649/.

2. Sydney, "70 Instagram Captions Perfect for Nashville," Kind You, June 14, 2019, https://kindyou.com/nashville-captions/.

3. Joe Rhodes, "The Heartbeat, and the Twang, of a City," New York Times, October 5, 2012, https://www.nytimes.com/2012/10/07/arts/television/nashville-the-tv-series-starring-the-city.html.

4. Alan Frio, "Nashville's Tourism Boom Translates into Cold Hard Cash," WSMV News 4, March 17, 2019, https://www.wsmv.com/news/nashville-s-tourism-boom-translates-into-cold-hard-cash/article_0bbc4d6c-4922-11e9-92aa-0b1a498318db.html.

5. Peter Keating, "The Numbers: No Team Delivers Fans More Value Than the Preds," ESPN, October 23, 2017, http://www.espn.com/nhl/story/_/id/21051370/nhl-numbers-show-nashville-predators-best-franchise-sports.

6. Jamie McGee, "Amazon in Nashville: Company to Bring 5,000 Corporate Jobs to Operations Center," Tennessean, November 13, 2018, https://www.tennessean.com/story/money/nation-now/2018/11/13/amazon-nashville-operations-center/1987289002/.

7. "Nashville NFL Draft Breaks Records across the Board," News Channel 5, May 22, 2019, https://www.newschannel5.com/news/nashville-nfl-draft-breaks-records-across-the-board.

8. Alex Carrick, "The 5 U.S. and 3 Canadian Cities with Best Jobs Markets," Daily Commercial News, April 10, 2019, https://canada.constructconnect.com/dcn/news/economic/2019/04/5-u-s-3-canadian-cities-best-jobs-markets.

9. Peter Lane Taylor, "Nashville Is One of America's Hottest Cities Right Now and It's Not Just the

Hockey," Forbes, June 2, 2017, https://www.forbes.com/sites/petertaylor/2017/06/02/nashville-is-on-a-red-hot-roll-and-its-not-just-the-predators/#2f80ede27a58.

10 Roger Ebert, review of Nashville, directed by Robert Altman, January 1, 1975, https://www.rogerebert.com/reviews/nashville-1975.

11 "Nashville Awards," IMDb, https://www.imdb.com/title/tt0073440/awards.

12 "AFI's 100 Years … 100 Movies—10th Anniversary Edition," American Film Institute, 2007, https://www.afi.com/100years/movies10.aspx.

13 Ridley, Jim. "Look Back in Anger: Robert Altman's Nashville, 20 Years Later." Nashville Scene, November 9, 1995, https://www.nashvillescene.com/news/article/13000170/look-back-in-anger-robert-altmans-nashville-20-years-later.

14 Ridley, "Look Back in Anger."

15 Dave Paulson, "As 'Nashville' Says Goodbye, It Leaves a Mark on the Real Music City," Tennessean, July 25, 2018, https://www.tennessean.com/story/entertainment/music/2018/07/25/tv-show-nashville-season-6-cmt/789804002/.

16 Kim Severson, "Nashville's Latest Big Hit Could Be the City Itself," New York Times, January 8, 2013, https://www.nytimes.com/2013/01/09/us/nashville-takes-its-turn-in-the-spotlight.html.

17 Jamie McGee, "Nashville's Rainmaker: How Butch Spyridon Made Music City a Top Destination," Tennessean, January 5, 2018, https://www.tennessean.com/story/money/2018/01/05/nashvilles-rainmaker-how-butch-spyridon-made-music-city-top-destination/941037001/.

18 Severson, "Nashville's Latest Big Hit."

19 Frio, "Nashville's Tourism Boom."

20 Nashville Area Chamber of Commerce, Nashville 2018 Regional Economic Guide, 2018, https://s3.amazonaws.com/nashvillechamber.com/Economic-Development/Resources+%26+Brochures+Page/2018+Regional+Profile/2018+Nashville+Regional+Economic+Development+Guide.pdf.

21 Jason Lamb, "Report: Nashville Still Growing 100 People Per Day," News Channel 5, March 28, 2017, https://www.newschannel5.com/news/report-nashville-still-growing-100-people-per-day.

22 Samantha Sharf, "Full List: America's Fastest-Growing Cities 2018," Forbes, February 28, 2018, https://www.forbes.com/sites/samanthasharf/2018/02/28/full-list-americas-fastest-growing-cities-2018/#7f26227e7feb.

23 Samantha Sharf, "Full List: America's Fastest-Growing Cities 2017," Forbes, February 10, 2017, https://www.forbes.com/sites/samanthasharf/2017/02/10/full-list-americas-fastest-growing-cities-2017/#71f90e013a36.

24 Jason Lamb, "'It' City vs. 'Our City': Cherry Blossoms Highlight Underlying Conflict in Nashville Development," News Channel 5, April 1, 2019, https://www.newschannel5.com/news/it-city-vs-our-city-cherry-blossoms-highlight-underlying-conflict-in-nashville-development.

25 Tony Gonzalez, "Uprooted Cherry Trees In Nashville Spark Protest Against NFL Draft," All Things Considered, NPR, April 3, 2019, https://www.npr.org/2019/04/03/709573941/uprooted-cherry-trees-in-nashville-spark-protest-against-nfl-draft.

26 Mariah Timms and Andy Humbles, "Nashville to Cut Down Cherry Trees to Make Way for NFL Draft Stage," Tennessean, March 30, 2019, updated April 2, 2019, https://www.tennessean.com/story/news/2019/03/30/nashville-cherry-trees-removed-for-nfl-draft-stage/3317812002/.

27 Lamb, "'It' City vs. 'Our City.'"

28 "Nashville NFL Draft Breaks Records."

29 Zannie Giraud Voss and Glenn Voss, with Brooke Awtry and Jennifer Armstrong, "The Top 40 Most Vibrant Arts Communities in America (2018)," Southern Methodist University DataArts, July 2, 2018, https://dataarts.smu.edu/artsresearch2014/articles/blog-white-papers/most-vibrant-arts-communities-america-2020.

30 Nashville Convention & Visitors Corp., "The Parthenon," Nashville Music City, accessed August 16, 2019, https://www.visitmusiccity.com/local-business/parthenon.

31 This sidebar features just a small sample of the many awards and accolades the city has won, as found at Nashville Convention & Visitors Corp., "Accolades & Honors," Nashville Music City, accessed August 16, 2019, https://www.visitmusiccity.com/accolades-honors.

32 Nashville Area Chamber of Commerce, 2018 Regional Economic Guide, 16.

33 Nashville Area Chamber of Commerce, 2018 Regional Economic Guide, 18.

34 Derek Silva, "The Best Cities for New College Grads in 2019," SmartAsset, April 17, 2019, https://smartasset.com/checking-account/the-best-cities-for-new-college-grads-in-2019.

35 Carrick, "5 U.S. and 3 Canadian Cities with Best Jobs Markets."

36 Jesse Knutson, "Nashville Hosts Convention of Convention Planners," News Channel 5, January 10, 2018, https://www.newschannel5.com/news/nashville-hosts-convention-of-convention-planners.

37 McGee, "Nashville's Rainmaker."

38 Margaret Littman, "Ernest Tubb's 'Midnite Jamboree' Hits Pause," Rolling Stone, April 1, 2015, https://www.rollingstone.com/music/music-country/ernest-tubbs-midnite-jamboree-hits-pause-75449/.

39 "Grand Ole Opry," Wikipedia, accessed June 7, 2021, https://en.wikipedia.org/wiki/Grand_Ole_Opry.

40 Friskics-Warren et al., "Why Is Nashville Called Music City?"

41 Burchard, "The Remarkable History of the Ryman."

42 Bill Friskics-Warren, Jim Ridley, Paul Griffith, Ron Wynn, and Danny Solomon, "Why Is Nashville Called Music City?," Nashville Scene, August 22, 2002, https://www.nashvillescene.com/arts-culture/article/13007578/why-is-nashville-called-music-city.

43 "L&C Tower," Nashville Downtown Partnership, accessed June 19, 2019, https://www.nashvilledowntown.com/go/landc-tower

44 Burchard, "The Remarkable History of the Ryman."

45 "History of Nashville, Tennessee," Wikipedia, accessed July 2, 2019, https://en.wikipedia.org/wiki/History_of_Nashville,_Tennessee.

46 Ketch Secor, interview by the authors, February 5, 2018.

47 Cynthia Cumfer, Separate Peoples, One Land: The Minds of Cherokees, Blacks, and Whites on the Tennessee Frontier (Chapel Hill: University of North Carolina Press, 2007), 132.

48 Stanley F. Horn, "Nashville During the Civil War," Tennessee Historical Quarterly 4, no. 1 (March 1945): 11.

49 Horn, "Nashville During the Civil War," 11.

50 "Nashville Sit-Ins," Wikipedia, accessed July 23, 2019, https://en.wikipedia.org/wiki/Nashville_sit-ins.

51 "Nashville Sit-Ins."

52 "Nashville Sit-Ins."

53 "Nashville Sit-Ins."

54 "Diane Nash," Wikipedia, accessed June 4, 2019, https://en.wikipedia.org/wiki/Diane_Nash.

55 "Complete Coverage: The Civil Rights Movement in Nashville," Tennessean, March 2, 2017, https://www.tennessean.com/story/news/local/2017/03/02/complete-coverage-civil-rights-movement-nashville/98648442/.

56 "Civil Rights Movement in Nashville."

57 "Civil Rights Movement in Nashville."

58 Morgan Goldsmith, "4 speeches Dr. Martin Luther King, Jr. delivered in Nashville," Urbaanite Nashville, accessed June 14, 2021, https://urbaanite.com/mlk-nashville-nashville-speeches/.

59 The bulk of this sidebar, unless otherwise indicated, is adapted from Randy Wilson, "Maxwell House Coffee History," FoodEditorial.co, accessed April 19, 2019, https://www.streetdirectory.com/food_editorials/beverages/coffee/maxwell_house_coffee_history.html.

60 "Maxwell House Hotel," Wikipedia, accessed July 14, 2019, https://en.wikipedia.org/wiki/Maxwell_House_Hotel.

61 "Sales of the Leading Regular Ground Coffee Brands in the United States in 2018 (in Million U.S. Dollars)," Statista, https://www.statista.com/statistics/188315/top-ground-coffee-brands-in-the-united-states/.

62 Nina Cardona, "How Does the Music City Center Compare to Previous Nashville Building Projects?," Nashville Public Radio, May 16, 2013, https://www.newschannel5.com/news/nashville-hosts-convention-of-convention-planners.

63 "Best Convention City Winners: 2014 10Best Readers' Choice Travel Awards," 10Best, USA Today, 2014, https://www.10best.com/awards/travel/best-convention-city/.

64 "Cvent's Top 50 Meeting Destinations in the US," Cvent, accessed August 3, 2019, https://www.cvent.com/microsites/cvents-2019-top-meeting-destinations/cvents-top-50-meeting-destinations-in-the-us.

65 "History of Cotton Candy," Candy History, accessed April 19, 2019, http://www.candyhistory.net/candy-origin/cotton-candy-history/.

66 Juli Thanki, "141 Years Later, Fisk Jubilee Singers Return to England," Tennessean, May 21, 2015, https://www.tennessean.com/story/entertainment/music/2015/05/21/years-later-fisk-jubilee-singers-return-england/27673883/.

67 Friskics-Warren et al., "Why Is Nashville Called Music City?"

68 Thanki, "141 Years Later."

69 Talia Cuddeback, "Nashville Is Officially the Friendliest City in America," HuffPost, July 14, 2016, https://www.huffpost.com/entry/the-rudest-city-in-america-might-surprise-you_n_57866880e4b08608d3327b7e.

70 Taylor, "Nashville Is One of America's Hottest Cities."

71 "Nashville, Tennessee," U.S. News & World Report, accessed August 3, 2019, https://realestate.usnews.com/places/tennessee/nashville.

72 "Belmont University," U.S. News & World Report, accessed August 3, 2019, https://www.usnews.com/best-colleges/belmont-3479.

73 Stephanie Horan, "The Best Cities for Young Professionals – 2019 Edition," SmartAsset, August 21, 2019, https://smartasset.com/mortgage/best-cities-for-young-professionals-2019.

74 Carrick, "5 U.S. and 3 Canadian Cities with Best Jobs Markets."

75 Claudette Riley, "Nashville Ranks Seventh in Growth of Young Professionals," Tennessean, October 20, 2014, https://www.tennessean.com/story/news/local/2014/10/20/nashville-ranks-seventh-growth-young-professionals/17632289/.

76 Adam Sichko, "Counting Cranes: Nashville's Skies among the Busiest on the Continent," Nashville Business Journal, January 30, 2018, https://www.bizjournals.com/nashville/news/2018/01/30/counting-cranes-nashvilles-skies-among-the-busiest.html.

77 Julieta Martinelli, "Out-of-State Investment in Local Tech Startups Is Booming, but Tennessee Investors Lag Behind," Nashville Public Radio, June 8, 2017, https://wpln.org/post/out-of-state-investment-in-local-tech-startups-is-booming-but-tennessee-investors-lag-behind/.

78 PwC and the Urban Land Institute, Emerging Trends in Real Estate 2019 (Washington, DC: PwC and the Urban Land Institute, 2018), https://www.pwc.com/us/en/asset-management/real-estate/assets/pwc-emerging-trends-in-real-estate-2019.pdf.

79 Leslie James, "The Best Places to Buy a Vacation Rental Home in 2018," AirDNA, August 30, 2018, https://www.airdna.co/blog/best-places-to-buy-a-vacation-rental-home-2018.

80 Adam Sichko, "Renata Soto to Leave Conexión Américas," Nashville Business Journal, December 7, 2018, https://www.bizjournals.com/nashville/news/2018/12/07/renata-soto-to-leave-conexi-n-am-ricas.html.

81 Brad Schmitt, "Renata Soto Grew Up Aiding Immigrants," Tennessean, December 9, 2014, https://www.tennessean.com/story/news/2014/12/08/renata-soto-started-helping-immigrants-girl/20122227/.

82 Mary Hance, "11 Things You Should Know about Nashville's Diversity: Nashville Is More Culturally Rich Than You Might Think," Tennessean, September 30, 2017, https://www.tennessean.com/story/life/shopping/ms-cheap/2017/09/30/11-things-you-should-know-nashvilles-diversity/699228001/.

83 Jason Gonzales, "Nashville Schools Have More Than 120 Languages," Tennessean, November 13, 2015, https://www.tennessean.com/picture-gallery/news/2015/11/13/nashville-schools-have-more-than-120-languages/75664508/.

84 Robbie Brown, "In Nashville, a Ballot Measure That May Quiet All but English," New York Times, January 10, 2009, https://www.nytimes.com/2009/01/11/us/11english.html.

85 Robbie Brown, "Nashville Won't Make English Official Language," New York Times, January 22, 2009, https://www.nytimes.com/2009/01/23/us/23english.html.

86 Steven Hale, "Five Years after English Only Vote, Opponents Celebrate Win," Nashville Scene, January 22, 2014, https://www.nashvillescene.com/news/article/13052262/five-years-after-english-only-vote-opponents-celebrate-win.

87 Brown, "Nashville Won't Make English Official Language."

88 Karl Dean, in conversation with authors, December 17, 2018.

89 Karen Grigsby, "20 Things to Know about the 2010 Nashville Flood," Tennessean, April 30, 2015, https://www.tennessean.com/story/news/local/2015/04/30/nashville-flood-20-things-to-know/26653901/.

90 "Climate—Nashville, Tennessee," US Climate Data, accessed August 5, 2019, https://www.usclimatedata.com/climate/nashville/tennessee/united-states/ustn0357.

91 Grigsby, "20 Things to Know."

92 Brian Reisinger, "Case Study: Hands On Nashville Faces Flood with Consistency, New Ideas," Nashville Business Journal, August 8, 2010, https://www.bizjournals.com/nashville/stories/2010/08/09/smallb5.html.

93 Reisinger, "Case Study."

94 Grigsby, "20 Things to Know."

95 Grigsby, "20 Things to Know."

96 Jack Silverman, "Two Years Ago Today: The Nashville Flood," Nashville Scene, May 1, 2012, https://www.nashvillescene.com/news/article/13043007/two-years-ago-today-the-nashville-flood.

97 Silverman, "Two Years Ago Today."

98 Don Johnson, "Nashville Area Has The 4th Strongest Economy In America: Report," Patch, May 27, 2018, https://patch.com/tennessee/nashville/nashville-area-has-4th-strongest-economy-america-report.

99 Nashville Area Chamber of Commerce, 2018 Regional Economic Guide, 5.

100 Nashville Area Chamber of Commerce, 2018 Regional Economic Guide, 8.

101 Carrick, "5 U.S. and 3 Canadian Cities with Best Jobs Markets."

102 "These Are the 50 Best Places in America for Starting a Business," Inc., accessed August 15, 2019, https://www.inc.com/surge-cities/best-places-start-business.html.

103 "Nashville, Tennessee," U.S. News & World Report.

104 Entrepreneurs' Organization, "EO Nashville," accessed August 15, 2019, https://www.eonetwork.org/nashville.

105 Nashville Entrepreneur Center, home page, accessed August 15, 2019, https://www.ec.co/.

106 Severson, "Nashville's Latest Big Hit."

107 Geert De Lombaerde, "Freddie Mac Says Nashville Still Hottest Housing Market in US," Nashville Post, December 1, 2016, https://www.nashvillepost.com/business/development/residential-real-estate/article/20845554/freddie-mac-says-nashville-still-hottest-housing-market-in-us.

108 Kevin McKenzie, "Nashville Overtakes Memphis as Tennessee's Largest City," Commercial Appeal, May 25, 2017, https://www.commercialappeal.com/story/news/2017/05/25/nashville-overtakes-memphis-tennessees-largest-city/342624001/.

109 Taylor, "Nashville Is One of America's Hottest Cities."

110 Taylor, "Nashville Is One of America's Hottest Cities."

111 Mary Hance, "Nashville Tourism Exec Reflects on Music City's 'Explosion' during 47-Year Career," Tennessean, June 27, 2019, https://www.tennessean.com/story/life/shopping/ms-cheap/2019/06/27/nashville-tourism-growth-terry-clements-qa/1501535001/.

112 John Buntin, "Musing City: What Kind of Place Does Nashville Want to Be?," Governing, July 2018, https://www.governing.com/topics/urban/gov-nashville.html.

113 Stacey Lastoe, "There's a New Bachelorette Capital, and It's Not Vegas," CNN, May 1, 2019, https://www.cnn.com/travel/article/bachelorette-party-nashville-tennessee/index.html.

114 Marq Burnett, "Nashville named one of the world's 20 top travel destinations," Nashville Business Journal, December 9, 2019, https://www.bizjournals.com/nashville/news/2019/12/09/nashville-named-one-of-the-worlds-20-top-travel.html.

115 Frio, "Nashville's Tourism Boom."

116 Melanie Layden, "Thousands of Hotel Rooms Under Construction in Nashville," News 4, July 10, 2019, https://www.wsmv.com/news/thousands-of-hotel-rooms-under-construction-in-nashville/article_ab27e360-a35f-11e9-9def-47c1bf12941d.html.

117 Staff, "Region Ranks High in Tech Talent Growth," Nashville Post, September 3, 2018, https://www.nashvillepost.com/business/technology/article/21020600/region-ranks-high-in-tech-talent-growth.

118 Martinelli, "Out-of-State Investment in Local Tech Startups."

119 McGee, "Amazon in Nashville."

120 Nashville Area Chamber of Commerce, 2018 Regional Economic Guide, 7.

121 Nashville Area Chamber of Commerce, 2018 Regional Economic Guide, 8.

122 Nashville Area Chamber of Commerce, 2018 Regional Economic Guide, 6.

123 Nashville Area Chamber of Commerce, 2018 Regional Economic Guide, 10.

124 Nashville Area Chamber of Commerce, 2018 Regional Economic Guide, 10.

125 David Briley, interview with authors, February 5, 2018.

126 McGee, "Amazon in Nashville."

127 Joel Stinnett, "Lyft's Nashville Office Has Hired Double What It Expected," Nashville Business Journal, August 15, 2018, https://www.bizjournals.

com/nashville/news/2018/08/15/lyfts-nashville-office-has-hired-double-what-it.html.

128 Sandy Mazza, "Major Accounting Firm EY Announces New $22M Nashville Office, Bringing 600 Jobs," Tennessean, November 13, 2018, https://www.tennessean.com/story/news/2018/11/13/ey-announces-22-m-nashville-office-bringing-600-jobs/1987436002/.

129 Jesse Knutson, "Gibson to Move Headquarters to Downtown Nashville," NewsChannel5, July 14, 2019, https://www.newschannel5.com/news/gibson-to-move-headquarters-to-downtown-nashville.

130 Getahn Ward, "How Nashville Nearly Lost Bridgestone Americas Headquarters," Tennessean, December 16, 2016, https://www.tennessean.com/story/money/real-estate/2016/12/16/how-nashville-nearly-lost-bridgestone-americas-headquarters/95470790/.

131 Nashville Area Chamber of Commerce, 2018 Regional Economic Guide, 8.

132 Megan Henney, "Nashville Eyes Pipeline to Wall Street after Securing Amazon, AllianceBernstein Deals," FoxBusiness, June 28, 2019, https://www.foxbusiness.com/markets/alliancebernstein-amazon-deals-nashville-wall-street-pipeline.amp.

133 Geert De Lombaerde and William Williams, "Tech Titan Plans Massive Local Presence," Nashville Post, March 1, 2019, https://www.nashvillepost.com/business/technology/article/21049285/tech-titan-plans-massive-local-presence.

134 Nashville Area Chamber of Commerce, 2018 Regional Economic Guide, 8.

135 Nashville Area Chamber of Commerce, 2018 Regional Economic Guide, 8.

136 Frist Foundation, home page, accessed August 15, 2019, http://www.fristfoundation.org/.

137 Ryan Darrow, "Dollar General," Tennessee Encyclopedia, Tennessee Historical Society, last updated March 1, 2018, https://tennesseeencyclopedia.net/entries/dollar-general/.

138 Darrow, "Dollar General."

139 Darrow, "Dollar General"; Seth Robertson, "$2 million Investment Establishes Turner Family Community Enterprise Clinic at Vanderbilt Law School," Vanderbilt News, August 22, 2017, https://news.vanderbilt.edu/2017/08/22/2-million-investment-establishes-turner-family-community-enterprise-clinic-at-vanderbilt-law-school/.

140 Darrow, "Dollar General."

141 "#195 Ingram Industries," Forbes, October 24, 2018, https://www.forbes.com/companies/ingram-industries/#498a5f923b8b.

142 E. Thomas Wood, "The Empire Strikes Back," Nashville Scene, June 6, 1996, https://www.nashvillescene.com/news/article/13000642/the-empire-strikes-back.

143 GayNelle Doll and James M. Patterson, "Martha's Mettle," Vanderbilt Magazine, September 2, 2011, https://news.vanderbilt.edu/vanderbiltmagazine/marthas-mettle/.

144 Wood, "Empire Strikes Back."

145 Bill Carey, "A Rich Life," Nashville Scene, December 13, 2001, https://www.nashvillescene.com/news/article/13006498/a-rich-life.

146 Doll and Patterson, "Martha's Mettle."

147 William H. Honan, "Vanderbilt U. Receives a Gift of $300 Million," New York Times, December 1, 1998, https://www.nytimes.com/1998/12/01/us/vanderbilt-u-receives-a-gift-of-300-million.html.

148 "#63 Ingram Family," Forbes, accessed August 15, 2019, https://www.forbes.com/profile/ingram/#16c833b1b93f; "Leadership," Ingram, accessed August 15, 2019, https://www.ingramcontent.com/about/leadership.

149 MLSsoccer staff, "Nashville MLS Expansion Team Unveils Name, Crest," MLS, February 20, 2019, https://www.mlssoccer.com/post/2019/02/20/nashville-mls-expansion-team-unveils-name-crest.

150 Joe Rexrode, "2017 Tennessean Sports Person of the Year: John Ingram Led Charge That Brought MLS to Nashville," Tennessean, December 30, 2017, https://www.tennessean.com/story/sports/2017/12/30/sports-person-year-john-ingram-led-charge-brought-mls-nashville/992115001/.

151 "Redfin CEO: We're Printing Money Much Faster Than We Can Build," CNBC, January 23, 2018, https://www.cnbc.com/video/2018/01/23/redfin-ceo-were-printing-money-much-faster-than-we-can-build-houses.html.

152 Sandy Mazza, "Investors Nationwide to Pounce on Nashville Real Estate in 2020," Tennessean, November 26, 2019, https://www.tennessean.com/story/money/homes/2019/11/26/nashville-real-estate-investors-nationwide-ready-pounce-2020/4273079002/.

153 Bill Hobbs, foreword to 505 (self-pub.).

154 Hobbs, 505.

155 Hobbs, 505.

156 Hobbs, 505.

157 Nashville Downtown Partnership, "2018 Annual Report," https://www.nashvilledowntown.com/_files/2018-NDP-Annual-Report.pdf.

158 Bendix Anderson, "Downtown Nashville's New Billion-Dollar Gateway: Nashville Yards," Urban Land, March 28, 2019, https://urbanland.uli.org/development-business/downtown-nashvilles-new-billion-dollar-gateway-nashville-yards/.

159 "Nashville Crane Watch," Nashville Business Journal, updated February 19, 2020, https://www.bizjournals.com/nashville/maps/nashville-crane-watch.

160 Milt Capps, "Urban Nashville: Steve Turner, V.U. Launch Research Center," Nashville Post, April 5, 2007, https://www.nashvillepost.com/business/education/article/20400853/urban-nashville-steve-turner-vu-launch-research-center.

161 Details about the Westhaven project were provided by Matthew D. Magallanes (Vice President, Business Development, Southern Land Company) in an email message to the authors, November 19, 2019.

162 Hobbs, 505.

163 Nashville Downtown Partnership, "2018 Annual Report."

164 Anderson, "New Billion-Dollar Gateway."

165 Anderson, "New Billion-Dollar Gateway."

166 Anderson, "New Billion-Dollar Gateway."

167 Details about the River North development were provided by Donald J. Allen (Principal, Monroe Investment Partners) in an email message to the authors, November 5, 2019.

168 Dave Paulson, "National Museum of African American Music Receives $1 Million from Regions, Mike Curb Foundations," Tennessean, February 19, 2019, https://www.tennessean.com/story/entertainment/music/2019/02/19/national-museum-african-american-music-receives-1-million-regions-mike-curb/2906941002/.

169 Sandy Mazza, "Mega-Developments Are Hoping to Make Downtown Nashville Greener," Tennessean, July 12, 2018, https://www.tennessean.com/story/money/2018/07/12/nashville-developers-add-green-space-downtown-urban-areas/738104002/.

170 "Broadwest," accessed October 8, 2019, https://broadwestnashville.com/.

171 Anderson, "New Billion-Dollar Gateway."

172 Joey Garrison, "Nashville Council Approves $15M in Infrastructure Work for Future Home of Amazon Hub," Tennessean, February 6, 2019, https://www.tennessean.com/story/news/2019/02/06/nashville-approves-15-m-infrastructure-future-home-amazon-hub/2777894002/.

173 Nashville Area Chamber of Commerce, 2018 Regional Economic Guide, 37.

174 Margaret Littman, "Why Nashville Is Still America's Music City," Next City, December 1, 2014, https://nextcity.org/features/view/why-nashville-is-still-americas-music-city.

175 Andy Greene, Kory Grow, Brittany Spanos, Patrick Doyle, and Hank Shteamer, "Jack White vs. the Black Keys: A Beef History," Rolling Stone, September 14, 2015, https://www.rollingstone.com/music/music-lists/jack-white-vs-the-black-keys-a-beef-history-56863/.

176 Clint Carter, "How Underground Nashville Bands Are Reclaiming Music City," Rolling Stone, July 14, 2017, https://www.rollingstone.com/music/music-features/how-underground-nashville-bands-are-reclaiming-music-city-203593/.

177 Friskics-Warren et al., "Why Is Nashville Called Music City?"

178 Dora Ball, "How to Make the Most of Nashville If You Don't Like Country Music," Lonely Planet, February 2018, https://www.lonelyplanet.com/usa/nashville/travel-tips-and-articles/how-to-make-the-most-of-nashville-if-you-dont-like-country-music/40625c8c-8a11-5710-a052-1479d27635da.

179 Seth Riddle, email to authors, December 10, 2019.

180 Littman, "Still America's Music City."

181 Littman, "Still America's Music City."

182 Ashley King, "Apple Music Is Expanding into Nashville—and Revitalizing an Old Sock Factory in the Process," Digital Music News, December 18, 2018, https://www.digitalmusicnews.com/2018/12/18/apple-music-nashville/.

183 Danny Ross, "6 Reasons Why Musicians Love the New Nashville," Forbes, March 29, 2017, https://www.forbes.com/sites/dannyross1/2017/03/29/6-reasons-to-love-the-new-nashville/#ffba5c355386.

184 Littman, "Still America's Music City."

185 Riddle, email to authors, December 10, 2019.

186 Nashville Area Chamber of Commerce, 2018 Regional Economic Guide, 36.

187 Emily Yahr, "Nashville Songwriters Are Like Family: Here's What Happens When Things Get Complicated," Washington Post, August 10, 2017, https://www.washingtonpost.com/entertainment/music/nashville-songwriters-are-like-family-heres-what-happens-when-things-get-complicated/2017/08/09/d3bc543e-77ef-11e7-8839-ec48ec4cae25_story.html.

188 Nashville Area Chamber of Commerce, 2018 Regional Economic Guide, 36.

189 Yahr, "Nashville Songwriters."

190 Littman, "Still America's Music City."

191 Littman, "Still America's Music City."

192 "EA Moves Videogame Production to Nashville," Nashville Music Scoring, December 7, 2017, http://www.nashvillemusicscoring.com/index.php/ea-moves-videogame-production-to-nashville.

193 Jon Burlingame, "Welcome to Nashville: The New Scoring Destination," Variety, July 19, 2018, https://variety.com/2018/music/news/nashville-scoring-destination-1202876071/.

194 Nashville Area Chamber of Commerce, 2018 Regional Economic Guide, 37.

195 Merriam-Webster, s.v. "Americana," accessed May 11, 2019, https://www.merriam-webster.com/dictionary/Americana.

196 Martin Chilton, "Americana: How Country and Roots Music Found a 'Brand New Dance,'" uDiscover Music, May 1, 2018, https://www.udiscovermusic.com/in-depth-features/americana-music-country-roots-history/.

197 Chilton, "Americana."

198 Chilton, "Americana."

199 Chilton, "Americana."

200 Chilton, "Americana."

201 Ross, "6 Reasons."

202 Chilton, "Americana."

203 Will Welch, "Meet Three Country Badasses Who Are Shaking Up the Nashville Establishment," GQ, January 7, 2016, https://www.gq.com/story/meet-the-country-badasses-from-nashville.

204 Welch, "Three Country Badasses."

205 Welch, "Three Country Badasses."

206 Nashville Area Chamber of Commerce, 2018 Regional Economic Guide, 45.

207 Nashville Area Chamber of Commerce, 2018 Regional Economic Guide, 36.

208 "Bridgestone Arena Ranked Sixth in United States by Pollstar Magazine," Bridgestone Arena, December 20, 2018, https://www.bridgestonearena.com/news/detail/bridgestone-arena-ranked-sixth-in-united-states-by-pollstar-magazine.

209 "Bridgestone Arena Ranked Sixth."

210 Littman, "Still America's Music City."

211 Littman, "Still America's Music City."

212 Nate Rau, "Tootsie's Changed Downtown Nashville's Tune," USA Today, October 21, 2015, https://www.usatoday.com/story/travel/nation-now/2015/10/21/tootsies-orchid-lounge-nashville-country-music/74303038/.

213 Cindy Watts, "Country Music and Nashville's Honky-Tonk Row Grew Up Together," Tennessean, November 13, 2017, https://www.tennessean.com/story/entertainment/music/2017/11/13/country-music-and-nashvilles-honky-tonk-row-grew-up-together/768926001/.

214 Adam Gold, "How the Honky-Tonks and Dives of 1960s Created Nashville's Lower Broad," Vice, March 13, 2019, https://www.vice.com/en_us/article/panvx7/deep-dive-nashville-downtown.

215 Gold, "How the Honky-Tonks."

216 "Top 25 Museums—United States," TripAdvisor, accessed August 7, 2019, https://www.tripadvisor.com/TravelersChoice-Museums-cTop-g191.

217 Country Music Hall of Fame, "2018 Annual Report," available at https://countrymusichalloffame.org/about/.

218 Dave Paulson, "Mumford and Sons Break Bridgestone Arena Record, Perform at Grimey's," Tennessean, March 25, 2019, https://www.tennessean.com/story/entertainment/music/2019/03/25/mumford-and-sons-break-bridgestone-arena-record-perform-grimeys/3267788002/.

219 Littman, "Still America's Music City."

220 "Founders Story," Musicians on Call, accessed August 7, 2019, https://www.musiciansoncall.org/founders-story/.

221 Jon Freeman, "Jason Isbell, Sheryl Crow Urge Action at Tennessee Voting Rally," Rolling Stone, October 20, 2018, https://www.rollingstone.com/politics/politics-news/jason-isbell-sheryl-crow-tennessee-voting-rally-745174/.

222 Mike "Grimey" Grimes, interview with authors, January 31, 2019.

223 Mike "Grimey" Grimes, interview with authors, January 31, 2019.

224 "Economic Impact Study," Nashville Health Care Council, June 2018, https://healthcarecouncil.com/nashville-health-care-industry/industry-research/economic-impact-study/.

225 "Economic Impact Study."

226 "Economic Impact Study."

227 Holly Fletcher, "How Big Is Health Care's Economic Impact in Nashville? $38.8B," Tennessean, August 18, 2015, https://www.tennessean.com/story/money/industries/health-care/2015/08/18/how-big-health-cares-economic-impact-nashville-388b/31564125/.

228 Alyssa Rege, "8 Largest For-Profit Health Systems in US," Becker's Hospital Review, January 24, 2017, https://www.beckershospitalreview.com/population-health/8-largest-for-profit-health-systems-in-us.html.

229 "HCA Healthcare at a Glance," HCA Healthcare, accessed May 18, 2019, https://hcahealthcare.com/about/hca-at-a-glance.dot.

230 Brett Kelman, "HCA: 50 Years Ago, a Chicken-Fried Idea Launched Nashville's Most Important Company," Tennessean, August 16, 2018, updated August 17, 2018, https://www.tennessean.com/story/money/industries/health-care/2018/08/16/hca-50-thomas-frist-jack-massey-launched-nashville-healthcare-industry/763946002/.

231 Kelman, "HCA."

232 "10 HCA Healthcare Hospitals Ranked among Nation's Top 100," HCA Today Blog, March 9, 2019, https://hcatodayblog.com/2019/03/09/10-hca-healthcare-hospitals-ranked-among-nations-top-100/.

233 Kelman, "HCA."

234 Kelman, "HCA."

235 "Family Tree," Nashville Health Care Council, June 30, 2018, https://healthcarecouncil.com/news-publications/family-tree/; Rege, "8 Largest."

236 "Nashville: The Health Care Industry Capital," Nashville Health Care Council, accessed August 8, 2019, https://healthcarecouncil.com/nashville-health-care-industry/.

237 Rege, "8 Largest."

238 Rege, "8 Largest."

239 Vanderbilt University, "Vanderbilt Injects $9.5 billion into Tennessee Economy, Report Says," Vanderbilt News, March 27, 2017, https://news.vanderbilt.edu/2017/03/27/vanderbilt-injects-9-5-billion-into-tennessee-economy/.

240 Holly Fletcher, "VUMC Gets Its Largest Grant to Lead Precision Medicine Initiative," Tennessean, July 7, 2016, https://www.tennessean.com/story/money/industries/health-care/2016/07/07/vumc-lands-grant-for-date-collection-under-federal-precision-medicine-initiative/86795692/.

241 Ashlea Ebeling, "World's Largest Healthcare Companies 2019," Forbes, May 15, 2019, https://www.forbes.com/sites/ashleaebeling/2019/05/15/worlds-largest-healthcare-companies-2019/.

242 John McBryde, "Health Care in Nashville, TN Is Forever Vibrant," Livability, May 10, 2016, https://livability.com/tn/nashville/health/health-care-in-nashville-tn-is-forever-vibrant.

243 "2017/2018 Family Tree," Nashville Health Care Council, https://healthcarecouncil.com/wp-content/uploads/2018/09/NHCC_tree_2018_PRINT.pdf.

244 Jamie McGee, "Great Recession: Nashville's Opportunities, Challenges 10 Years Later," Tennessean, August 28, 2018, https://www.tennessean.com/story/money/2018/08/28/great-recession-nashville-10-years-later/824196002/.

245 McGee, "Great Recession."

246 US Bureau of Labor Statistics, "Healthcare Occupations," Occupational Outlook Handbook, accessed April 12, 2019, https://www.bls.gov/ooh/healthcare/home.htm.

247 Holly Fletcher, "Investors Bet Big on Nashville's Young Health Care Firms," Tennessean, August 7, 2016, https://www.tennessean.com/story/money/Industries/health-care/2016/08/07/healthcare-led-nashville-venture-capital-community-last-decade/88065726/.

248 Fletcher, "Investors Bet Big."

249 Tommy Ragsdale, interview with authors, March 28, 2018.

250 Ragsdale, interview.

251 Ragsdale, interview.

252 Ragsdale, interview.

253 "Comparison between U.S. States and Sovereign States by GDP," Wikipedia, accessed August 5, 2019, https://en.wikipedia.org/wiki/Comparison_between_U.S._states_and_sovereign_states_by_GDP.

254 "History of Metro," Metro Government of Nashville & Davidson County, Tennessee, https://www.nashville.gov/Government/History-of-Metro.aspx.

255 Part Hardy, "The Consolidation of City and County Governments: A Look at the History and Outcome-Based Research of These Efforts," Municipal Technical Advisory Service, Institute for Public Service, August 21, 2019, https://www.mtas.tennessee.edu/system/files/knowledgebase/original/Hardy_ConsolidationResearch_2019_final.pdf.

256 Buntin, "Musing City."

257 Nate Rau and Joey Garrison, "Richard Fulton, Former Nashville Mayor and Congressman, Dies at 91," Tennessean, November 28, 2018, https://www.tennessean.com/story/news/2018/11/28/richard-fulton-nashville-mayor-obituary/2118159002/.

258 Mary Hance, "Former Nashville Mayor Bill Boner Buys Bargain Bears to Give Away," Tennessean, March 7, 2017, https://www.tennessean.com/story/life/shopping/ms-cheap/2017/03/07/former-nashville-mayor-bill-boner-buys-bargain-bears-give-away/98818630/.

259 "Nashville Mayor," Our Campaigns, accessed February 5, 2019, https://www.ourcampaigns.com/RaceDetail.html?RaceID=6643.

260 "Nashville Mayor."

261 Phil Bredesen, "The Interview: The Man in the Middle," interview by Stephen George," *Nashville Scene*, January 6, 2011, https://www.nashvillescene.com/news/article/13036843/phil-bredesen-reflects-on-his-career-as-mayor-and-governor-his-lowest-moments-and-how-tennessee-democrats-can-survive.

262 "Nashville Mayor," Our Campaigns, accessed December 16, 2004, https://www.ourcampaigns.com/RaceDetail.html?RaceID=155092.

263 Staff, "After Purcell," Nashville Scene, April 27, 2006, https://www.nashvillescene.com/news/article/13013169/after-purcell.

264 Karl Dean, "Mayor Karl Dean: The Cream Interview," interview by Adam Gold, Nashville Scene, April 21, 2011, https://www.nashvillescene.com/music/article/13038142/mayor-karl-dean-the-cream-interview.

265 Staff, "Mayor Megan Barry Resigns after Pleading Guilty to Theft," Nashville Scene, March 6, 2018, https://www.nashvillescene.com/news/pith-in-the-wind/article/20995103/mayor-megan-barry-resigns-after-pleading-guilty-to-theft.

266 John D. Stoll, "Nashville Mayor's Unorthodox Promise: Slow Corporate Handouts," Wall Street Journal, October 25, 2019, https://www.wsj.com/articles/nashville-mayors-unorthodox-promise-slow-corporate-handouts-11572029641.

267 "Fiscal Stability Rankings," U.S. News & World Report, accessed October 19, 2019, https://www.usnews.com/news/best-states/rankings/fiscal-stability.

268 Tennessee Department of Economic and Community Development, "Tennessee Receives Triple Triple-A Rating," accessed August 10, 2019, https://tnecd.com/news/tennessee-receives-triple-triple-a-rating/.

269 Bill Lee, speech at Pinnacle Bank event, Omni Hotel, Nashville, TN, October 1, 2019.

270 "Tax Comparison—Florida Verses Tennessee," Real Estate Scorecard, accessed August 10, 2019, https://realestatescorecard.com/library/story/taxes/tax-comparison-florida-verses-tennessee.

271 Adam McCann, "2019's Tax Burden by State," WalletHub, April 2, 2019, https://wallethub.com/edu/states-with-highest-lowest-tax-burden/20494/.

272 Dave Flessner, "Tennessee Has Lowest State, Local Tax Burden for Average Resident," Times Free Press, March 14, 2018, https://www.timesfreepress.com/news/business/aroundregion/story/2018/mar/14/tennessee-hlowest-state-and-local-taxes-avera/465859/.

273 Flessner, "Tennessee Has Lowest State, Local Tax Burden."

274 Flessner, "Tennessee Has Lowest State, Local Tax Burden."

275 Judith Byrd, "Metro Nashville Government Earns Strong Bond Ratings Again from Moody's and S&P," Nashville.gov, October 5, 2018, https://www.nashville.gov/News-Media/News-Article/ID/7974/Metro-Nashville-Government-Earns-Strong-Bond-Ratings-Again-from-Moodys-and-SP.aspx.

276 Byrd, "Metro Nashville Government Earns Strong Bond Ratings."

277 Matthew Wiltshire, seminar at Stites & Harbison, Nashville, TN, March 21, 2019.

278 Samuel Stebbins, "Tax Policy: States with the Highest and Lowest Taxes," Tennessean, April 6, 2018, https://www.tennessean.com/story/money/taxes/2018/04/06/states-highest-and-lowest-taxes-3-6/482944002/.

279 Office of the Mayor Megan Barry, "Housing Nashville: Nashville & Davidson County's Housing Report," 2017, retrieved from https://www.nashville.gov/Mayors-Office/Housing.aspx.

280 Office of the Mayor, "Housing Nashville."

281 Office of the Mayor, "Housing Nashville."

282 Office of the Mayor, "Housing Nashville."

283 "At a Glance," Rebuilding Together Nashville, accessed August 11, 2019, https://www.rtnashville.org/.

284 Kaitlin Dastugue, email to authors, February 4, 2020.

285 Kaitlin Dastugue, "Private-Public Partnerships Can Solve Nashville's Affordable Housing Crisis," Tennessean October 1, 2019, www.tennessean.com/story/opinion/2019/10/01/private-public-partnerships-can-solve-nashville-affordable-housing-crisis/3822944002/.

286 Yihyun Jeong and Mike Reicher, "Nashville Mayor David Briley Announces $500M Affordable Housing Push," Tennessean, March 26, 2019, https://www.tennessean.com/story/news/2019/03/26/nashville-commit-500-m-affordable-housing-initiative/3268463002/.

287 Jeong and Reicher, "Affordable Housing Push."

288 Thomas Mulgrew, "Mayor Briley Celebrates Approval of Most Recent Barnes Fund Grant Recipients," Nashville.gov, May 2, 2019, https://www.nashville.gov/News-Media/News-Article/ID/8534/Mayor-Briley-Celebrates-Approval-Of-Most-Recent-Barnes-Fund-Grant-Recipients.aspx.

289 Erika Lathon, "Cayce Homes $600 Million Redevelopment Could Attract High-Dollar Tenants to Public Housing," Fox 17 Nashville, December 22, 2016, https://fox17.com/news/local/cayce-homes-600-million-redevelopment-could-attract-high-dollar-tenants-to-public-housing.

290 Sarah Larson, "'The Promise,' a Stellar Podcast about Life in Nashville's Public Housing," New Yorker, May 3, 2018, https://www.newyorker.com/culture/podcast-dept/the-promise-a-stellar-podcast-about-life-in-nashvilles-public-housing.

291 Knight, "Recruiting a New Kind of Tenant."

292 Staff, "Runaway Train," Nashville Post, September 2, 2016, https://www.nashvillepost.com/business/nashville-post-magazine/article/20832634/runaway-train.

293 Eleanor Kennedy, "Take a Look at the New Concourse Headed to Nashville International Airport," Nashville Business Journal, June 20, 2018, https://www.bizjournals.com/nashville/news/2018/06/20/take-a-look-at-the-new-concourse-headed-to.html.

294 "Over 17 Million Passengers Pass through Nashville Airport," Associated Press, July 18, 2019, https://apnews.com/article/053ee545e13746e2bdf4ee6e4b95dcf4.

295 Kennedy, "New Concourse Headed to Nashville International Airport."

296 Nate Rau, "Nashville's Airport Is Getting a Major Overhaul, Including New International Arrivals Facility," Tennessean, November 14, 2018, https://www.tennessean.com/story/money/2018/11/14/nashville-airport-bna-new-terminal-lobby/2002452002/.

297 Jamie McGee, "Nashville Airport First in U.S. to OK Uber, Lyft," Tennessean, September 25, 2014, https://www.usatoday.com/story/travel/flights/2014/09/25/nashville-airport-first-in-us-to-allow-uber-lyft/16221841/.

298 Nashville Downtown Partnership, "2018 Annual Report."

299 Kriston Capps, "Nashville's Transit Plan Just Got Trounced," City Lab, May 2, 2018, https://www.citylab.com/transportation/2018/05/what-went-wrong-with-nashvilles-transit-plan/559436/.

300 Miranda Peterson and Cathleen Kelly, "Making Nashville a More Livable and Sustainable City for All," Center for American Progress, March 9, 2017, https://www.americanprogress.org/issues/green/reports/2017/03/09/427682/making-nashville-livable-sustainable-city/.

301 Melonee Hurt, "Nashville Hot Chicken, the History behind the South's 'It' Dish," Style Blueprint, accessed June 7, 2019, https://styleblueprint.com/everyday/nashville-hot-chicken/.

302 Nashville Area Chamber of Commerce, 2018 Regional Economic Guide, 7.

303 "Captain D's," Wikipedia, accessed August 7, 2019, https://en.wikipedia.org/wiki/Captain_D%27s.

304 "O'Charley's," Wikipedia, accessed July 26, 2019, https://en.wikipedia.org/wiki/O%27Charley%27s.

305 "Shoney's," Wikipedia, accessed July 5, 2019, https://en.wikipedia.org/wiki/Shoney%27s.

306 "J. Alexander's," Wikipedia, accessed July 8, 2019, https://en.wikipedia.org/wiki/J._Alexander%27s.

307 Brad Schmitt, "Nashville's Dining Scene Explodes," Tennessean, May 22, 2016, https://www.tennessean.com/story/life/2016/05/22/nashvilles-dining-scene-explodes/82987810/.

308 Andrew Knowlton and Julia Kramer, "The East Nasty Sandwich from Biscuit Love Is the Best Sandwich of 2015," Bon Appétit, August 4, 2015, https://www.bonappetit.com/restaurants-travel/best-new-restaurants/article/best-sandwich.

309 Meghan Kraft, "This Classic Nashville Biscuit House Was Just Named the Best Breakfast in the City," Only in Your State, February 26, 2018, https://www.onlyinyourstate.com/tennessee/nashville/biscuit-house-spring-2018/.

310 Kristin Tice Studeman, "The 13 Hardest Restaurant Reservations in America Right Now," Vogue, April 4, 2016, https://www.vogue.com/article/hardest-restaurant-reservations-america-2016.

311 Schmitt, "Nashville's Dining Scene Explodes."

312 Kim Severson, "The Food Scene in East Nashville," New York Times, June 18, 2012, https://www.nytimes.com/2012/06/20/dining/the-food-scene-in-east-nashville.html.

313 Margaret Littman, "How Nashville Is Becoming an Inclusive Magnet for Women Chefs and Restaurant Owners," Fortune, May 4, 2019, https://fortune.com/2019/05/04/nashville-women-restaurants-chefs/.

314 Littman, "Inclusive Magnet for Women Chefs."

315 Brad Schmitt, "Jimmy Kimmel: 'People Are Talking' about Nashville Food," Tennessean, November 3, 2014, https://www.tennessean.com/story/life/food/2014/11/03/jimmy-kimmel-people-talking-nashville-food/18419005/.

316 "Let the Black Keys' Dan Auerbach Show You How to Eat Like a Rock Star in Nashville," Bon Appétit, January 17, 2012, https://www.bonappetit.com/columns/the-foodist/article/let-the-black-keys-dan-auerbach-show-you-how-to-eat-like-a-rock-star-in-nashville.

317 D. Patrick Rodgers, "Nashville Lands Five James Beard Award Nominations," Nashville Scene, February 27, 2019, https://www.nashvillescene.com/food-drink/bites/article/21048994/nashville-lands-five-james-beard-award-nominations.

318 "Awards Search: Nashville," James Beard Foundation, accessed August 13, 2019, https://www.jamesbeard.org/awards/search?year=&keyword=nashville.

319 "Awards Search: Nashville."

320 "About Us," Varallo's Restaurant, accessed November 19, 2019, https://varallosrestaurant.business.site/.

321 "Mission," Nashville Food Truck Association, accessed June 7, 2021, https://www.nashvillefta.org/mission.

322 "Nashville Food Trucks," Roaming Hunger, accessed August 12, 2019, https://roaminghunger.com/food-trucks/tn/nashville/.

323 Vivek Surti, "How a Novice Chef Created the Supper Club Series Nashville Loves," interview by Steve Cavendish, Nashville Scene, October 19, 2017, https://www.nashvillescene.com/food-drink/features/article/20979588/how-a-novice-chef-created-the-supper-club-series-nashville-loves.

324 Surti, "The Supper Club Series Nashville Loves."

325 Surti, "The Supper Club Series Nashville Loves."

326 "About," Tailor, accessed August 13, 2019, https://www.tailornashville.com/about.

327 Anna Hensel, "How 2 Brothers Are Giving Nashville a New Kind of Cool, One Burger Joint and Mini Golf Course at a Time," Inc., June 28, 2016, https://www.inc.com/anna-hensel/strategic-hospitality-how-benjamin-and-max-goldberg-are-transforming-nashville.html.

328 Hensel, "2 Brothers."

329 Hensel, "2 Brothers."

330 Kimberly Tharel, "The Nashville Craft Whiskey Trail," Whisky Advocate, December 11, 2017, http://whiskyadvocate.com/nashville-craft-whiskey-trail/.

331 Tharel, "The Nashville Craft Whiskey Trail."

332 "Our Story," Nelson's Green Brier Distillery, accessed August 13, 2019, https://greenbrierdistillery.com/nelsonsgreenbrierhistory.

333 "Our Story."

334 Chris Chamberlain, "Nelson's Green Brier Distillery Wins Double Gold at SF World Spirits Competition," Nashville Scene, April 1, 2019, https://www.nashvillescene.com/food-drink/bites/article/21062145/nelsons-green-brier-distillery-wins-double-gold-at-sf-world-spirits-competition.

335 "Our Story."

336 Tharel, "The Nashville Craft Whiskey Trail."

337 Tharel, "The Nashville Craft Whiskey Trail."

338 Tharel, "The Nashville Craft Whiskey Trail."

339 Leila Beem Núñez, "Coffee County Native Finds Success in Craft Distilling," Manchester Times, July 20, 2017, https://www.manchestertimes.com/news/local/capturing-the-american-spirit/article_a08445a1-ad69-5615-876b-313f569c4101.html.

340 "Story," Corsair, accessed August 13, 2019, http://www.corsairdistillery.com/story.

341 Tharel, "The Nashville Craft Whiskey Trail."

342 "Distilleries," Tennessee Whiskey Trail, accessed August 13, 2019, https://www.tnwhiskeytrail.com/distilleries/.

343 Wil Fulton, Andy Kryza, and Matt Lynch, "The 10 Best Drinking Cities in America Right Now," Thrillist, September 29, 2018, https://www.thrillist.com/drink/nation/best-drinking-cities-in-america.

344 Matthew Leimkuehler, "Nashville Brewery Wins Big at Global Craft Beer Competition," Tennessean, October 7, 2019, https://www.tennessean.com/story/entertainment/music/2019/10/07/great-american-beer-festival-east-nashville-beer-works-wins-big/3897385002/.

345 "The World's 50 Best Bars 2019," William Reed Business Media, https://www.worlds50bestbars.com/fifty-best-bars-list-2019/?ist=6.

346 Jennifer Justus, "A Perfect Mix," Southwest, December 2018, https://issuu.com/southwestmag/docs/december2018.

347 Michael Gallagher, "Forget 'It City,' Nashville Named Best Sports City," Nashville Post, December 17, 2019, https://www.nashvillepost.com/sports/commentary/article/21106836/forget-it-city-nashville-named-best-sports-city.

348 Rudy Kalis, "My Story: Covering Nashville's Favorite Hockey Team," Nashville Predators, May 30, 2019, https://www.nhl.com/predators/news/my-story-covering-nashvilles-favorite-hockey-team/c-307613194.

349 Kalis, "My Story."

350 Kalis, "My Story."

351 George Plaster, "My Story: How We Helped Save the Predators," Nashville Predators, May 17, 2019, https://www.nhl.com/predators/news/my-story-how-we-helped-save-the-predators/c-307450188

352 Plaster, "My Story."

353 Nashville Predators, "Predators Holdings LLC purchases Nashville Predators, Powers Management," December 7, 2007, https://www.nhl.com/predators/news/predators-holdings-llc-purchases-nashville-predators-powers-management/c-439366.

354 Keating, "The Numbers"; "#25 Nashville Predators," Forbes, December 2018, https://www.forbes.com/teams/nashville-predators/#3599a8f36f67.

355 Tal Pinchevsky, "Nashville Took the Party Up a Notch for Memorable Game 3," ESPN, June 4, 2017, https://www.espn.com/nhl/story/_/id/19530898/2017-stanley-cup-finals-wild-crazy-game-3-scene-nashville.

356 National Mortgage Bankers Association lunch, Nashville, TN, August 9, 2018.

357 Keating, "The Numbers."

358 Cole Johnson, "Is Bridgestone Arena the Loudest Place in the NHL?," WKRN.com, June 2, 2017, https://www.wkrn.com/sports/nashville-predators/is-bridgestone-arena-the-loudest-place-in-the-nhl/.

359 Jim Norman, "Football Still Americans' Favorite Sport to Watch," Gallup, January 4, 2018, https://news.gallup.com/poll/224864/football-americans-favorite-sport-watch.aspx.

360 Joey Garrison, "Why Major League Soccer Picked Nashville for Expansion," Tennessean, December 20, 2017, https://www.tennessean.com/story/news/2017/12/20/why-major-league-soccer-picking-nashville-expansion/966403001/.

361 Joey Garrison and Mike Organ, "MLS Grants Nashville Expansion Club, Propelling Music City from Underdog to 'Soccer City,'" Tennessean, December 20, 2017, https://www.tennessean.com/story/sports/nashvillesc/2017/12/20/mls-expansion-nashville-announcement-live-stream/947951001/.

362 Garrison and Organ, "MLS Grants Nashville Expansion Club."

363 Garrison and Organ, "MLS Grants Nashville Expansion Club."

364 Satchel Price, "Why Do Predators Fans Throw Catfish on the Ice at the Stanley Cup Final?," SB Nation, June 11, 2017, https://www.sbnation.com/2017/5/29/15710698/why-do-predators-fans-throw-catfish-2017-nhl-playoffs.

365 Chuck Schilken and Helene Elliott, "Charges against Man Who Threw a Dead Catfish onto the Ice during Stanley Cup Finals Will Be Dropped," Los Angeles Times, May 30, 2017, https://www.latimes.com/sports/sportsnow/la-sp-catfish-arrest-stanley-cup-20170530-story.html.

366 J. R. Lind, "Nashville Predators Playoff Ticket Prices Soar: Report," Patch, April 11, 2018, https://patch.com/tennessee/nashville/nashville-predators-playoff-ticket-prices-soar-report.

367 Garrison, "Why Major League Soccer Picked Nashville."

368 Garrison, "Why Major League Soccer Picked Nashville."

369 Steven Hale, "Metro Council Approves Soccer Stadium," Nashville Scene, November 7, 2017, https://www.nashvillescene.com/news/pith-in-the-wind/article/20981995/metro-council-approves-soccer-stadium-nashville-john-ingram-mls.

370 David Boclair, "Nashville SC Expands, Delays Stadium Plan," Nashville Scene, March 21, 2019, https://www.nashvillescene.com/news/sports/article/21060925/nashville-sc-expands-delays-stadium-plan.

371 Luis Torres, "Why Nashville SC's MLS Team Decided It Won't Play at Fairgrounds Stadium until 2022," Tennessean, March 21, 2019, https://www.tennessean.com/story/sports/nashvillesc/2019/03/21/nashville-sc-mls-stadium-ian-ayre-fairgrounds/3235867002/.

372 Garrison, "Why Major League Soccer Picked Nashville."

373 Rau, Organ, and Goad, "How Nashville Got the 2019 NFL Draft."

374 MLSsoccer staff, "Nashville MLS Expansion Team Unveils Name, Crest."

375 MLSsoccer staff, "Nashville MLS Expansion Team Unveils Name, Crest."

376 Rau, Organ, and Goad, "How Nashville Got the 2019 NFL Draft."

377 Rau, Organ, and Goad, "How Nashville Got the 2019 NFL Draft."

378 Rau, Organ, and Goad, "How Nashville Got the 2019 NFL Draft."

379 Rau, Organ, and Goad, "How Nashville Got the 2019 NFL Draft."

380 Rau, Organ, and Goad, "How Nashville Got the 2019 NFL Draft."

381 "History of the Tennessee Titans," Wikipedia, accessed August 6, 2019, https://en.wikipedia.org/wiki/History_of_the_Tennessee_Titans.

382 "Music City Miracle," Wikipedia, accessed July 30, 2019, https://en.wikipedia.org/wiki/Music_City_Miracle.

383 Jim Wyatt, "Titans Owner Amy Adams Strunk Honored as 2019 Tennessean of the Year by Tennessee Sports Hall of Fame," Tennessee Titans, June 15, 2019, https://www.titansonline.com/news/titans-owner-amy-adams-strunk-honored-as-2019-tennessean-of-the-year.

384 Rikka, "The Parthenon: A Slice of Ancient Greece in Nashville, Tennessee," Deviating the Norm (blog), June 15, 2016, http://www.deviatingthenorm.com/blogarchive/2016/6/15/parthenonnash.

385 Rikka, "The Parthenon."

386 Rikka, "The Parthenon."

387 Nashville Convention & Visitors Corp., "The Parthenon," Nashville Music City, 2019, https://www.visitmusiccity.com/local-business/parthenon.

388 Nashville Area Chamber of Commerce, 2018 Regional Economic Guide, 18.

389 Nashville Area Chamber of Commerce, 2018 Regional Economic Guide, 18.

390 "Vanderbilt University," U.S. News & World Report, accessed August 15, 2019, https://www.usnews.com/best-colleges/vanderbilt-3535.

391 Vanderbilt University, "Quick Facts," accessed August 15, 2019, https://www.vanderbilt.edu/about/facts/.

392 Joel Stinnett, "Jeff Bezos Visits Nashville to Launch New Program in Metro Schools," Nashville Business Journal, September 11, 2019, https://www.bizjournals.com/nashville/news/2019/09/11/jeff-bezos-visits-nashville-to-launch-new-program.html.

393 Nashville Area Chamber of Commerce, 2018 Regional Economic Guide, 8.

394 Vanderbilt University, "Vanderbilt Injects $9.5 billion into Tennessee Economy."

395 "Fisk University," U.S. News & World Report, accessed August 15, 2019, https://www.usnews.com/best-colleges/fisk-3490.

396 April Hefner, "Belmont University Draws Record 8,318 Students for Fall 2018," Belmont University, August 23, 2018, https://news.belmont.edu/belmont-university-draws-record-8318-students-for-fall-2018/.

397 Hefner, "Belmont University."

398 Hefner, "Belmont University."

399 "Belmont University," U.S. News & World Report, accessed August 3, 2019, https://www.usnews.com/best-colleges/belmont-3479.

400 Andy Humbles, "Belmont University to Bid for 2020 Presidential Debate," Tennessean, October 8, 2018, https://www.tennessean.com/story/news/politics/2018/10/08/belmont-university-nashville-2020-presidential-debate/1533491002/.

401 Thom Duffy, "Billboard's 2019 Top Music Business Schools: Taking Classes from the Grammys to SXSW," Billboard, March 25, 2019, https://www.billboard.com/articles/business/8503707/billboard-top-music-business-schools-2019.

402 "Belmont Bruins Men's Basketball," Wikipedia, accessed July 8, 2019, https://en.wikipedia.org/wiki/Belmont_Bruins_men%27s_basketball.

403 Kim Chaudoin, "Lipscomb University Named One of Fastest-Growing Private Doctoral Universities in the Nation," Lipscomb University, August, 28, 2018, https://www.lipscomb.edu/news/lipscomb-university-named-one-fastest-growing-private-doctoral-universities-nation.

404 Chaudoin, "Lipscomb University."

405 Chaudoin, "Lipscomb University."

406 Kasie Corley, "Lipscomb University Continues to Rise in State, National Rankings in Accounting, Veteran Friendliness," Lipscomb University, April, 4, 2018, https://www.lipscomb.edu/news/lipscomb-university-continues-rise-state-national-rankings-accounting-veteran-friendliness.

407 Nashville Community Education, "Fall 2019 Class Catalog," Fall 2019, https://www.nashville.gov/Portals/0/SiteContent/CommunEd/docs/Fall%20Catalog%20Small%20Size.pdf.

408 Nashville Community Education, "Fall 2019 Class Catalog."

409 Shalina Chatlani, "Students in Tennessee Now Have a Shot at Free Four-Year College," Nashville Public Radio, March 14, 2019, https://www.nashvillepublicradio.org/post/students-tennessee-now-have-shot-free-four-year-college#stream/0.

410 "Stratford STEM Magnet School Upper Campus," Metro Nashville Public Schools, accessed August 15, 2019, https://schools.mnps.org/stratford-stem-magnet-high-school#about.

411 "McGavock High School," Metro Nashville Public Schools, accessed August 15, 2019, https://schools.mnps.org/mcgavock-high-school.

412 "Mayor's Education Initiatives," Nashville.gov, accessed August 15, 2019, https://www.nashville.gov/Mayors-Office/Education.aspx; Gonzales, "More Than 120 Languages."

413 "Hume-Fogg Academic Magnet School," Niche, accessed August 15, 2019, https://www.niche.com/k12/hume-fogg-academic-magnet-school-nashville-tn/.

414 "Hume Fogg Magnet High School," U.S. News & World Report, accessed August 15, 2019, https://www.usnews.com/education/best-high-schools/tennessee/districts/metropolitan-nashville-public-schools/hume-fogg-magnet-high-school-18154.

415 "Martin Luther King Jr. Magnet High School," Niche, accessed August 15, 2019, https://www.niche.com/k12/martin-luther-king-jr-magnet-high-school-nashville-tn/.

416 "Martin Luther King Jr. Magnet School," U.S. News & World Report, accessed August 15, 2019, https://www.usnews.com/education/best-high-schools/tennessee/districts/metropolitan-nashville-public-schools/martin-luther-king-jr-magnet-school-18163.

417 "Martin Luther King Jr. Magnet School," U.S. News & World Report; "Hume Fogg Magnet High School," U.S. News & World Report.

418 Amanda Ronan, "How Valor Collegiate Academy is Rethinking SEL," EdSurge, March 14, 2017, https://www.edsurge.com/news/2017-03-14-how-valor-collegiate-academy-is-rethinking-sel.

419 "University School of Nashville," Niche, accessed August 15, 2019, https://www.niche.com/k12/university-school-of-nashville-nashville-tn/.

420 "The 50 Best Private Day Schools in the United States," Best Schools, accessed August 15, 2019, https://thebestschools.org/features/best-private-day-schools-america/.

421 "Metro Schools Unveils School Improvement Plan," Metro Nashville Public Schools, September 24, 2018, https://news.mnps.org/metro-schools-unveils-school-improvement-plan/.

422 Elissa Kim, interview with authors, February 20, 2018.

423 "Nashville Education Facts," Scarlett Family Foundation, https://www.scarlettfoundation.org/friends-followers/nashville-education-facts/.

424 Vince Durnan, interview with authors, January 16, 2018.

425 "KIPP Nashville Video," Snapshot Interactive, accessed August 15, 2019, https://snapshotinteractive.com/project/kipp-nashville-video/.

426 Lizzy Alfs, "The Mall at Green Hills Debuts $200M Overhaul with New Wing, More Stores and Parking," Tennessean, June 21, 2019, https://www.tennessean.com/story/money/2019/06/21/mall-green-hills-nashville-new-stores-renovation/1476864001/.

427 Donna Vissman, "7 Things You Need to Know about RH Nashville," Williamson Source, June 29, 2018, https://williamsonsource.com/7-things-you-need-to-know-about-rh-nashville/.

428 Kyren Harvey, "Regal Cinemas Adds ScreenX to 2 Theaters in Nashville," Tennessean, May 29, 2019, https://www.tennessean.com/story/news/local/2019/05/29/screen-x-nashville-movie-theaters-regal-opry-mills/1269423001/.

429 Nashville Convention & Visitors Corp., "Belcourt Theatre," Nashville Music City, accessed August 16, 2019, https://www.visitmusiccity.com/local-business/belcourt-theatre.

430 Caroline Sutton, "CMA Fest 2019 Has Another Record-Breaking Year, Generating $65M for City of Nashville," News Channel 5, July 18, 2019, https://www.newschannel5.com/news/cma-fest-2019-has-another-record-breaking-year-generating-65m-for-city-of-nashville.

431 "Tomato Art Fest," Nashville Guru, August 8, 2019, http://nashvilleguru.com/35956/tomato-fest.

432 Anthony Bourdain, "Episode Intel from Nashville," Anthony Bourdain: Parts Unknown, accessed August 14, 2019, https://explorepartsunknown.com/nashville/episode-intel-from-nashville/.

433 Butch Spyridon, "Nashville's Recent Growing Pains Are a Reflection of How Far the City Has Come," Tennessean, July 5, 2019, https://www.tennessean.com/story/opinion/2019/07/05/nashvilles-growth-also-comes-growing-pains/1628134001/.

434 Taylor, "Nashville Is One of America's Hottest Cities."

435 Jason Hall, "Nashville 'Let Freedom Sing!' Sets New Attendance Record," Fox 17 Nashville, July 4, 2019, https://fox17.com/news/local/nashville-let-freedom-sing-sets-new-attendance-record.

436 Jenna Scherer, "The Best 4th of July Fireworks in the USA," Condé Nast Traveler, June 27, 2018, https://www.cntraveler.com/galleries/2014-07-03/the-10-biggest-fireworks-displays-in-the-us.

CLIMBING THE CHARTS